THE DAILY STUDY BIBLE

(OLD TESTAMENT)

General Editor: John C.L. Gibson

I & II SAMUEL

I & II SAMUEL

DAVID F. PAYNE

THE WESTMINSTER PRESS
PHILADELPHIA

Published by
The Saint Andrew Press
Edinburgh, Scotland
and
The Westminster Press®
Philadelphia, Pennsylvania

Printed in the U.S.A.

3   4   5   6

Library of Congress Cataloging in Publication Data

Payne, David F. (David Frank), 1931–
I & II Samuel.

(The Daily study Bible series)
Bibliography: p.
1. Bible. O.T. Samuel—Commentaries. 2. Bible.
O.T. Samuel—Study. I. Title. II. Title: I and
II Samuel. III. Title: 1 & 2 Samuel. IV. Series: Daily
study Bible series (Westminster Press)
BS1325.3.P39   1982   222'.4077   82-16009
ISBN 0-664-21806-7
ISBN 0-664-24573-0 (pbk.)

GENERAL PREFACE

This series of commentaries on the Old Testament, to which this volume on *Samuel* belongs, has been planned as a companion series to the much-acclaimed New Testament series of the late Professor William Barclay. As with that series, each volume is arranged in successive headed portions suitable for daily study. The Biblical text followed is that of the Revised Standard Version or Common Bible. Eleven contributors share the work, each being responsible for from one to three volumes. The series is issued in the hope that it will do for the Old Testament what Professor Barclay's series succeeded so splendidly in doing for the New Testament—make it come alive for the Christian believer in the twentieth century.

Its two-fold aim is the same as his. Firstly, it is intended to introduce the reader to some of the more important results and fascinating insights of modern Old Testament scholarship. Most of the contributors are already established experts in the field with many publications to their credit. Some are younger scholars who have yet to make their names but who in my judgment as General Editor are now ready to be tested. I can assure those who use these commentaries that they are in the hands of competent teachers who know what is of real consequence in their subject and are able to present it in a form that will appeal to the general public.

The primary purpose of the series, however, is *not* an academic one. Professor Barclay summed it up for his New Testament series in the words of Richard of Chichester's prayer—to enable men and women "to know Jesus Christ more clearly, to love Him more dearly, and to follow Him more nearly." In the case of the Old Testament we have to be a little more circumspect than that. The Old Testament was completed long before the time of Our Lord, and it was (as it still is) the sole Bible of the Jews, God's first people, before it became part of the Christian Bible. We must take this fact seriously.

Yet in its strangely compelling way, sometimes dimly and sometimes directly, sometimes charmingly and sometimes embarrassingly, it holds up before us the things of Christ. It should not be forgotten that Jesus Himself was raised on this Book, that He based His whole ministry on what it says, and that He approached His death with its words on His lips. Christian men and women have in this ancient collection of Jewish writings a uniquely illuminating avenue not only into the will and purposes of God the Father, but into the mind and heart of Him who is named God's Son, who was Himself born a Jew but went on through the Cross and Resurrection to become the Saviour of the world. Read reverently and imaginatively the Old Testament can become a living and relevant force in their everyday lives.

It is the prayer of myself and my colleagues that this series may be used by its readers and blessed by God to that end.

New College
Edinburgh

JOHN C.L. GIBSON
General Editor

CONTENTS

CONTENTS

INTRODUCTION

THE TITLE

The books of Samuel, which were originally one single book, are named after the chief character of the first chapters of 1 Samuel, the prophet Samuel. Altogether there are three main characters; the other two were the first kings of Israel, Saul and David. According to the story, it was Samuel who anointed both Saul and David as king, so in a certain respect he stood over both of them, and his name is not an inappropriate title for the whole work. All the same, it may not have been the earliest title. When the Greek translation known as the Septuagint was made, in the last century or two before Christ, what we know as "Samuel" and "Kings" were called the four books of "Reigns", a title which is even more suitable.

THE CONTENTS

The books of Samuel are part of the whole series of historical books with which the Old Testament begins; in particular, the books of Joshua, Judges, Samuel and Kings belong very closely together. The full story begins with the Creation in Genesis and ends with the Babylonian Exile in Kings. In this wider setting, the books of Samuel discuss the important transitional period when Israel adopted a monarchic constitution. Thus 1 Samuel begins with the last of the "Judges", Eli and Samuel himself; then the story is told of Israel's first king, Saul, who was in some ways a false start to the monarchy; and 2 Samuel goes on to outline the reign of David, who was the founder of the dynasty in Judah and who set the standards for his successors and descendants to follow. The books of Samuel are closely linked with the book of Judges, which tells the story of the earlier political leaders known as "Judges", and with Kings. which concludes the narrative of David himself and then describes the reigns of his successors, from Solomon onwards.

All the historical books of the Old Testament are anonymous. Since the history contained in Joshua, Judges, Samuel and Kings ends with the Babylonian Exile of the sixth century B.C., it follows that the final edition of these books was not made until that century; but the final writer (or perhaps writers) must have had many earlier documents which he could use. In many chapters of 1 and 2 Samuel the sixth-century writer's hand cannot be detected at all, so he was much more of a compiler than an author. However, he did select his material carefully, and he added to it or adapted it when he chose, so it is best to think of him as an editor. Two obvious editorial touches can be seen in 1 Sam. 9:9 and 2 Sam. 13:18; but in general it is a matter of some dispute how much the editor himself wrote, or for that matter whether or not there was an earlier edition and an earlier editor, perhaps towards the end of the eighth century B.C.

It is uncertain how many documents were available to the editors. Some, perhaps the majority, of the individual episodes reported in 1 and 2 Samuel circulated at first as individual stories. Old lists and archives no doubt provided the data about the families and officials of Saul and David (cp. 1 Sam. 14:49ff.; 2 Sam. 3:2–5; 8:15–18; 20:23ff.) as well as the names of David's leading soldiers (2 Sam. 23:24–39). Poems such as the Song of Hannah (1 Sam. 2:1–10) and the Elegy of David (2 Sam. 1:19–27) were probably taken from collections of poetry. Little more can be said with any degree of certainty; a better approach to the material seems to be to divide the books of Samuel into major sections. There seem to be good grounds for thinking that several main sections, if not all, were built up separately, out of the early material available. The major sections are:

(i)   Samuel's early years (1 Sam. 1:1–4:1(a))
(ii)   The wanderings of the ark (1 Sam. 4:1(b)–7:1)
(iii) The start of the monarchy (1 Sam. 7:2–12:25)

(iv) The decline of Saul and the rise of David (1 Sam. 13:1–31:13)
(v) David's early years as king (2 Sam. 1:1–8:18)
(vi) The court history of David (2 Sam. 9:1–20:26)
(vii) Appendix, containing six separate subsections (2 Sam. 21:1–24:25).

THE PURPOSE OF SAMUEL

Why was Samuel written, and for whom? The frequent description of Genesis-Chronicles as the "historical" books of the Old Testament tends to beg both questions; it is often taken for granted that the purpose of all these books was to record history, "what actually happened", for the benefit of posterity as a whole. Up to a point this traditional view may not be far wrong; every nation likes to know something about its past, and especially about its founders and its heroes. Undoubtedly countless generations of Israelites, Jews and Christians have found these stories about the birth of the monarchy in ancient Judah full of interest and inspiration; and there is no good reason to doubt that the original writers felt the same motivation, and set out to pass on historical information to their contemporaries and to posterity.

How accurate their information was is another question, which again brings us into a much-debated area of enquiry. Where the books of Kings are concerned, there is available to the modern scholar a wide range of documents and archaeological finds by which he can test the biblical material; but it is unfortunate that very little in Samuel can be tested in this way. We cannot even *prove* that Samuel or Saul existed— though nobody seriously doubts that they did. It is not surprising, therefore, to find that scholars differ considerably in their assessment of historicity. Did David kill Goliath, or is the tale a legend? Was David innocent of complicity in the death of Abner and others, or is the story as told in 2 Samuel something of a "whitewash", a wholesale piece of propaganda? There is no way of being sure; but it is at least clear that if we reject the biblical data at certain points we shall have nothing left but our imagination to fall back on—there is no alternative source of information. However, few scholars would deny that in any case the books of Samuel as a whole contain a great deal of valuable historical information, and perhaps we cannot hope for more than this.

Samuel, then, can properly be described as "historical"; but it would be wrong to suppose that to convey history was the sole purpose of the writer. Perhaps "biography" would be a better description of his work—provided that we are aware that one of the major personalities and actors was God himself. The story is not simply about Samuel's virtues, Saul's defects and David's successes, but about God's activities during an important phase of Israel's history. The books of Samuel are not just history but theology too. It follows almost inevitably that the material contained in Samuel is as much a sermon as a history lesson. The author saw a divine purpose in his people's past history and he was convinced that there were morals to be drawn from that history, lessons applicable to his own contemporaries.

We may sum up these lessons under four heads:

(i) God overrules in human affairs, small and great, and plays an active role in them.

(ii) God always acts in the best interests of his people. He may and does punish them when they deserve it (in other words, when they are disobedient to his will), but his ultimate purposes are for their well-being and prosperity.

(iii) To fulfil his purposes for them, God has designed appropriate leadership for his people. David, that outstanding king in a golden age, stood as proof of this fact, and provided both a model and a promise for the future.

(iv) God is present with his people, and frequently reveals his presence, in a variety of ways—in the sanctuary, through the voice of prophets, and not least in actions in history for their benefit, especially delivering them from their enemies.

THE MESSAGE OF SAMUEL

If indeed the books of Samuel took their final shape in the sixth century B.C., it is easy to see how suitable these lessons were for the original readers, Jews suffering hardship of one sort or another during the depressing and humiliating years of the Babylonian Exile. They had lost their temple and their capital city, for both lay in ruins; and they had lost their political independence together with the dynasty of David. Many of them had even lost their homes and homeland, finding themselves many hundreds of miles away in exile. To them came the reassuring message that God was still active, if behind the scenes, and still had his own people's interests at heart and in mind. At present there was no king on Israel's throne, but David's family survived, and one day—in God's good time— the Messiah would arise from it and lead Israel into an era of wonderful peace and prosperity. Buoyed up with such hopes, in the meantime they should look out for the signs of God's presence, obey his laws, and avoid all the bad examples of disobedience to God which the books of Samuel described for them.

If such a message was particularly designed for exilic Jewish readers, it proved to be no less well suited for the Jewish people in the centuries that followed. Many of them devoutly trusted in God, obeyed his laws, and waited expectantly for his Messiah. In the same spirit the first Christians gladly embraced the fulfilment of the promise in the person of Jesus of Nazareth. With the Church there came a broader concept of the people of God, together with the conviction that the work of the Messiah had already begun and that the Messianic kingdom was already in being. Nevertheless we still look for the consummation of that kingdom, and in our troubled times we may have much in common with the exilic Jews of old. For the Christian, neither apathy nor stoical resignation is the right response to frightening circumstances; a living trust in the reality of God and in his designs for our world is the necessary basis both of hope and co-operation in the building of his kingdom.

The books of Samuel provide above all a study in leadership, as this commentary seeks to show. This study will often remind us of Christ, as we contrast his kingship with the worst and even the best of human rulers. But since we are called to reign with him (Rev. 5:9f.), there are also practical lessons to be learned for all those who aspire to leadership, on however lowly and insignificant a level, in society and not least in Christian churches and communities. In many different ways, the books of Samuel reveal a great deal about ideal leadership.

THE FIRST BOOK OF SAMUEL

HANNAH AT SHILOH

1 Samuel 1:1-18

[1]There was a certain man of Ramathaim-zophim of the hill country of Ephraim, whose name was Elkanah the son of Jeroham, son of Elihu, son of Tohu, son of Zuph, an Ephraimite. [2]He had two wives; the name of the one was Hannah, and the name of the other Peninnah. And Peninnah had children, but Hannah had no children.

[3]Now this man used to go up year by year from his city to worship and to sacrifice to the Lord of hosts at Shiloh, where the two sons of Eli, Hophni and Phinehas, were priests of the Lord. [4]On the day when Elkanah sacrificed, he would give portions to Peninnah his wife and to all her sons and daughters; [5]and, although he loved Hannah, he would give Hannah only one portion, because the Lord had closed her womb. [6]And her rival used to provoke her sorely, to irritate her, because the Lord had closed her womb. [7]So it went on year by year; as often as she went up to the house of the Lord, she used to provoke her. Therefore Hannah wept and would not eat. [8]And Elkanah, her husband, said to her, "Hannah, why do you weep? And why do you not eat? And why is your heart sad? Am I not more to you than ten sons?"

[9]After they had eaten and drunk in Shiloh, Hannah rose. Now Eli the priest was sitting on the seat beside the door-post of the temple of the Lord. [10]She was deeply distressed and prayed to the Lord, and wept bitterly. [11]And she vowed a vow and said, "O Lord of hosts, if thou wilt indeed look on the affliction of thy maidservant, and remember me, and not forget thy maidservant, but wilt give to thy maidservant a son, then I will give him to the Lord all the days of his life, and no razor shall touch his head."

[12]As she continued praying before the Lord, Eli observed her mouth. [13]Hannah was speaking in her heart; only her lips moved, and her voice was not heard; therefore Eli took her to be a drunken woman. [14]And Eli said to her, "How long will you be drunken? Put

away your wine from you." [15]But Hannah answered, "No, my lord, I am a woman sorely troubled; I have drunk neither wine nor strong drink, but I have been pouring out my soul before the Lord. [16]Do not regard your maidservant as a base woman, for all along I have been speaking out of my great anxiety and vexation." [17]Then Eli answered, "Go in peace, and the God of Israel grant your petition which you have made to him." [18]And she said, "Let your maidservant find favour in your eyes." Then the woman went her way and ate, and her countenance was no longer sad.

The first person we meet is called Elkanah, a man who lived with his family in the central part of the land of Israel. His town was Ramathaim-zophim (or Ramah for short), in the tribal territory of Ephraim. We are not told when he lived, but in the Hebrew Bible the books of Samuel follow immediately after the book of Judges, which gives a picture of the situation at the time. Israel had no king: "every man did what was right in his own eyes" (Judg. 21:25), but there were local leaders such as "elders" in towns and villages, and also priests at the sanctuaries. Eli must have been an important priest, because the sanctuary of Shiloh, some kilometres north of Ramah, was especially important. In the background lurked the Philistines, a real threat to Israel, but they will not come into the story till chapter 4. The date was roughly 1025 B.C.

Elkanah was probably quite well off, since he was able to maintain two wives; polygamy was not very common in Israel, but was perfectly legal. We can see from the unhappy situation that developed in this household why monogamy became the New Testament and the Christian ideal. Of course, rifts and quarrels can occur in any family, big or small, but jealousy is especially liable to happen where there are rival wives. Hannah was very vulnerable because she had no children; childlessness nearly always creates unhappiness in a married woman, but it was much worse in a society where children provided a status symbol, and where medical science did not exist. It seems as if Elkanah tried to make up for her unhappiness, but in doing so he only caused Peninnah to become jealous and unkind. Things came to a head at a festival time, when the family was visiting

Shiloh. At an annual sacred festival (probably the feast of Tabernacles each autumn) families would present animals for sacrifice and after the ceremony they would feast on the meat available; the priest kept some of it, but much of each animal would be returned to the owner. Meat was seldom eaten, so it was a rare treat. From this food Elkanah gave Hannah a special *portion*, probably; the Hebrew of verse 5 is difficult, but "a double portion" (New International Version) makes better sense than *only one portion*.

Peninnah was angry and spiteful, and Hannah felt publicly disgraced. If this quarrel had not happened at Shiloh the result might have been different; but in Shiloh Hannah knew that she had access to the very presence of God, in *the house of the Lord*, the temple there. Nowadays most people would not think of the inability to bear children as a religious matter at all—it would be referred to medical specialists. But both the writer of verse 5 and Hannah herself believed it was a matter of God's will. The two approaches do not rule each other out; Hannah and her contemporaries were in no position to consult medical men, but we today can freely consult both doctors and the God who overrules in human affairs, and we should be as foolish to ignore the second as the first. Jesus saw how God could be glorified through the healing of human disabilities (John 9:1–3).

Hannah's earnest prayer was accompanied by a *vow*. All too easily such vows can be attempts to buy God's favour, but hers was truly unselfish, since it would mean giving away her son. He would be dedicated to God's service and would live at the sanctuary itself.

Uncut hair (verse 11) was a symbol visible to everyone of consecration to God's service in consequence of a special vow. The custom was age-old in Samuel's time, and was not limited to the Israelites. The most important biblical passage about this institution is Num. 6, which indicates that as a rule a man (or woman) made such a vow with regard to himself, not for his child. However, Judg. 13.3ff. gives another instance of a child being specially consecrated to God before his birth. The

technical term for a person consecrated in this way was a
"nazirite", and an old Hebrew manuscript among the Dead Sea
Scrolls expressly calls the unborn Samuel a "nazirite" at the end
of verse 22. As a rule such vows were of limited duration, but
Samuel was to be exceptional, dedicated to God's service for his
full lifetime. Very possibly a contrast is intended with Samson,
a nazirite who did not fully maintain his consecrated state.

Eli at first mistook her deep emotion for drunkenness; once
she had convinced him to the contrary, he added his blessing to
her prayer, confirming her certainty that it would be answered.
Samuel's future was thus planned before his birth. If his mother
had not been barren in the first years of marriage, his future
would have been very different; he might have become a well-
to-do farmer in the hills of Ephraim but he would never have
been a great Israelite leader. Equally, if Hannah's
disappointment had led her into idolatry, magic, or merely
stoical resignation, his future would have been very different, if
indeed he had been born at all. God overruled, but he looked
for the human co-operation of a devout woman.

SAMUEL'S BIRTH

1 Samuel 1:19–28

[19]They rose early in the morning and worshipped before the Lord;
then they went back to their house at Ramah. And Elkanah knew
Hannah his wife, and the Lord remembered her; [20]and in due time
Hannah conceived and bore a son, and she called his name Samuel,
for she said, "I have asked him of the Lord."

[21]And the man Elkanah and all his house went up to offer to the
Lord the yearly sacrifice, and to pay his vow. [22]But Hannah did not
go up, for she said to her husband, "As soon as the child is weaned, I
will bring him, that he may appear in the presence of the Lord, and
abide there for ever." [23]Elkanah her husband said to her, "Do what
seems best to you, wait until you have weaned him; only, may the
Lord establish his word." So the woman remained and nursed her
son, until she weaned him. [24]And when she had weaned him, she
took him up with her, along with a three-year-old bull, an ephah of

flour, and a skin of wine; and she brought him to the house of the Lord at Shiloh; and the child was young. ²⁵Then they slew the bull, and they brought the child to Eli. ²⁶And she said, "Oh, my lord! As you live, my lord, I am the woman who was standing here in your presence, praying to the Lord. ²⁷For this child I prayed; and the Lord has granted me my petition which I made to him. ²⁸Therefore I have lent him to the Lord; as long as he lives, he is lent to the Lord."

And they worshipped the Lord there.

The unhappiness of Hannah's early married life was forgotten when *the Lord remembered her*—her rival Peninnah is never mentioned again. Her sense of God's direct involvement in her life transformed it. To us the opposite of "remembering" is forgetting; in Hebrew thought its opposite would be more like neglecting, i.e. a practical matter. It was as if God had neglected her problems in the past; but now he responded promptly to her prayer and gave her the gift of a son *in due time* (which probably refers simply to the nine months between conception and birth). So to Hannah and to the biblical writer alike, the birth of Samuel was a miracle. The Bible presents us with a number of miraculous births: Isaac and Joseph begin the list in Genesis, and it continues into the New Testament with John the Baptist. In each case the point being made is that the man who was to achieve so much for God's people was wholly a gift from God. Samuel's later deeds for Israel were not due to his talents, primarily, nor to his training, but to the fact that God provided him—at a watershed and a crisis point in Israel's history.

Weaning (verse 22) took much longer in the East (and still does in some countries) than is normal in modern western society, so a year or two passed before Hannah fulfilled her vow. Even so, Samuel was still only a very young child when he was taken to Eli at Shiloh and left with him, dedicated to the service of God. Throughout the chapter it is emphasized how carefully Elkanah and his family carried out the requirements of their religion. It was very different from Christian practice— with its annual visit to the place of worship, taking along a sacrificial animal or two and other components of the offerings to be made. We must remember that Israel was an agricultural community, that sanctuaries were relatively few and spaced out, and that travel was slow and laborious. Farmers and peasants could not possibly have attended temples every week. Devout people, therefore, will have been all the more concerned to attend at the proper times; note how Hannah felt the need to explain to her husband why she was staying at home on one occasion (verse 22). Samuel, however, was now to live in the Shiloh temple itself.

In physical reality, then, the chapter ends with the youthful Samuel taking up residence in the temple. What this meant in theological terms is expressed in three verses which use several words drawn from the same Hebrew verb *sha-al*, chosen for its similarity to the name Samuel (Hebrew *Shemu-el*). It has long been observed that the last of these words, which is translated *lent* in verse 28, is *sha-ul*, exactly the same word as the name of King Saul, Samuel's younger contemporary. This is obviously no coincidence. After a good start, Saul was to prove a failure, rejected by God; the writer wants the reader to see that Samuel was, so to speak, the true Saul, the national leader who was wholly God's man from first to last.

These Hebrew wordplays can be grouped together as follows:
  (i) *I have asked him of the Lord* (verse 20)
  (ii) *My petition which I made* (verse 27)
  (iii) *I have lent him . . . he is lent* (verse 28).
The first and second of these statements by Hannah relate to Samuel's birth; there would have been no Samuel but for her prayer and God's gracious response to it. The third statement relates to the whole of Samuel's future life; he was Hannah's child but she made him over on permanent "loan" to God. God had given him; Hannah gave him back; and Samuel's very name was a reminder of these things. We should not overlook the sacrifice made by Hannah; but her loss was to be Israel's gain, and she felt amply compensated. In any case, a parent's ultimate duty to his or her children is to fit them for service to others and then to release them. To bind children to one's own apron-strings can only stunt their development and is likely to rob both them and society in general.

THE SONG OF HANNAH

1 Samuel 2:1–10

[1]Hannah also prayed and said,
  "My heart exults in the Lord;
  my strength is exalted in the Lord.
My mouth derides my enemies,
  because I rejoice in thy salvation.

[2]"There is none holy like the Lord,
  there is none besides thee;
  there is no rock like our God.
[3]Talk no more so very proudly,
  let not arrogance come from your mouth;
for the Lord is a God of knowledge,
  and by him actions are weighed.
[4]The bows of the mighty are broken,
  but the feeble gird on strength.
[5]Those who were full have hired themselves out for bread,
  but those who were hungry have ceased to hunger.
The barren has borne seven,
  but she who has many children is forlorn.
[6]The Lord kills and brings to life;
  he brings down to Sheol and raises up.
[7]The Lord makes poor and makes rich;
  he brings low, he also exalts.
[8]He raises up the poor from the dust;
  he lifts the needy from the ash heap,
to make them sit with princes
  and inherit a seat of honour.
For the pillars of the earth are the Lord's,
  and on them he has set the world.

[9]"He will guard the feet of his faithful ones;
  but the wicked shall be cut off in darkness;
  for not by might shall a man prevail.
[10]The adversaries of the Lord shall be broken to pieces;
  against them he will thunder in heaven.

> The Lord will judge the ends of the earth;
>   he will give strength to his king,
>   and exalt the power of his anointed."

The Song of Hannah is an Israelite hymn very similar to many poems in the book of Psalms. Modern versions of the Bible helpfully print it in poetic form. Two typical features of Hebrew poetry can easily be observed in translation. One is what is known as "parallelism": nearly every line has a "parallel", in other words another line which responds to it, reinforcing the contents of the first line. Often the second line says much the same thing in different words (verse 6 offers a good example); sometimes it provides a contrast (verse 4 is an example of this). Sometimes such parallels are found in half lines too (as in verse 6); and sometimes there may be more than two parallels (e.g. verse 2). The other feature is by no means unique to Hebrew poetry; poetic language makes frequent use of metaphors and figurative speech. It is a mistake to take it too literally. In this poem *the pillars of the earth* (verse 8) are of course not literal; nor are the barren woman's *seven* children (verse 5). Very often in Hebrew poetry these two features together have the effect of producing a black-and-white picture, which would be misleading and even untrue if taken too literally. It is not true, and never was, that every once-barren woman bears precisely seven children, nor that every mother of a big family becomes *forlorn* (verse 5). What is true is that God can exalt the humble and humiliate the proud.

The Song of Hannah recalls only two details of chapter 1, the hostility of her rival and her own barrenness, together with the fact that God had eliminated both these problems. Samuel's birth was a blessing not only for Hannah but also for the nation, and the Song of Hannah is really a poem of *national* exultation. The real *enemies* (verse 1) were the Philistines, whom we shall first meet in chapter 4; their arrogance can be seen in the challenge of Goliath (17:8,10,43–45). However, the birth of Samuel heralded their defeat and the beginning of a strong kingship in Israel. This hope was certain, because the God who promised it was no local god of a minor people but the Almighty universal God, the Lord of life and of death (verse 6) and the Creator (verse 8). So those now faithful to him, however *feeble*, *forlorn* and *needy* in present circumstances, had a bright and joyful future.

The Song of Hannah has yet another dimension. The Philistines, of course, passed from the scene of history many hundreds of years ago; the Song offered hope to Israelites who were suffering from later powerful invaders like the Assyrians and Babylonians. They in turn perished. The New Testament is more concerned with spiritual enemies, and with the ultimate triumph not of one nation over another but of right over wrong, of God's cause over demonic forces (see especially Eph. 6:10-17). In this struggle one is on the right side not by the accident of birth but by choice and decision. The Song of Hannah fits this interpretation equally well, putting the *faithful* in stark contrast to the *wicked* (verse 9), and depicts God as weighing all human actions (verse 3).

The central character of the poem is God himself; the detailed portrayal of him in this passage shows the richness of Israelite faith. Of all that is said about God in this poem nothing is more important and distinctive than verse 2, which has three points to make about him:

(i) *He is holy*. The Hebrew word for *holy* (*qadosh*) is not too easily translated into twentieth century secular English. Its primary sense is the opposite of "profane"; in other words, it is a term which makes a radical distinction between two modes of being. God is separate from everything which is profane or unholy. In particular, he is distinguished from everything and everybody else by two attributes, his power and his moral perfection. In both respects he commands awe and elicits the reverence and devotion of his worshippers.

(ii) *He is incomparable*. The claim that God is without equal was a natural one in an environment where many deities, male and female, were revered. Israel, especially in its rise from small, humble and almost hopeless beginnings to the status of a unified and strong state (under David), could gratefully assert that her God's power was unrivalled. This is only a step from the assertion that no other god exists. Our environment today is very different, with atheism rather than polytheism as the rival to Christianity; even so, it is still worth remembering—and asserting from time to time—that our God's power is incomparable. The powers of science, or of economics, or the stars, or fate, are all insignificant when set beside his supreme control.

(iii) *He is trustworthy*. The word *rock* was a familiar metaphor for God, to express the solid, unchangeable refuge which he provided for his people. His power was not some blind, impersonal and irresistible force; his actions, though often mysterious in purpose, were always for the ultimate good of his own people Israel. The past experience of God's unfailing help in times of great difficulty gave Israel and her psalmists faith and confidence as they looked into the future.

ELI'S SONS

1 Samuel 2:11–26

[11]Then Elkanah went home to Ramah. And the boy ministered to the Lord, in the presence of Eli the priest.

[12]Now the sons of Eli were worthless men; they had no regard for the Lord. [13]The custom of the priests with the people was that when any man offered sacrifice, the priest's servant would come, while the meat was boiling, with a three-pronged fork in his hand, [14]and he would thrust it into the pan, or kettle, or cauldron, or pot; all that the fork brought up the priest would take for himself. So they did at Shiloh to all the Israelites who came there. [15]Moreover, before the fat was burned, the priest's servant would come and say to the man who was sacrificing, "Give meat for the priest to roast; for he will not accept boiled meat from you, but raw." [16]And if the man said to him, "Let them burn the fat first, and then take as much as you wish," he would say, "No, you must give it now; and if not, I will take it by force." [17]Thus the sin of the young men was very great in the sight of the Lord; for the men treated the offering of the Lord with contempt.

¹⁸Samuel was ministering before the Lord, a boy girded with a linen ephod. ¹⁹And his mother used to make for him a little robe and take it to him each year, when she went up with her husband to offer the yearly sacrifice. ²⁰Then Eli would bless Elkanah and his wife, and say, "The Lord give you children by this woman for the loan which she lent to the Lord"; so then they would return to their home.

²¹And the Lord visited Hannah, and she conceived and bore three sons and two daughters. And the boy Samuel grew in the presence of the Lord.

²²Now Eli was very old, and he heard all that his sons were doing to all Israel, and how they lay with the women who served at the entrance to the tent of meeting. ²³And he said to them, "Why do you do such things? For I hear of your evil dealings from all the people. ²⁴No, my sons; it is no good report that I hear the people of the Lord spreading abroad. ²⁵If a man sins against a man, God will mediate for him; but if a man sins against the Lord, who can intercede for him?" But they would not listen to the voice of their father; for it was the will of the Lord to slay them.

²⁶Now the boy Samuel continued to grow both in stature and in favour with the Lord and with men.

The scene of the action remains in Shiloh, with only occasional references to Ramah; but the centre of the stage is now held by Eli and his family, while Samuel's parents drop into the background. By skilful moving of the spotlight, the biblical story-teller lets us see the two families, especially the sons, in vivid contrast. Samuel's family is now seen as humble but happy, united and devout—with a son to be proud of, in Samuel himself. Eli's two sons, on the other hand, were not only disobedient to their father but also a cause of public scandal. They were guilty of two practices which brought them and the whole priesthood into disrepute:

(i) *Greed* (verses 12–17). The background to this paragraph was the normal Israelite sacrificial practice. The sacrifices which worshippers brought to the shrines were edible, and a portion of each sacrifice was intended for the priests who officiated. Evidently Eli's sons were "improving" on previous custom, in their own interests, by choosing beforehand the choice pieces of meat. Meat was a luxury item in a peasant economy, and they were living off the fat of the land. Their arrogance was as great as their greed.

(ii) *Sexual immorality* (verse 22). This sin speaks for itself; the background may be the fact that at Canaanite shrines there were ritual prostitutes, and it may be that Eli's sons were importing pagan as well as immoral practices to Shiloh. The Canaanites (i.e. the inhabitants of Palestine before the Israelites had settled there) still possessed a number of shrines where they practised their religion, which had many sexual rites. They believed that human fertility and the fertility of the soil were linked together in some magical way. In any case, the flagrant misconduct of Eli's sons caused a scandal.

It must be remembered that Eli was not simply the chief priest at Shiloh; serving at the most important Israelite shrine, he was a man of considerable political importance, indeed a leader ("judge") of Israel (cp. 4:18). Yet he could not control his own sons! There was therefore a leadership crisis in Israel; physically the very elderly Eli was no longer fit to rule, and his sons were obviously morally unfit. But Samuel was growing up there at Shiloh, and was well liked by all the Israelite worshippers who came there (verse 26). More important than the people's approval, however, were God's decisions. He too viewed Samuel with favour, but had already determined that Eli's sons must die; verse 25 does not mean that they were unable to change their minds and their behaviour, but that their refusal to do so was no impediment to God's plans for the future. Their father warned them that their sins were unforgivable: they were the very men whose responsibility it was to intercede for others, and there was no way in which anyone else could intercede with God for them—they were the senior priests. They were quite deliberately flouting God.

In a book which is all about leadership, Eli's sons are object lessons, prime examples of the unsuitability to lead a nation. To this day, arrogant assertiveness and self-seeking are temptations to all those in positions of great power in society. Israel did not have much in the way of constitutional safeguards; but they had a God who guided their fortunes.

A PROPHETIC MESSAGE

1 Samuel 2:27–36

[27]And there came a man of God to Eli, and said to him, "Thus the Lord has said, 'I revealed myself to the house of your father when they were in Egypt subject to the house of Pharaoh. [28]And I chose him out of all the tribes of Israel to be my priest, to go up to my altar, to burn incense, to wear an ephod before me; and I gave to the house of your father all my offerings by fire from the people of Israel. [29]Why then look with greedy eye at my sacrifices and my offerings which I commanded, and honour your sons above me by fattening yourselves upon the choicest parts of every offering of my people Israel?' [30]Therefore the Lord the God of Israel declares: 'I promised that your house and the house of your father should go in and out before me for ever'; but now the Lord declares: 'Far be it from me; for those who honour me I will honour, and those who despise me shall be lightly esteemed. [31]Behold, the days are coming, when I will cut off your strength and the strength of your father's house, so that there will not be an old man in your house. [32]Then in distress you will look with envious eye on all the prosperity which shall be bestowed upon Israel; and there shall not be an old man in your house for ever. [33]The man of you whom I shall not cut off from my altar shall be spared to weep out his eyes and grieve his heart; and all the increase of your house shall die by the sword of men. [34]And this which shall befall your two sons, Hophni and Phinehas, shall be the sign to you: both of them shall die on the same day. [35]And I will raise up for myself a faithful priest, who shall do according to what is in my heart and in my mind; and I will build him a sure house, and he shall go in and out before my anointed for ever. [36]And every one who is left in your house shall come to implore him for a piece of silver or a loaf of bread, and shall say, "Put me, I pray you, in one of the priest's places, that I may eat a morsel of bread."'"

Eli's ineffective protests to his sons were followed by a prophetic denunciation. The phrase *a man of God* was a less technical term for a prophet; people recognized that there were men in their midst who had a special relationship with what we should call the supernatural. We tend to think of prophets as being a purely Old Testament phenomenon, we tend to limit their activities to a later period than this, and we tend to view them as writers who predicted the future. However, they were in fact a widespread phenomenon in the ancient world, over many centuries, and their primary function was the spoken, not the written, word. The Bible itself mentions prophets of other religions (e.g. 1 Kings 18:19) and tells of prophets active in the New Testament era (e.g. Acts 21:7-14). Their activities were varied, but the unnamed prophet of this chapter was typical of the so-called "writing prophets" of the Old Testament, in that he did foretell something of the future, at the same time denouncing evil and pronouncing judgment.

The purpose of the writer in describing his words in such detail is to indicate in advance to the reader that the important historical events which the books of Samuel will describe were no accident but fully planned by God. Eli had a noble and long ancestry (as verses 27f. acknowledge), and the downfall of his family must have been very traumatic for Israelites of the time, especially as it was accompanied by invasion and domination by a foreign enemy, the Philistines. There was a lesson here for readers of the book during the Babylonian Exile, who also had just lived through very distressing times, and had lost the dynasty (David's descendants) who had given them stability of leadership for four centuries. Applying the moral of these verses, devout readers could see that the same God had both foreseen and foreordained the major change of political circumstances which had come upon them—and had foretold it through several prophets' messages.

The condemnation of Eli takes the standpoint that he was implicated in his sons' guilt. As a family they had been singularly honoured for a couple of centuries (the ancestor of verse 27 must be either Aaron or Levi), but greed and self-seeking now characterized them. So God rejected the family which had rejected him. While Israel would see prosperity (a hope for the reader!), those who had failed him would suffer hardship or even death (verses 31-33). Eli's own two sons, Hophni and Phinehas, were to die, and the priesthood was destined for a better man; here the prophecy looks beyond Samuel to Zadok (cp. 2 Sam.8:17) whose family would hold the Jerusalem high-priesthood for some eight centuries. The last verse of the chapter recognizes that Eli's family would not die out altogether, but it would become completely subservient, a second-class priesthood.

This section, then, teaches that God was at work in the downfall of Eli's family and in its replacement. We must not overlook the importance of the priesthood in Israelite eyes. In the West people today often think of clergymen as ineffective bystanders, helpless to influence political realities in any way; the recent history of Iran, by contrast, demonstrates the colossal importance of religious leadership in less secular countries and societies. Israel would have been utterly bereft and demoralized if it had lost its chief priestly family without any replacement.

At the same time, the reader is reminded that God does not raise one family and demote another on some mere whim of the moment. If God's *decisions* are at times mysterious, his *principles* of action are not. The governing principle here is expressed plainly in verse 30: *those who honour me I will honour, and those who despise me shall be lightly esteemed.* On this verse Stuart Holden has written, "To honour God does not necessarily imply doing great things for Him. It is rather the consistently maintained attitude of heart which refers every choice to His judgment, measures every value by His standard, and endeavours to make every incident of life contribute towards the glorifying of His Name."

SAMUEL BECOMES A PROPHET

1 Samuel 3:1–4:1(a)

¹Now the boy Samuel was ministering to the Lord under Eli. And the word of the Lord was rare in those days; there was no frequent vision.
²At that time Eli, whose eyesight had begun to grow dim, so that he could not see, was lying down in his own place; ³the lamp of God

had not yet gone out, and Samuel was lying down within the temple of the Lord, where the ark of God was. 4Then the Lord called, "Samuel! Samuel!" and he said, "Here I am!" 5and ran to Eli, and said, "Here I am, for you called me." But he said, "I did not call; lie down again." So he went and lay down. 6And the Lord called again, "Samuel!" And Samuel arose and went to Eli, and said, "Here I am, for you called me." But he said, "I did not call, my son; lie down again." 7Now Samuel did not yet know the Lord, and the word of the Lord had not yet been revealed to him. 8And the Lord called Samuel again the third time. And he arose and went to Eli, and said, "Here I am, for you called me." Then Eli perceived that the Lord was calling the boy. 9Therefore Eli said to Samuel, "Go, lie down; and if he calls you, you shall say, 'Speak, Lord, for thy servant hears.'" So Samuel went and lay down in his place.

10And the Lord came and stood forth, calling as at other times, "Samuel! Samuel!" And Samuel said, "Speak, for thy servant hears." 11Then the Lord said to Samuel, "Behold, I am about to do a thing in Israel, at which the two ears of every one that hears it will tingle. 12On that day I will fulfil against Eli all that I have spoken concerning his house, from beginning to end. 13And I tell him that I am about to punish his house for ever, for the iniquity which he knew, because his sons were blaspheming God, and he did not restrain them. 14Therefore I swear to the house of Eli that the iniquity of Eli's house shall not be expiated by sacrifice or offering for ever."

15Samuel lay until morning; then he opened the doors of the house of the Lord. And Samuel was afraid to tell the vision to Eli. 16But Eli called Samuel and said, "Samuel, my son." And he said, "Here I am." 17And Eli said, "What was it that he told you? Do not hide it from me. May God do so to you and more also, if you hide anything from me of all that he told you." 18So Samuel told him everything and hid nothing from him. And he said, "It is the Lord; let him do what seems good to him."

19And Samuel grew, and the Lord was with him and let none of his words fall to the ground. 20And all Israel from Dan to Beer-sheba knew that Samuel was established as a prophet of the Lord. 21And the Lord appeared again at Shiloh, for the Lord revealed himself to Samuel at Shiloh by the word of the Lord. 1And the word of Samuel came to all Israel.

In chapter 3 Samuel passes from boyhood to manhood.

Up till now he appears as rather passive, content to remain in the background; but by the end of chapter 3 he has emerged as a nationally known figure. (*Dan* and *Beer-sheba* were the most northerly and southerly towns inside the borders of Israel; see Map 1.) This development was not due, primarily at least, to his strength of personality, but to the fact that he experienced the call to be a prophet. He was being groomed for priestly activities, to carry out the rituals of the sanctuary, to offer sacrifices, to give counsel to worshippers, and to tend the sacred ark of the covenant (mentioned in verse 3; see chapter 5 for a description of it). In later years he did carry out some priestly functions, we are told, but he was first and foremost a prophet.

The prophet too was a religious functionary, who might be attached to a sanctuary, as Samuel was at first, but he differed in important respects from the priest. His primary business was the word of God, which came to him through visions, dreams, supernatural experiences, and in a variety of ways. Priests normally became priests by being born into a priestly family; but to become a prophet, one had to experience a personal call to office. This chapter tells the story, then, of Samuel's call: he heard the voice of God repeatedly (so that there could be no mistake about it), and apparently also had a vision of God (verse 10). Eli too was able to bear witness that Samuel heard the call of God; so there could be no doubting the reality and authenticity of this call. Other prophets' calls were important (see Isa. 6 and Jer. 1), but Samuel's was all the more important, since he would not only advise and guide individual Israelites but would himself become the leader of the whole nation in a testing, transitional phase of its history. The anonymous prophet of chapter 2, by contrast, was a mere spokesman of God, with no responsibility but to convey the message; but Samuel was to be God's appointed national leader as well as his spokesman.

The first message of the new prophet concerned Eli. It not only confirmed the prophecy of 2:27–36, it also made it plain that the time of its fulfilment had now arrived. Eli is a dignified and resigned yet pathetic figure. His age and infirmity are underlined at the start of the chapter, and his moral weakness in coping with his sons is recalled in verse 13. He had been tried and found wanting as Israel's leader, and the time had come for the mantle of leadership to pass to another man. In those days of political change and uncertainty, the old age of national rulers was itself a problem; it became a problem once again when Samuel grew old (cp. 8:1–5). The inexorable passage of time eventually brings to an end even the most brilliant examples of leadership. But God showed his care for Israel; before Eli's death he had already provided better leadership, already known to the whole nation, in the person of Samuel. He would give them stability, comfort and reassurance in the dark days that lay just ahead; above all, he would be able, as a prophet, to make known to his fellow-countrymen God's will, God's wishes and God's instructions in all the various situations which were to arise.

Today's political leaders, of course, are not granted the role of prophets—we might wish that they were! But ordinary Christian people are no longer utterly dependent on priests and prophets; the Spirit of God and the mind of Christ are available to the simplest and most humble Christian man and woman.

A DISASTROUS DEFEAT

1 Samuel 4:1(b)–11

Now Israel went out to battle against the Philistines; they encamped at Ebenezer, and the Philistines encamped at Aphek. ²The Philistines drew up in line against Israel, and when the battle spread, Israel was defeated by the Philistines, who slew about four thousand men on the field of battle. ³And when the troops came to the camp, the elders of Israel said, "Why has the Lord put us to rout today before the Philistines? Let us bring the ark of the covenant of the Lord here from Shiloh, that he may come among us and save us from the power of our enemies." ⁴So the people sent to Shiloh, and brought from there the ark of the covenant of the Lord of hosts, who is enthroned on the cherubim; and the two sons of Eli, Hophni and Phinehas, were there with the ark of the covenant of God.

⁵When the ark of the covenant of the Lord came into the camp, all Israel gave a mighty shout, so that the earth resounded. ⁶And when the Philistines heard the noise of the shouting, they said, "What does this great shouting in the camp of the Hebrews mean?" And when they learned that the ark of the Lord had come to the camp, ⁷the Philistines were afraid; for they said, "A god has come into the camp." And they said, "Woe to us! For nothing like this has happened before. ⁸Woe to us! Who can deliver us from the power of these mighty gods? These are the gods who smote the Egyptians with every sort of plague in the wilderness. ⁹Take courage, and acquit yourselves like men, O Philistines, lest you become slaves to the Hebrews as they have been to you; acquit yourselves like men and fight."

¹⁰So the Philistines fought, and Israel was defeated, and they fled, every man to his home; and there was a very great slaughter, for there fell of Israel thirty thousand foot soldiers. ¹¹And the ark of God was captured; and the two sons of Eli, Hophni and Phinehas, were slain.

The scene shifts from the peace of the sanctuary at Shiloh to a battlefield, at *Aphek*: here the real world in which the Israelites then lived comes sharply into focus. *The Philistines* were a small but well-organized, energetic and aggressive nation whose territory lay on the south-western plains of Palestine. They had come originally from the Greek islands, and were experienced and well-equipped soldiers, more than a match for the Israelite farmers and peasants. After consolidating their position in Palestine for a hundred and fifty years or so, they were now determined to dominate the hilly areas inland where the Israelites lived for the most part. Aphek was on the edge of the coastal plain, so it is clear that an Israelite army, hastily assembled from their farms and smallholdings, was attempting to obstruct a Philistine invasion (see Map 2). The Philistines won the first engagement.

The Israelite leaders, who were tribal elders meeting as a council, saw the need for desperate measures. They did not blame the defeat on military inexperience or inadequate equipment, nor on poor generalship. The causes were not military but religious, they were sure, and it is a measure of their faith that they did not believe that Philistine gods had won the battle. On the other hand, they evidently believed that they could achieve God's favour, and victory with it, simply by mechanical means: if they fetched the ancient symbol of God's presence, the ark of the covenant, and took it into battle, God could do no other than give them victory. Even today, the boundary between religion and magic is all too easily crossed.

It is interesting to find that the Philistines knew the reputation of Israel's God and were disconcerted at the arrival of the ark of the covenant, brought from Shiloh by Eli's sons; but it only spurred them to greater efforts and to greater courage.

The second battle resulted in an even heavier defeat for Israel, with the death of the ark's custodians and, worst of all, the capture of the ark itself. Israel thus quickly learned the lesson that God's arm cannot be twisted; the ark was only a symbol, not an idol to be worshipped nor a sort of magic wand (see the next chapter for a fuller description of it).

Disasters—national, communal or personal—are part and parcel of life. We cannot tell as a rule what part they play in God's plans; and even if we could know, the physical sufferings and the sorrows of bereavement and loss would not in themselves be lessened. However, the Christian must always look beyond the present to the future; it is there that the explanation ultimately lies. We are more used nowadays to the scientific principle of cause and effect; in other words, it is yesterday that explains today. But in Christian experience, it may well be *tomorrow* that best explains today. As John Hick has written, "If there is any eventual resolution of the interplay between good and evil, any decisive bringing of good out of evil, it must lie beyond this world and beyond the enigma of death." For the Christian, certainly, "the best is yet to be".

AFTER THE BATTLE

1 Samuel 4:12–22

12A man of Benjamin ran from the battle line, and came to Shiloh the same day, with his clothes rent and with earth upon his head. [13]When he arrived, Eli was sitting upon his seat by the road watching, for his heart trembled for the ark of God. And when the man came into the city and told the news, all the city cried out. [14]When Eli heard the sound of the outcry, he said, "What is this uproar?" Then the man hastened and came and told Eli. [15]Now Eli was ninety-eight years old and his eyes were set, so that he could not see. [16]And the man said to Eli, "I am he who has come from the battle; I fled from the battle today." And he said, "How did it go, my son?" [17]He who brought the tidings answered and said, "Israel has fled before the Philistines, and there has also been a great slaughter among the people; your two sons also, Hophni and Phinehas, are dead, and the ark of God has been captured." [18]When he mentioned the ark of God, Eli fell over backward from his seat by the side of the gate; and his neck was broken and he died, for he was an old man, and heavy. He had judged Israel forty years.

[19]Now his daughter-in-law, the wife of Phinehas, was with child, about to give birth. And when she heard the tidings that the ark of God was captured, and that her father-in-law and her husband were dead, she bowed and gave birth; for her pains came upon her. [20]And about the time of her death the women attending her said to her, "Fear not, for you have borne a son." But she did not answer or give heed. [21]And she named the child Ichabod, saying, "The glory has departed from Israel!" because the ark of God had been captured and because of her father-in-law and her husband. [22]And she said, "The glory has departed from Israel, for the ark of God has been captured."

The story is vividly told how the news of the crushing defeat was brought from the battlefield to Shiloh, about thirty kilometres to the east of Aphek. Runners then used to carry urgent messages, and this man adopted visible signs of mourning so that everyone who saw him would at once know the tenor of his news. Eli was unable to see, however, and evidently the sanctuary must have been a little outside the town of Shiloh, so that the messenger had to bring him the news personally.

Thus the aged Eli heard the news of the threefold tragedy. The death of his two sons had been foretold but was still a cause for anguish; the disastrous defeat for Israel must also have crushed his spirit; but it was the news of the loss of the ark of the covenant which affected him most deeply. His own death was a direct result of it. In this fashion the Philistine victory ended an era for Israel, to which Eli had given leadership for so long (verse 18); note that the word *judge* in the Old Testament often refers to political rule rather than to the administration of law. So Israel suffered a fourth tragedy in the death of Eli, and a crisis of leadership was to develop; for the moment there was a political vacuum, although as the reader knows Samuel was there, already provided by God, to fill the gap.

The wife of Phinehas was of no political significance; we are not even told what her name was. Equally, the son born to her on her death-bed was not destined for greatness; we never hear of him again. This vivid little story is told for one reason only, namely because the name given to the child, *Ichabod*, was such a perfect commentary on the situation. Israelite women would at times name their children after some circumstance, major or minor, which obtained at the time of their birth; the most famous case is that of "Immanuel", cp. Isa. 7:14–16. Ichabod is such a name, although there is slight uncertainty as to its precise meaning. Possibly it meant "No-glory", but very probably it expressed a question, "Where [is the] glory?" In either case, God's provision of leadership and even the very symbol of God's presence had *departed from Israel*. The name Ichabod, then, voiced a hopeless question. The literal answer to it was that the ark had gone to the land of the Philistines, as chapter 5 will describe; but the name was more significant and prophetic than the dying woman could appreciate. What had been captured was no mere wooden box, no mere religious trophy or national emblem, but the symbol of God's *glory*.

The noun *glory* (Hebrew *kabod*) is another word familiar to us from the Bible and yet none too easy to translate meaningfully. In its usage it is not limited to the divine; it might signify the honour, majesty or splendour of a human being such as a great king. When associated with the ark of the covenant, *kabod* denoted the awesome splendour of God's invisible presence. Ichabod's mother no doubt meant to express her horror that God's presence had, as she thought, departed with the ark from Israel. But the glory of God was expressed not only in his presence in the sanctuary but particularly in his deeds in history, such as in the miraculous rescue of the fleeing Israelites at the Red Sea (Exod. 14:17f.). "Where is the glory?" was the question; the answer would speedily be seen by Israelites and Philistines alike, in the events which surrounded the ark while in Philistia, and in the permanent deliverance of Israel from the Philistines, which would gradually come about in the next twenty-five years or so.

In the New Testament too, the word *glory* can be used of God's deliverance for his people, namely their salvation, achieved by the work of Christ. Jesus, in fact, in himself brought to man in visible and tangible form both the living presence and the active power of God; as John 1:14 puts it, "The Word became flesh . . . we have beheld his glory, glory as of the only Son from the Father". For the Christian, glory is not so much an alternative term for "heaven", a future hope, as a living experience of God through Jesus Christ.

THE ARK AND ITS EFFECTS

1 Samuel 5:1-12

[1]When the Philistines captured the ark of God, they carried it from Ebenezer to Ashdod; [2]then the Philistines took the ark of God and brought it into the house of Dagon and set it up beside Dagon. [3]And when the people of Ashdod rose early the next day, behold, Dagon had fallen face downward on the ground before the ark of the Lord. So they took Dagon and put him back in his place. [4]But when they rose early on the next morning, behold, Dagon had fallen face downward on the ground before the ark of the Lord, and the head of Dagon and both his hands were lying cut off upon the threshold; only the trunk of Dagon was left to him. [5]This is why the priests of Dagon and all who enter the house of Dagon do not tread on the threshold of Dagon in Ashdod to this day.

[6]The hand of the Lord was heavy upon the people of Ashdod, and he terrified and afflicted them with tumours, both Ashdod and its

territory. 7And when the men of Ashdod saw how things were, they said, "The ark of the God of Israel must not remain with us; for his hand is heavy upon us and upon Dagon our god." 8So they sent and gathered together all the lords of the Philistines, and said, "What shall we do with the ark of the God of Israel?" They answered, "Let the ark of the God of Israel be brought around to Gath." So they brought the ark of the God of Israel there. 9But after they had brought it around, the hand of the Lord was against the city, causing a very great panic, and he afflicted the men of the city, both young and old, so that tumours broke out upon them. 10So they sent the ark of God to Ekron. But when the ark of God came to Ekron, the people of Ekron cried out, "They have brought around to us the ark of the God of Israel to slay us and our people." 11They sent therefore and gathered together all the lords of the Philistines, and said, "Send away the ark of the God of Israel, and let it return to its own place, that it may not slay us and our people." For there was a deathly panic throughout the whole city. The hand of God was very heavy there; 12the men who did not die were stricken with tumours, and the cry of the city went up to heaven.

(i)

In chapter 4 the ark was treated by the Israelites and Philistines alike as a potentially powerful symbol, but superficially it appeared to be quite passive, even useless. This sacred object suddenly fulfils its potential in chapter 5, and indeed occupies the centre of the stage in chapters 5 and 6. It is time, therefore, to consider what this object was and what it meant to Israel.

The ark was in shape a box or chest (as the name implies). It was primarily a container, and held the two tablets of the Law, cp. Deut. 10:1–5, with some other articles. It was placed in the innermost shrine of one Israelite sanctuary after another, including Shiloh and subsequently Jerusalem. It is not surprising, therefore, that to the Israelites it symbolized the presence of God, whom they worshipped by the name Yahweh (often translated as *the Lord*). Unlike all their neighbours, the Israelites did not make any idol or representation of their God. One concept of the ark was that it was the throne of Yahweh; the golden cherubim made for the ark (see the description in Exod. 25) were envisaged as his divine attendants.

During the Israelites' long period of wandering between Egypt and the Promised Land the ark was mobile, travelling with them; and it played a special role whenever an enemy confronted them or tried to obstruct them (see Num. 10:33–36). In earlier days, then, the ark had given Israel a visible and tangible focus, proof positive of God's presence and protection. No other nation shared in it, so it was also a national symbol, and probably gave some degree of unity to Israel in the Judges period, when the Israelite tribes tended to be very disunited.

By Samuel's time, then, there was a real danger that the ark might replace Yahweh as the object of Israel's worship. Its capture by the Philistines even had a salutary effect on Israel's thinking, for events proved that though the ark was lost, God's presence and power were still realities. On the other hand, God by no means abandoned the ark to its fate.

(ii)

It was common practice to place captured trophies, religious or otherwise, inside the victors' temples, so the ark was set in an important Philistine temple, dedicated to the local deity Dagon, god of corn and of the fertility of the ground. It was widely believed in the ancient world that each deity had his or her own sphere of influence—a city, a country, the sky, the sun, and so on. In Dagon's own temple, surely, Dagon ruled supreme . . . and yet the mere symbol of Yahweh's presence was enough first to topple, then to break, the very idol of Dagon itself. The God of Israel was supreme even in the heart of Philistine territory and in the centre of their pagan faith. Israel was a weak and rather divided nation; but her God was all-powerful, as she increasingly came to appreciate. Verse 5 may recall some very ancient cultic rite; but to the biblical writer, the rite was a permanent record of Dagon's weakness so long as Philistine rituals lasted. Indeed, those rituals have long since perished, but the God of Israel is worshipped today in every continent of the world.

(iii)

The Philistines had five major cities, and in this section we read how the ark rested in three of them—Ashdod, Gath and Ekron—and all three were afflicted by plague. Serious epidemics were frequent in the Mediterranean world; this one probably came in by sea (Ashdod was a port), and the reference to mice and to tumours strongly suggests that it was bubonic plague, a disease carried by rodents of which marked glandular swellings are a characteristic symptom. The biblical writer knew and cared nothing about the medical causes; his sole interest was theological, and he saw the epidemic as clear proof that the power of Yahweh, due to the presence of the ark, overwhelmed the Philistines. Victorious over Israel's armies, they were defeated and indeed reduced to utter *panic* (verses 9, 11) by Israel's God. The Philistines in fact agreed with the writer's outlook: for them too the cause of their troubles could only be religious.

If such an outlook was for many centuries a barrier to medical and scientific progress, that is a fact to be regretted; but if we in our age substitute a knowledge of scientific facts for an awareness of God's unseen power, we are no better off than our ancestors. On the contrary, we shall be guilty not of excusable *ignorance* but of deliberately *ignoring* the power, control and will of God in human affairs.

THE PHILISTINES' SUBMISSION

1 Samuel 6:1–9

¹The ark of the Lord was in the country of the Philistines seven months. ²And the Philistines called for the priests and the diviners and said, "What shall we do with the ark of the Lord? Tell us with what we shall send it to its place." ³They said, "If you send away the ark of the God of Israel, do not send it empty, but by all means return him a guilt offering. Then you will be healed, and it will be known to you why his hand does not turn away from you." ⁴And they said, "What is the guilt offering that we shall return to him?" They answered, "Five golden tumours and five golden mice, according to the number of the lords of the Philistines; for the same

plague was upon all of you and upon your lords. ⁵So you must make images of your tumours and images of your mice that ravage the land, and give glory to the God of Israel; perhaps he will lighten his hand from off you and your gods and your land. ⁶Why should you harden your hearts as the Egyptians and Pharaoh hardened their hearts? After he had made sport of them, did not they let the people go, and they departed? ⁷Now then, take and prepare a new cart and two milch cows upon which there has never come a yoke, and yoke the cows to the cart, but take their calves home, away from them. ⁸And take the ark of the Lord and place it on the cart, and put in a box at its side the figures of gold, which you are returning to him as a guilt offering. Then send it off, and let it go its way. ⁹And watch; if it goes up on the way to its own land, to Beth-shemesh, then it is he who has done us this great harm; but if not, then we shall know that it is not his hand that struck us, it happened to us by chance."

To the Philistines, the ark had been at first a prized military trophy; now it had become a liability, something in fact so dangerous that it was not even clear how to get rid of it. The description of the Philistines is here sympathetic: they are in deep trouble and anxiety, but are not in any position to consult Israel's God or Israelite priests and prophets who could advise them. In such circumstances, the steps taken were sensible and methodical, and show a considerable humility too. Ignorant of the true God, they could but resort to magic and to the practitioners of magic. The purpose of the golden objects mentioned in verse 4 was what is called "sympathetic magic": it was hoped and believed that the golden mice and tumours would, when they were taken out of Philistine territory, remove the real mice and tumours at the same time. The biblical writer does not challenge or mock their faith; on the contrary, God is seen to respond favourably to it. The important thing is the sincere desire to find out God's will and then to be obedient to it; for God does not condemn the weakness or folly of humankind, who are after all his creatures.

The passage strikes no missionary note. At the same time, the portrayal of foreign idolaters as men aware of and responsive to the true God when they needed "salvation" draws attention to our missionary responsibility. "How are they to hear without a preacher?" asked the Apostle Paul (Rom. 10:14). The great need of all men for the knowledge, guidance and salvation of God remains to this day.

In its historical setting, the passage stresses the fact that the powerful enemy of Israel set about returning the ark of their own volition: the Israelites did not have to perform prodigious feats of arms to retrieve it. Here was a message of hope and encouragement to the Jewish exiles in sixth century B.C. Babylonia, who had similarly lost their temple and important sacred items from it. Then too God overruled, so that the Persians in due course allowed the temple to be rebuilt and some at least of its treasures restored.

Faith, however, must repose in God himself, not in any sacred objects and articles, however traditional and treasured. No doubt Christians persecuted for their faith in societies hostile to Christianity have learned this lesson—or their faith would have lapsed. In the last resort neither Bible nor sacraments nor priesthood are absolutely essential to the Christian faith. That is why Jesus brushed aside questions about the right place to worship (John 4:19–24). Yet God in his grace permits us to possess many tangible signs of his presence and of his involvement with us. They are his gifts, for which we ought to be thankful; they should never become crutches or idols.

THE ARK COMES HOME

1 Samuel 6:10–7:2

[10]The men did so, and took two milch cows and yoked them to the cart, and shut up their calves at home. [11]And they put the ark of the Lord on the cart, and the box with the golden mice and the images of their tumours. [12]And the cows went straight in the direction of Beth-shemesh along one highway, lowing as they went; they turned neither to the right nor to the left, and the lords of the Philistines went after them as far as the border of Beth-shemesh. [13]Now the people of Beth-shemesh were reaping their wheat harvest in the

valley; and when they lifted up their eyes and saw the ark, they rejoiced to see it. [14]The cart came into the field of Joshua of Beth-shemesh, and stopped there. A great stone was there; and they split up the wood of the cart and offered the cows as a burnt offering to the Lord. [15]And the Levites took down the ark of the Lord and the box that was beside it, in which were the golden figures, and set them upon the great stone; and the men of Beth-shemesh offered burnt offerings and sacrificed sacrifices on that day to the Lord. [16]And when the five lords of the Philistines saw it, they returned that day to Ekron.

[17]These are the golden tumours, which the Philistines returned as a guilt offering to the Lord: one for Ashdod, one for Gaza, one for Ashkelon, one for Gath, one for Ekron; [18]also the golden mice, according to the number of all the cities of the Philistines belonging to the five lords, both fortified cities and unwalled villages. The great stone, beside which they set down the ark of the Lord, is a witness to this day in the field of Joshua of Beth-shemesh.

[19]And he slew some of the men of Beth-shemesh, because they looked into the ark of the Lord; he slew seventy men of them, and the people mourned because the Lord had made a great slaughter among the people. [20]Then the men of Beth-shemesh said, "Who is able to stand before the Lord, this holy God? And to whom shall he go up away from us?" [21]So they sent messengers to the inhabitants of Kiriath-jearim, saying, "The Philistines have returned the ark of the Lord. Come down and take it up to you." [1]And the men of Kiriath-jearim came and took up the ark of the Lord, and brought it to the house of Abinadab on the hill; and they consecrated his son, Eleazar, to have charge of the ark of the Lord. [2]From the day that the ark was lodged at Kiriath-jearim, a long time passed, some twenty years, and all the house of Israel lamented after the Lord.

The Philistines were delighted to get rid of the ark and the Israelites were delighted to get it back again: but the picture was much more complicated than this. The Philistines recede into the background again, for the moment; but the writer allows us to see that the sacred ark was just as potent a force in Israelite hands as in Philistine ones. The power of God was not something that Israel somehow tamed and confined in a box, any more than modern man can banish God to the churches, chapels and cathedrals they take care never to frequent.

The disaster at Beth-shemesh (6:19) was obviously totally unexpected by the Israelite people who lived there; they had, they supposed, been as cautious and devout in handling the ark as the Philistines had been since the start of the epidemic. For instance, they made sure that it was carried only by Levites, the sacred personnel specially entrusted with the care of sacred objects. Nowadays we should no doubt attribute the death of seventy people to the same epidemic that had ravaged neighbouring Philistine districts, but Israelite piety rightly saw, though nothing was known of germs and bacteria, that God is in control of the mysteries of life and death.

The explanation given was an interpretation after the event. It seems that some citizens were guilty of unseemly curiosity with regard to the ark, although it is not clear from the Hebrew whether they peered into it, as the RSV has it, or merely gazed at it. Another explanation is incorporated in the ancient Greek version (known as the Septuagint), and it has been adopted as original by many modern scholars and by the NEB: "The sons of Jeconiah did not rejoice with the rest of the men of Beth-shemesh when they welcomed the ark of the Lord, and he struck down seventy of them." In either case, we would be inclined to feel that the punishment far outweighed the fault, but the passage is at pains to stress the power of God and to warn any Israelites of later centuries who were heedless of him.

At any rate, the ark was temporarily settled at Kiriath-jearim, a step on its way to Jerusalem, but that was still some way in the future (cp. 2 Sam. 6). It may be that the Philistines, glad though they were to be rid of the ark, refused to permit it to be taken to any major Israelite sanctuary. If so, Israel's lamentation (7:2) is the more readily understood. Besides, Israel was still reeling from the effects of the two defeats in battle. The Philistine victories permitted them to impose their will over much of Israel's territory. The retrieval of the ark was a temporary cause for joy, but the Philistine domination was not lessened by it. Nevertheless, the return of the ark to Israelite soil was a sign of hope and promise. The "glory" had come back to Israel (cp. 4:22) and Israel could be sure that their God would not remain inactive for ever. The certainty of God's presence is always a sign of hope, however dark the circumstances may be.

SAMUEL IN CHARGE

1 Samuel 7:3-17

³Then Samuel said to all the house of Israel, "If you are returning to the Lord with all your heart, then put away the foreign gods and the Ashtaroth from among you, and direct your heart to the Lord, and serve him only, and he will deliver you out of the hand of the Philistines." ⁴So Israel put away the Baals and the Ashtaroth, and they served the Lord only.

⁵Then Samuel said, "Gather all Israel at Mizpah, and I will pray to the Lord for you." ⁶So they gathered at Mizpah, and drew water and poured it out before the Lord, and fasted on that day, and said there, "We have sinned against the Lord." And Samuel judged the people of Israel at Mizpah. ⁷Now when the Philistines heard that the people of Israel had gathered at Mizpah, the lords of the Philistines went up against Israel. And when the people of Israel heard of it they were afraid of the Philistines. ⁸And the people of Israel said to Samuel, "Do not cease to cry to the Lord our God for us, that he may save us from the hand of the Philistines." ⁹So Samuel took a sucking lamb and offered it as a whole burnt offering to the Lord; and Samuel cried to the Lord for Israel, and the Lord answered him. ¹⁰As Samuel was offering up the burnt offering, the Philistines drew near to attack Israel; but the Lord thundered with a mighty voice that day against the Philistines and threw them into confusion; and they were routed before Israel. ¹¹And the men of Israel went out of Mizpah and pursued the Philistines, and smote them, as far as below Beth-car.

¹²Then Samuel took a stone and set it up between Mizpah and Jeshanah, and called its name Ebenezer; for he said, "Hitherto the Lord has helped us." ¹³So the Philistines were subdued and did not again enter the territory of Israel. And the hand of the Lord was against the Philistines all the days of Samuel. ¹⁴The cities which the Philistines had taken from Israel were restored to Israel, from Ekron to Gath; and Israel rescued their territory from the hand of the Philistines. There was peace also between Israel and the Amorites.

¹⁵Samuel judged Israel all the days of his life. ¹⁶And he went on a

circuit year by year to Bethel, Gilgal, and Mizpah; and he judged Israel in all these places. [17]Then he would come back to Ramah, for his home was there, and there also he administered justice to Israel. And he built there an altar to the Lord.

Although the story of Samuel occupies nearly half of the first book of Samuel, this is the only chapter that gives a general picture of his role among the Israelites; earlier chapters have been concerned with his background and early years, and later chapters will concentrate on his relationship with Saul, to whom he handed over the leadership of Israel. For all the brevity of this chapter, it is evident that Samuel was for some considerable time the most important political figure in the land. He was primarily a prophet (verses 3f.); and he exercised some priestly functions (verses 9f.) plus a variety of judicial ones (verses 15ff.). The statement in verse 6 that he *judged the people of Israel* means that he also came to exercise political leadership, with his capital at Mizpah, and it was this development which spurred the Philistines into an invasion, since they were determined to establish themselves as the ruling power in the land.

The picture offered in this chapter is one of Samuel's prophetic denunciation of idolatry, of Israel's repentance, and of the resulting defeat of the Philistines, more by the power of God than by Israelite force of arms. One particular Israelite success is recounted, a success which reversed the earlier defeat at Ebenezer (see chapter 4) and gave new meaning to its name, literally "Stone of Help". We need not doubt the fact that this major victory did occur under Samuel's leadership, but one gets the impression that he himself was no soldier, and the picture of peace and security given in verses 13f. must be balanced by later passages showing that the Philistines still exercised no little influence in the hill-country: note, for instance, the presence of a Philistine garrison at Michmash in 13:23. It is really a picture of what should and would have been the case but for Israel's lack of trust in both Samuel himself and the God he served. Israelite unrest was very human and understandable against the background of the Philistine threats and encroachments, especially when Samuel offered nothing by way of military skills; but even so it amounted to rejection of God's provision for them. The victory associated with Ebenezer was created by a sort of miracle (verse 10); but the trouble with miracles is that they are unpredictable and cannot be planned or ordered. So at least the Israelites thought; and which of us, if we are honest, would have reacted differently? Yet faith in God demands a constant unwavering trust in his providential care.

Brief as the portrait of Samuel here is, it gives us a glimpse of the ideal ruler. He had been provided by God and trained by him; he now showed himself able to read his people's minds and capable of rebuking them effectively. He was decisive in word and action, and he was fully in touch with God. Nor is his concern to provide justice purely coincidental. Yet the irony was that such a ruler was precisely the man whom Israel rejected, as chapter 8 will show. Political unrest may mirror inadequate or oppressive leadership; on the other hand, it may well demonstrate the fatal flaws in human nature. Exactly the same may be true of unrest within any human community, including a local congregation.

THE DEMAND FOR A KING

1 Samuel 8:1-5

¹When Samuel became old, he made his sons judges over Israel. ²The name of his first-born son was Joel, and the name of his second, Abijah; they were judges in Beer-sheba. ³Yet his sons did not walk in his ways, but turned aside after gain; they took bribes and perverted justice.

⁴Then all the elders of Israel gathered together and came to Samuel at Ramah, ⁵and said to him, "Behold, you are old and your sons do not walk in your ways; now appoint for us a king to govern us like all the nations."

It seems that the situation in Beer-sheba (verses 1ff.)—a frontier town, whose affairs were not in any way of central importance in Israel—was seized on as a pretext to rebel against Samuel's leadership, for all its virtues. Tribal elders formed the political substructure of Israel, so their opinions could not be ignored nor dismissed out of hand. What they demanded was a king.

In a world where monarchies are a rarity and strike many people as anachronisms, it is none too easy to arrive at an objective view of this form of constitution. But kingship was commonplace in Israel's world—as the elders themselves were aware. Not far to the south-west lay a large and famous kingdom, Egypt; even better known to Israelites were the petty Canaanite kingdoms, the city-states dotted about inside Palestine. Jerusalem itself must have been one such kingdom before David captured it and made it part of Israel (cp. 2 Sam. 5). The chief virtues of an institution like monarchy were stability and centralization. The stability derived from the position of the king at the head of society, giving it both a nucleus and an ideal, and more particularly from the principle of dynastic succession, which ensured continuity when kings aged and died. Centralization had its benefits in terms of efficiency, strength and a unified approach to problems.

In contrast, Israel's history up to this point had seen much disunity, with each tribe going its own way, and consequent weakness, while in terms of leadership there had never been any real continuity. The "judges" had arisen haphazardly and unpredictably—in the elders' view of the matter, at any rate. In many ways, therefore, a monarchy made good sense; but the demand for one left God entirely out of account. The book of Judges teaches that Israel's weakness had been due for the most part to idolatry, which had been punished by God, and her strength had been the gift of God to his people. The elders now wished to sidestep such lessons of history simply by political machinery; subsequent history was to demonstrate their mistake.

No nation has ever found some magical constitutional formula to solve every social and political problem; but a people that seeks above all to honour and obey God possesses an inner stability and serenity which allow it to confront universal and permanent problems with both courage and compassion, and with a considerable measure of success.

The same principles apply to smaller human groups as well. Different churches and denominations have developed a variety of systems of government; none is perfect, simply because human beings are so imperfect. But when and where God is recognized as the real ruler in his Church, there is a congregation which will prosper.

THE IMPLICATIONS OF A MONARCHY

1 Samuel 8:6–22

[6]But the thing displeased Samuel when they said, "Give us a king to govern us." And Samuel prayed to the Lord. [7]And the Lord said to Samuel, "Hearken to the voice of the people in all that they say to you; for they have not rejected you, but they have rejected me from being king over them. [8]According to all the deeds which they have done to me, from the day I brought them up out of Egypt even to this day, forsaking me and serving other gods, so they are also doing to you. [9]Now then, hearken to their voice; only, you shall solemnly warn them, and show them the ways of the king who shall reign over them."

[10]So Samuel told all the words of the Lord to the people who were asking a king from him. [11]He said, "These will be the ways of the king who will reign over you: he will take your sons and appoint them to his chariots and to be his horsemen, and to run before his chariots; [12]and he will appoint for himself commanders of thousands and commanders of fifties, and some to plough his ground and to reap his harvest, and to make his implements of war and the equipment of his chariots. [13]He will take your daughters to be perfumers and cooks and bakers. [14]He will take the best of your fields and vineyards and olive orchards and give them to his servants. [15]He will take the tenth of your grain and of your vineyards and give it to his officers and to his servants. [16]He will take your menservants and maidservants, and the best of your cattle and your asses, and put them to his work. [17]He will take the tenth of your flocks, and you shall be his slaves. [18]And in that day you will cry out because of your king, whom you have chosen for yourselves; but the Lord will not answer you in that day."

¹⁹But the people refused to listen to the voice of Samuel; and they said, "No! but we will have a king over us, ²⁰that we also may be like all the nations, and that our king may govern us and go out before us and fight our battles." ²¹And when Samuel had heard all the words of the people, he repeated them ·in the ears of the Lord. ²²And the Lord said to Samuel, "Hearken to their voice, and make them a king." Samuel then said to the men of Israel, "Go every man to his city."

The elders demanded a king; this at least was a healthier beginning than the sort of situation we find exemplified in Judg. 9, when a military adventurer tried to get power for himself and became king for a while, largely by setting his subjects against one another. The elders were quite content to let Samuel find the right man to become Israel's first king. We find Samuel directed by God, consenting to their wishes. It is emphatically stated, nonetheless, that the Israelites through their elders were rejecting not only Samuel but God himself; and the argument of the chapter seems to be that, in permitting them to have the king they requested, God was in a sense punishing them—a punishment to fit the crime! Kingship was in fact a double-edged affair, and two contrasting views of monarchy are offered to the reader in this chapter.

(i) The elders were more interested in the *functions* of monarchy: a king would provide military organization, co-ordination and efficiency (verse 20). They were not so naive as to imagine that a king would win every battle for them, but they no doubt sensed the need for a standing army and a permanent staff of military officers. It was a fact that the Israelites outnumbered the Philistines and, given adequate weapons, training and administration, they would in due course be able to defeat this major enemy—without any need for them to call on God for special help. To achieve this desirable end the elders were willing to accept any disadvantages which might come with the advent of kingship. They must have realized that for a start they would be obliged to relinquish some of their own political power and influence, but considered this to be a sacrifice worth making.

(ii) Samuel, by contrast, drew attention to the inherent *nature* of monarchy: a king would *give* certain benefits, undeniably, but it was beyond question that he would *take*. *Take* is the keyword of verses 11–18. Kingship would have to be paid for. The army which the people desired would involve conscription and taxation, necessarily; but over and beyond such inevitable costs, kings would want pomp and ceremony and the best of everything. The worst feature of all would be the forced labour described in verse 17 as slavery; this institution was later to be a major factor in the break-up of the Israelite kingdom at the end of Solomon's reign (see 1 Kings 12:1–20).

It may be that Samuel's description of monarchy has been amplified by the biblical writer in the light of the actual deeds of Israelite kings such as Solomon; on the other hand, there is ample evidence that such a description well fitted kings and kingdoms outside Israel already in Samuel's era. The chapter makes it clear, in any case, that the Israelites chose a monarchic constitution, warts and all, of their own free will. If kings proved to be a mixed blessing, Israel could never blame her God for imposing a monarchy on her. Yet through this sinful choice God would show his grace by giving Israel a great king (David) and ultimately the Messianic ideal: see the comments on 2 Sam. 7:1–17.

The worst feature of the elders' demand, in the biblical writer's eyes, was their desire to be *like all the nations* (verse 20). The ancient Israelites, and of course modern Christians too, are only human beings and as such there is a natural resistance within them to any suggestion that they should be totally different from all other men. Nor does God intend that his people should be *totally* different; he himself has made all men of the same flesh and blood. But to his own people he has given special gifts and higher standards, and it is tragic when they spurn these for no better reason than to be like other people. Jesus in the Sermon on the Mount might have been responding to the Israelite elders of Samuel's time when he said, "Be concerned above everything else with the Kingdom of God and with what he requires of you" (Matt. 6:33, *Good News Bible*).

SAUL COMES ON THE SCENE

1 Samuel 9:1–14

¹There was a man of Benjamin whose name was Kish, the son of Abiel, son of Zeror, son of Becorath, son of Aphiah, a Benjaminite, a man of wealth; ²and he had a son whose name was Saul, a handsome young man. There was not a man among the people of Israel more handsome than he; from his shoulders upward he was taller than any of the people.

³Now the asses of Kish, Saul's father, were lost. So Kish said to Saul his son, "Take one of the servants with you, and arise, go and look for the asses." ⁴And they passed through the hill country of Ephraim and passed through the land of Shalishah, but they did not find them. And they passed through the land of Shaalim, but they were not there. Then they passed through the land of Benjamin, but did not find them.

⁵When they came to the land of Zuph, Saul said to his servant who was with him, "Come, let us go back, lest my father cease to care about the asses and become anxious about us." ⁶But he said to him, "Behold, there is a man of God in this city, and he is a man that is held in honour; all that he says comes true. Let us go there; perhaps he can tell us about the journey on which we have set out." ⁷Then Saul said to his servant, "But if we go, what can we bring the man? For the bread in our sacks is gone, and there is no present to bring to the man of God. What have we?" ⁸The servant answered Saul again, "Here, I have with me the fourth part of a shekel of silver, and I will give it to the man of God, to tell us our way." ⁹(Formerly in Israel, when a man went to inquire of God, he said, "Come, let us go to the seer"; for he who is now called a prophet was formerly called a seer.) ¹⁰And Saul said to his servant, "Well said; come, let us go." So they went to the city where the man of God was.

¹¹As they went up the hill to the city, they met young maidens coming out to draw water, and said to them, "Is the seer here?" ¹²They answered, "He is; behold, he is just ahead of you. Make haste; he has come just now to the city, because the people have a sacrifice today on the high place. ¹³As soon as you enter the city, you will find him, before he goes up to the high place to eat; for the people will not eat till he comes, since he must bless the sacrifice;

afterward those eat who are invited. Now go up, for you will meet him immediately." ¹⁴So they went up to the city. As they were entering the city, they saw Samuel coming out toward them on his way up to the high place.

Israel's first king was not to be David but Saul, to whom the reader is now introduced. The earliest readers, like ourselves, were thoroughly familiar with the fact that Saul was the man who first became king over Israel; so the story holds no surprise for the reader, but instead emphasizes what a surprise the sequence of events was to Saul himself. It was a series of chances which brought him face to face with Samuel; but the reader, ancient and modern, is expected to realize for himself that God overruled in all these apparently trivial circumstances. Saul's whole concern was with some lost donkeys, and the only reason for him to search out Samuel was that prophets were men who by divine power could "see" what other people could not. (Hence the old name for prophets, mentioned in verse 9.)

On the face of it, the story treats the great prophet as if he were some mere local, little-known character. There is a dramatic reason for this feature of the narrative; the narrator uses this dramatic device to underline the point that, far from seeking the limelight, neither Saul nor his servant knew or recognized Samuel. On the one side Saul was a man hunting for donkeys who instead found a kingdom; and on the other side there was Samuel, who was looking for a suitable king and found a young man of remarkable political unawareness. Yet so it was meant to be.

It is important to note that, in spite of the gloomy analysis of kingship given in chapter 8, and in spite of the glaring defects that Saul was later to exhibit, this chapter presents him in a very good light, beginning with his outstanding physique and appearance (which seem to have been important matters in those days). He was a good man, and his later achievements show that he was in many respects an able man. One interesting aspect of his background is that his tribe was Benjamin (verse 1); this small tribe could never have aspired to dominate other larger tribes. Its position (see Map 1) made it a sort of neutral buffer-zone between the two powerful rivals Ephraim and Judah. A king from Benjamin, then, could well be expected to reduce rivalries and help to unify Israel in the struggle against the Philistines. Everything, indeed, seemed to be favourable; Saul could have been the ideal king for Israel, and at this point in time there was nothing to stop him achieving true greatness. It was not to be; but the fault "is not in our stars, but in ourselves", as Shakespeare has Cassius say to Brutus.

It is worth pausing to consider what our contemporaries would expect to see in a new political leader. A measure of ambition and drive, certainly; proven qualities of intellectual ability and leadership; and some degree of political experience, at least. Saul displayed none of these characteristics as yet, though (as events were to prove) he was by no means without ability. The important thing was that he was a man whom God could use. Ambition, self-confidence and experience can have the effect of making a man deaf to God's guidance.

PROPHET AND KING

1 Samuel 9:15-27

15Now the day before Saul came, the Lord had revealed to Samuel: 16"Tomorrow about this time I will send to you a man from the land of Benjamin, and you shall anoint him to be prince over my people Israel. He shall save my people from the hand of the Philistines; for I have seen the affliction of my people, because their cry has come to me." 17When Samuel saw Saul, the Lord told him, "Here is the man of whom I spoke to you! He it is who shall rule over my people." 18Then Saul approached Samuel in the gate, and said, "Tell me where is the house of the seer?" 19Samuel answered Saul, "I am the seer; go up before me to the high place, for today you shall eat with me, and in the morning I will let you go and will tell you all that is on your mind. 20As for your asses that were lost three days ago, do not set your mind on them, for they have been found. And for whom is all that is desirable in Israel? Is it not for you and for all your father's house?" 21Saul answered, "Am I not a Benjaminite, from the least of

the tribes of Israel? And is not my family the humblest of all the
families of the tribe of Benjamin? Why then have you spoken to me
in this way?"

²²Then Samuel took Saul and his servant and brought them into
the hall and gave them a place at the head of those who had been
invited, who were about thirty persons. ²³And Samuel said to the
cook, "Bring the portion I gave you, of which I said to you, 'Put it
aside.'" ²⁴So the cook took up the leg and the upper portion and set
them before Saul; and Samuel said, "See, what was kept is set before
you. Eat; because it was kept for you until the hour appointed, that
you might eat with the guests."

So Saul ate with Samuel that day. ²⁵And when they came down
from the high place into the city, a bed was spread for Saul upon the
roof, and he lay down to sleep. ²⁶Then at the break of dawn Samuel
called to Saul upon the roof, "Up, that I may send you on your way."
So Saul arose, and both he and Samuel went out into the street.

²⁷As they were going down to the outskirts of the city, Samuel said
to Saul, "Tell the servant to pass on before us, and when he has
passed on stop here yourself for a while, that I may make known to
you the word of God."

In this passage Saul is the man destined to be king, though he
does not yet know it and is puzzled about the reception given to
him. Samuel is above all presented as a prophet here; he will
have to relinquish political leadership to Saul, but his position
as a prophet is confirmed. Three things prove his prophetic
status, and they are features which distinguish him from a king:

(a) The future was revealed to him (verses 15f.).

(b) Events unknown to others were revealed to him (verse
20).

(c) *The word of God*, that is to say God's instructions for
another man, was given through him.

These features made the prophet unique and invaluable, both
to the whole nation and especially to the kings of Israel. Samuel
was in fact the prophetic prototype for the period of the
monarchy, and the existence of the office of prophet was a
divine gift to each king, beginning with Saul. Each king would
have the privilege of access to the mind and the guidance of
God—provided that he was willing to hear and to heed them.

On the other hand, this God-given arrangement for the benefit of the nation reduced somewhat the autocratic status of kingship. The king would always feel the necessity of consulting the prophet, and indeed at times would be obliged to obey him. In this sense Israel's new monarchy was a "constitutional" one, with the prophets exercising a brake on the absolute powers of the kings. The ideal of government for Israel was the king and the prophet acting in concord and unity. Then the king could fulfil his own role of leadership, not least in battle (verse 16).

The role of the king is assessed positively in this chapter, especially in verse 16, in contrast with the negative estimate of monarchy in 8:11-18. The contrast is somewhat surprising to the reader, and the great majority of scholars explain it in terms of different traditions (or documents, perhaps) underlying these chapters. However, there is realism in this two-fold evaluation of monarchy; both good and bad lay in store for Israel under the kings. Their predominant role in the first generation or two, however, was to be the positive one of ridding Israel permanently of the Philistine menace. In this way, acting through the kings (through Saul and David, to be precise), God performed his age-old role as the saviour of Israel. As verse 16 indicates, Israel was marked not only by demands for a king and complaints against Samuel but also by a heartfelt cry for help against Philistine raids and encroachment, felt more by some tribes than by others. By one and the same gift of kingship God would answer prayer and punish disbelief. Such is the ambiguity of history; it takes both faith in God and also spiritual insight to see the principles of God's activity in all human history.

THE ANOINTING OF SAUL

1 Samuel 10:1-16

¹Then Samuel took a vial of oil and poured it on his head, and kissed him and said, "Has not the Lord anointed you to be prince over his people Israel? And you shall reign over the people of the Lord and

you will save them from the hand of their enemies round about. And this shall be the sign to you that the Lord has anointed you to be prince over his heritage. ²When you depart from me today you will meet two men by Rachel's tomb in the territory of Benjamin at Zelzah, and they will say to you, 'The asses which you went to seek are found, and now your father has ceased to care about the asses and is anxious about you, saying, "What shall I do about my son?"' ³Then you shall go on from there further and come to the oak of Tabor; three men going up to God at Bethel will meet you there, one carrying three kids, another carrying three loaves of bread, and another carrying a skin of wine. ⁴And they will greet you and give you two loaves of bread, which you shall accept from their hand. ⁵After that you shall come to Gibeathelohim, where there is a garrison of the Philistines; and there, as you come to the city, you will meet a band of prophets coming down from the high place with harp, tambourine, flute, and lyre before them, prophesying. ⁶Then the spirit of the Lord will come mightily upon you, and you shall prophesy with them and be turned into another man. ⁷Now when these signs meet you, do whatever your hand finds to do, for God is with you. ⁸And you shall go down before me to Gilgal; and behold, I am coming to you to offer burnt offerings and to sacrifice peace offerings. Seven days you shall wait, until I come to you and show you what you shall do."

⁹When he turned his back to leave Samuel, God gave him another heart; and all these signs came to pass that day. ¹⁰When they came to Gibe-ah, behold, a band of prophets met him; and the spirit of God came mightily upon him, and he prophesied among them. ¹¹And when all who knew him before saw how he prophesied with the prophets, the people said to one another, "What has come over the son of Kish? Is Saul also among the prophets?" ¹²And a man of the place answered, "And who is their father?" Therefore it became a proverb, "Is Saul also among the prophets?" ¹³When he had finished prophesying, he came to the high place.

¹⁴Saul's uncle said to him and to his servant, "Where did you go?" And he said, "To seek the asses; and when we saw they were not to be found, we went to Samuel." ¹⁵And Saul's uncle said, "Pray, tell me what Samuel said to you." ¹⁶And Saul said to his uncle, "He told us plainly that the asses had been found." But about the matter of the kingdom, of which Samuel had spoken, he did not tell him anything.

After the slow build-up of chapter 9, the narrator abruptly

brings us to the climax of the whole affair: Samuel anoints Saul to be king. At this stage it was a private and indeed secret action; Samuel took care to be unobserved by others (9:27), and Saul did not even tell his closest relatives what had happened (verse 16). In other words, it was a symbolic act, making him king in God's sight but not yet in the nation's. (It is possible that the word translated *prince* in verse 1 means "king-designate", "king-to-be".)

The ritual of anointing a man to be king was afterwards very important in Israelite thought and understanding. As verse 1 expresses it, the king was understood to be anointed by God himself; by this visible and irrevocable sign God consecrated a man, setting him apart for a special office. Priests too were consecrated by the rite of anointing, and this parallel makes it clear that kingship was not so much a secular and political office as a sacred and holy one. It may be significant that in Egyptian culture it was the custom to anoint vassal kings, i.e. minor kings who owed allegiance to the great king of Egypt; in this light we may see the king of Israel not as a king in his own right but as the vassal of Yahweh, who is envisaged as the true king of Israel. Towards his subjects, however, the Israelite king stood in God's place—chosen and marked out by God to exercise God's rule among them.

To Saul, such a role in Israel was doubly unexpected: in the first place, a monarchy itself was a new institution, and secondly, he had had no expectations of becoming a judge or even a tribal elder as yet, let alone a king. This is the reason why Samuel offered him several *signs* as proof that he would indeed be king. The most important sign was to be an inward one, a personal experience which would change him *into another man* (verse 6).

This experience was more typical of a prophet than a king; in prophetic company, Saul too found himself *prophesying*, under the compulsion of *the spirit of God.* In this context we are probably to understand that he was caught up in a form of ecstatic speech and dancing; at any rate his actions were startling to everyone who saw him, and the bystanders' remarks (verses 11f.) seem to have been not only puzzled but somewhat sarcastic. The experience was intended as a sign to Saul himself but one which would not enlighten anyone else.

Verse 8 is introduced quite casually; it lays a basis for the events described in chapter 13, but here it serves as a reminder, in passing, that Saul, despite the high office for which he had now been designated, was still subject to God's instructions given through Samuel, whose priestly functions were not transferred to Saul.

As Saul embarked on his career as king, then, he had a gift from God and an obligation towards God. *From* God, he received that transformation of his inner self without which no man can adequately serve God; *towards* God he had the duty of careful obedience. These two requirements remain as important as ever for any Christian; and they are all the more vital for any Christian who finds himself in a position of responsibility or leadership.

THE PEOPLE MEET THEIR KING

1 Samuel 10:17–27

17Now Samuel called the people together to the Lord at Mizpah; 18and he said to the people of Israel, "Thus says the Lord, the God of Israel, 'I brought up Israel out of Egypt, and I delivered you from the hand of the Egyptians and from the hand of all the kingdoms that were oppressing you.' 19But you have this day rejected your God, who saves you from all your calamities and your distresses; and you have said, 'No! but set a king over us.' Now therefore present yourselves before the Lord by your tribes and by your thousands."

20Then Samuel brought all the tribes of Israel near, and the tribe of Benjamin was taken by lot. 21He brought the tribe of Benjamin near by its families, and the family of the Matrites was taken by lot; finally he brought the family of the Matrites near man by man, and Saul the son of Kish was taken by lot. But when they sought him, he could not be found. 22So they inquired again of the Lord, "Did the man come hither?" and the Lord said, "Behold, he has hidden himself among the baggage." 23Then they ran and fetched him from there; and when he stood among the people, he was taller than any of the people from his shoulders upward. 24And Samuel said to all the people, "Do you see him whom the Lord has chosen? There is none like him among all the people." And all the people shouted, "Long live the king!"

25Then Samuel told the people the rights and duties of the kingship; and he wrote them in a book and laid it up before the Lord. Then Samuel sent all the people away, each one to his home. 26Saul also went to his home at Gibe-ah, and with him went men of valour whose hearts God had touched. 27But some worthless fellows said, "How can this man save us?" And they despised him, and brought him no present. But he held his peace.

At this point in the story, only Samuel and Saul knew that, under divine guidance (9:16), it had already been decided who should be Israel's first king. Everybody else knew only that Samuel had reluctantly consented to arrange that there should be a king; as far as the general populace was concerned, therefore, the second half of chapter 10 is the direct sequel to chapter 8. (It may indeed have been the immediate sequel to it in the source document used by the compiler and author of the books of Samuel.) Samuel called together a national assembly at Mizpah, reminded the people of their sinful demand for a king, and indicated that the time had now come when their request was to be granted. We might have expected him to produce Saul, present him to the people, and declare that God had designated him as their king; instead, Saul is kept completely in the background—in fact, he has hidden himself!—and a king is found by the drawing of lots.

To us, this seems a totally random method, by no means calculated to discover the best man for the job. Throughout the Old Testament, however, it is recognized that through the drawing of lots human choice is excluded, and so God is freely permitted to choose and to overrule. In the words of Samuel in verse 24, accordingly, God was seen to *choose* Saul by this mechanism, and the people in general, with only a few exceptions, gladly assented to the choice.

It certainly seems a startling coincidence that the one man

whom Samuel had already anointed should have been found by lottery from the thousands of eligible Israelites. Many scholars doubt the historicity of this passage; another approach might be to suppose that Samuel was able somehow to manipulate the lottery. Whatever explanation we may prefer, there is no doubt that the author of Samuel was convinced that God was fully behind the choice of Saul as king; God not only revealed it to Samuel beforehand but confirmed it now by the lottery. This conviction is all the more remarkable when we consider that within a very short space of time Saul was to be rejected by God (13:14). It is certain that all the traditions about Saul which were utilized by the author of Samuel were unanimous that God had chosen him and made him king.

From the very start, as verse 25 shows, the monarchy was constitutional: the kings would have both *rights and duties*. We might see in the document mentioned here a sort of bill of rights for the people, held in the very safe keeping of a sanctuary (that is the meaning of the phrase *before the Lord*). Here was an important brake upon the development of absolute power. Strictly speaking, *rights and duties* is used to translate a single word (*mishpat*) in Hebrew, which in other contexts might mean "custom" or "ways", as in 8:11. Such a document must however have been a legal one, not a mere description of the ways in which kings are prone to act; so "regulations" (NIV) is probably the nearest English equivalent to *mishpat*.

Whatever the natural tendencies and inclinations of an individual king, he had prescribed for him duties as well as privileges. Even in terms of Christian leadership, it is no bad thing that the *rights and duties* of the minister, priest or pastor should be clearly if flexibly defined; 1 Tim. 3 is worth consideration in this regard.

SAUL'S FIRST VICTORY

1 Samuel 11:1-15

[1]Then Nahash the Ammonite went up and besieged Jabesh-gilead; and all the men of Jabesh said to Nahash, "Make a treaty with us,

and we will serve you." [2]But Nahash the Ammonite said to them, "On this condition I will make a treaty with you, that I gouge out all your right eyes, and thus put disgrace upon all Israel." [3]The elders of Jabesh said to him, "Give us seven days respite that we may send messengers through all the territory of Israel. Then, if there is no one to save us, we will give ourselves up to you." [4]When the messengers came to Gibe-ah of Saul, they reported the matter in the ears of the people; and all the people wept aloud.

[5]Now Saul was coming from the field behind the oxen; and Saul said, "What ails the people, that they are weeping?" So they told him the tidings of the men of Jabesh. [6]And the spirit of God came mightily upon Saul when he heard these words, and his anger was greatly kindled. [7]He took a yoke of oxen, and cut them in pieces and sent them throughout all the territory of Israel by the hand of messengers, saying, "Whoever does not come out after Saul and Samuel, so shall it be done to his oxen!" Then the dread of the Lord fell upon the people, and they came out as one man. [8]When he mustered them at Bezek, the men of Israel were three hundred thousand, and the men of Judah thirty thousand. [9]And they said to the messengers who had come, "Thus shall you say to the men of Jabesh-gilead: 'Tomorrow, by the time the sun is hot, you shall have deliverance.'" When the messengers came and told the men of Jabesh, they were glad. [10]Therefore the men of Jabesh said, "Tomorrow we will give ourselves up to you, and you may do to us whatever seems good to you." [11]And on the morrow Saul put the people in three companies; and they came into the midst of the camp in the morning watch, and cut down the Ammonites until the heat of the day; and those who survived were scattered, so that no two of them were left together.

[12]Then the people said to Samuel, "Who is it that said, 'Shall Saul reign over us?' Bring the men, that we may put them to death." [13]But Saul said, "Not a man shall be put to death this day, for today the Lord has wrought deliverance in Israel." [14]Then Samuel said to the people, "Come, let us go to Gilgal and there renew the kingdom." [15]So all the people went to Gilgal, and there they made Saul king before the Lord in Gilgal. There they sacrificed peace offerings before the Lord, and there Saul and all the men of Israel rejoiced greatly.

It is evident from 10:27 that not everybody in Israel was willing at first to accept the new institution of a monarchy; chapter 11 tells how it came about that the whole nation rallied behind Saul. The chapter ends with a united Israel rejoicing in victory and in the gift of an able king.

The chapter begins with a reminder of the wider background. As can be seen in the book of Judges, Israel was subject to the inroads and depredations of a variety of tribes and peoples. The Philistines were the most threatening enemy, but others could apply severe pressure on a more local scale. The Ammonites were a small state in southern Transjordan (see Map 1), and the details given here show that they were bent on conquering the Israelite territory that lay to the north of them. If the Israelite city of Jabesh-gilead had fallen to them, Israel could well have lost the whole of her possessions east of the River Jordan.

Saul had evidently gone back to his farm at Gibeah, in no hurry to exert himself in Israel. So when the Ammonite attack on Jabesh took place, he had formed no standing army; he was no different, except for the proud title of king, from such men as Gideon or Samson in the book of Judges. He now showed that he was no *less* than a "judge"; like them, he had a powerful experience of *the spirit of God* within him, which transformed him into a real leader and commander of men. His dramatic and symbolic action (verse 7) was immediately effective throughout the whole of Israel, which after all was free to disregard his orders if it chose. The first thing that he commanded, then, was obedience; any leader must have an innate—or implanted—sense of authority, to which ordinary folk respond. Secondly, he commanded unity. Without unity, the Israelite tribes were relatively weak and at the mercy of other peoples in the vicinity; but numerically the Israelites could master any local enemy, even the Philistines, if only they were united and co-ordinated. Thirdly, Saul provided military leadership, taking command in the situation of battle against the Ammonites. The result of these three achievements by Saul was a swift and total victory.

By this means Saul proved that he really was a king, and his royal position was now ratified or *renewed*. We have in verses 12–15 the third stage and the third ceremony in the process of

Saul's acquisition of the status of king; the long-drawn-out process in itself indicates how disunited Israel had been and how important it was for Saul to be accepted by the whole nation. Good leadership can only be based on the stable foundation of willing and obedient followers.

A minor but not insignificant detail is Saul's generous treatment of his earlier critics (verse 13). Too many rulers in history have been merciless and vindictive towards opponents, and all the more so when they have had clear popular support for such brutality. But forgiveness is God's way, as the Lord's Prayer constantly reminds us—and it may also be the greater wisdom. The best way of eliminating enemies is to turn them into allies.

A REMINDER OF PAST EVENTS

1 Samuel 12:1–11

¹And Samuel said to all Israel, "Behold, I have hearkened to your voice in all that you have said to me, and have made a king over you. ²And now, behold, the king walks before you; and I am old and grey, and behold, my sons are with you; and I have walked before you from my youth until this day. ³Here I am; testify against me before the Lord and before his anointed. Whose ox have I taken? Or whose ass have I taken? Or whom have I defrauded? Whom have I oppressed? Or from whose hand have I taken a bribe to blind my eyes with it? Testify against me and I will restore it to you." ⁴They said, "You have not defrauded us or oppressed us or taken anything from any man's hand." ⁵And he said to them, "The Lord is witness against you, and his anointed is witness this day, that you have not found anything in my hand." And they said, "He is witness."

⁶And Samuel said to the people, "The Lord is witness, who appointed Moses and Aaron and brought your fathers up out of the land of Egypt. ⁷Now therefore stand still, that I may plead with you before the Lord concerning all the saving deeds of the Lord which he performed for you and for your fathers. ⁸When Jacob went into Egypt and the Egyptians oppressed them, then your fathers cried to the Lord and the Lord sent Moses and Aaron, who brought forth your fathers out of Egypt, and made them dwell in this place. ⁹But

they forgot the Lord their God; and he sold them into the hand of Sisera, commander of the army of Jabin king of Hazor, and into the hand of the Philistines, and into the hand of the king of Moab; and they fought against them. ¹⁰And they cried to the Lord, and said, 'We have sinned, because we have forsaken the Lord, and have served the Baals and the Ashtaroth; but now deliver us out of the hand of our enemies, and we will serve thee.' ¹¹And the Lord sent Jerubbaal and Barak, and Jephthah, and Samuel, and delivered you out of the hand of your enemies on every side; and you dwelt in safety."

Samuel's role was not yet finished, although he was now an old man (verse 2); but Saul's rise to be king meant that Samuel must relinquish some of the offices and functions which he had previously exercised—certainly military leadership and political rule, and no doubt also judicial functions. The administration and organization of the realm were now Saul's business.

(i) Samuel's first response was in effect a personal apologia, a defence of his past career (verses 1–5). We are not told the occasion on which he had the opportunity to present his challenging questions to *all Israel*, but we may judge that it was at some national ceremony. This may have been at one of the great festivals, when great crowds would go to one of the sanctuaries of Israel, just as Elkanah's family had gone to Shiloh every year (cp. 1:3). Equally, it may have been a more political occasion; there is much evidence to suggest that there were in Israel ceremonies of covenant renewal by the people, probably annually, and it is very likely that the king played an important role in them. The king, if so, would have been under obligation to show how far he had both adhered to and maintained the laws of the covenant. In this chapter it is not the king but Samuel who, on relinquishing political leadership, demands that the people acknowledge that his period of rule had been marked by justice and equity. Here, as in 8:11–18, a keyword is the verb *take*: if kingship was to be characterized by the tendency to take rather than to give, it was otherwise with the prophet. As he stepped down from high office, Samuel's hands were empty (verse 5). In these verses, then, we are given another portrait of good leadership, presented in terms of contrast.

(ii) Next Samuel offered a review of the nation's history (verses 6–11). In this respect too there is good reason to think that Samuel was following, or perhaps helping to establish, normal patterns of practice at such ceremonies. Many Old Testament figures would have agreed with the opinion that a nation which forgets its history will commit the same errors over and over again.

All reviews of history are necessarily selective. This one picks out three themes for Israel's consideration:

(a) God had consistently helped Israel in the vicissitudes of her history. His acts in history are summed up as *saving deeds* (verse 7). This fact ought to produce gratitude for the past and faith for the future: in the words of a well-known hymn, "We'll praise Him for all that is past, and trust Him for all that's to come."

(b) God had made himself responsible for providing leadership. The great national leaders of the past, from Moses to the judges, had all been chosen by God just when they were needed. (It is not impossible that Samuel named himself in verse 11, but perhaps *Samuel* is a slip of an ancient scribe's pen for "Samson".)

(c) Israel had all too often forgotten and neglected God; in particular, her history was stained by idolatry (verse 10). Here lay the cause of all her past problems, for God invariably punished disobedience on a national scale.

Human nature is apt to take the credit for successes and to find scapegoats for failures. Both attitudes are just as likely to be wrong. The Christian, at least, should always be thankful to God for every good thing in life, and quick to blame himself for the failures and failings which from time to time have marred his happiness and well-being.

FACING THE FUTURE

1 Samuel 12:12-25

[12]"And when you saw that Nahash the king of the Ammonites came against you, you said to me, 'No, but a king shall reign over us,' when the Lord your God was your king. [13]And now behold the king whom you have chosen, for whom you have asked; behold, the Lord has set a king over you. [14]If you will fear the Lord and serve him and hearken to his voice and not rebel against the commandment of the Lord, and if both you and the king who reigns over you will follow the Lord your God, it will be well; [15]but if you will not hearken to the voice of the Lord, but rebel against the commandment of the Lord, then the hand of the Lord will be against you and your king. [16]Now therefore stand still and see this great thing, which the Lord will do before your eyes. [17]Is it not wheat harvest today? I will call upon the Lord, that he may send thunder and rain; and you shall know and see that your wickedness is great, which you have done in the sight of the Lord, in asking for yourselves a king." [18]So Samuel called upon the Lord, and the Lord sent thunder and rain that day; and all the people greatly feared the Lord and Samuel.

[19]And all the people said to Samuel, "Pray for your servants to the Lord your God, that we may not die; for we have added to all our sins this evil, to ask for ourselves a king." [20]And Samuel said to the people, "Fear not; you have done all this evil, yet do not turn aside from following the Lord, but serve the Lord with all your heart; [21]and do not turn aside after vain things which cannot profit or save, for they are vain. [22]For the Lord will not cast away his people, for his great name's sake, because it has pleased the Lord to make you a people for himself. [23]Moreover as for me, far be it from me that I should sin against the Lord by ceasing to pray for you; and I will instruct you in the good and the right way. [24]Only fear the Lord, and serve him faithfully with all your heart; for consider what great things he has done for you. [25]But if you still do wickedly, you shall be swept away, both you and your king."

Samuel showed himself a true prophet when he brought the history lesson up to date in verses 12f. Israel could not claim that this generation was innocent of the disobedience to God which had characterized their ancestors. The recent demand for a king itself constituted a rejection of the rule of God. Here we find the same assessment of monarchy, or rather of the demand for a monarchy, as in chapter 8. The sequence of events is not quite the same, however, since chapter 8 describes the demand for a king at some earlier date than the attacks of the Ammonites (which are recorded in chapter 11); we could perhaps explain this by assuming that the Ammonite inroads were felt over a considerable period before they culminated in the siege of Jabesh-gilead. In any case, there is no reason to doubt the general statement that the Israelites' adoption of a monarchy was a direct response to foreign military pressures.

The question which remained unanswered was this. How did Israel now stand before God, who had after all permitted them to have a king and had indeed found a king for them? The answer is clearly and unambiguously stated in verses 14f. The nation had a choice: with its king it could now resolve to be obedient to God, or it could rebel against him. It is to be noted that the king and nation are viewed as standing together: both could obey or both could disobey. Today, especially in the West, we have a heightened sense of the individual and of individual responsibility; but it is as true as it ever was that a nation does indeed have a certain communal existence, which its leaders embody (whether they give a lead to their people or tend to follow their wishes). For instance, a nation may become embroiled in a foolish war; if so, there is a sense in which the whole of the nation must bear the responsibility, and certainly will have to share the sufferings involved.

A sign of *thunder and rain* was given (verse 18); such weather conditions are almost unheard of at the time of the *wheat harvest* in Palestine. The sign confirmed the truth of Samuel's words, and the people acknowledged that they had acted wrongly (verses 16-19). What, then, was the future to bring? Samuel again set two choices before them. Obedience to God's covenant was still open to them, and they could renounce idolatry if they were prepared to do so. On the other hand, disobedience was an option—a choice which would bring in its train exile and the loss of the very monarchy which they thought would give them victory. There is in verse 25 a glance forward to the Babylonian Exile of the sixth century B.C., when this twin disaster actually occurred.

But there were two good reasons for hope. (a) Israel not only had kings now—for good or ill—but also prophets, Samuel the first of them, who would serve the nation faithfully. They would do two things: they would intercede with God for their people, and they would clearly and unambiguously reveal God's will to the people (verse 23). (b) However fallible and forgetful Israel might be, God had himself chosen them for his own purposes, and he could never demean his own reputation by abandoning them (verse 22). So the message to them was *Fear not* (verse 20); despite past sins and present sinfulness the future offered much hope and promise.

PHILISTINE SUPREMACY

1 Samuel 13:1-7, 15(b)-23

¹Saul was ... years old when he began to reign; and he reigned ... and two years over Israel.

²Saul chose three thousand men of Israel; two thousand were with Saul in Michmash and the hill country of Bethel, and a thousand were with Jonathan in Gibe-ah of Benjamin; the rest of the people he sent home, every man to his tent. ³Jonathan defeated the garrison of the Philistines which was at Geba; and the Philistines heard of it. And Saul blew the trumpet throughout all the land, saying, "Let the Hebrews hear." ⁴And all Israel heard it said that Saul had defeated the garrison of the Philistines, and also that Israel had become odious to the Philistines. And the people were called out to join Saul at Gilgal.

⁵And the Philistines mustered to fight with Israel, thirty thousand chariots, and six thousand horsemen, and troops like the sand on the seashore in multitude; they came up and encamped in Michmash, to the east of Beth-aven. ⁶When the men of Israel saw that they were in straits (for the people were hard pressed), the people hid themselves in caves and in holes and in rocks and in tombs and in cisterns, ⁷or crossed the fords of the Jordan to the land

of Gad and Gilead. Saul was still at Gilgal, and all the people followed him trembling....

15And Saul numbered the people who were present with him, about six hundred men. 16And Saul, and Jonathan his son, and the people who were present with them, stayed in Geba of Benjamin; but the Philistines encamped in Michmash. 17And raiders came out of the camp of the Philistines in three companies; one company turned toward Ophrah, to the land of Shual, 18another company turned toward Beth-horon, and another company turned toward the border that looks down upon the valley of Zeboim toward the wilderness.

19Now there was no smith to be found throughout all the land of Israel; for the Philistines said, "Lest the Hebrews make themselves swords or spears"; 20but every one of the Israelites went down to the Philistines to sharpen his ploughshare, his mattock, his axe, or his sickle; 21and the charge was a pim for the ploughshares and for the mattocks, and a third of a shekel for sharpening the axes and for setting the goads. 22So on the day of the battle there was neither sword nor spear found in the hand of any of the people with Saul and Jonathan; but Saul and Jonathan his son had them. 23And the garrison of the Philistines went out to the pass of Michmash.

(*Note:* for commentary on verses 8–15a see the next section.)

The promises and warnings of chapter 12 provide the background to the whole reign of Saul, which is summarized in verse 1, in much the same way that later reigns are summarized in the books of Kings (see e.g. 1 Kings 15:1f., 9f.). Unfortunately two of the numbers have dropped out of the text, presumably because they became illegible in an early manuscript. We do not therefore know how long Saul was on the throne.

The first seven verses and the final part of the chapter (from the middle of verse 15), provide background of a different sort to the reign of Saul. Three aspects of the Philistine threat are important:

(i) *Their dominant presence.* It is clear from the narrative that the Philistines were free to march into Israelite territory when and where they chose. This time they marched to Michmash (see Map 2), in the very heart of Israelite territory, and no great distance from Saul's own hometown and capital, Gibeah. It is also clear that till now they had maintained a hold on Israel's territory by strategically-placed garrisons. The word translated *garrison* in verse 3 could mean "governor" (as the NEB renders it), but in any case the presence of a Philistine governor would demand a garrison to support and defend him and to enforce his authority, so the translation problem does not affect the issue.

(ii) *The size of their forces.* It is doubtful if the numbers listed in verse 5 are to be taken at face value; very probably the Hebrew word usually translated *thousand* here means a military "unit", perhaps a relatively small one. Even so, the Philistines could muster thirty units of chariots and six cavalry units, to say nothing of a vast array of infantry; against all this, Saul and his son Jonathan could muster no more than three infantry units altogether (verse 2). Evidently the Philistines already had a powerful standing army, but Israel, though a larger nation, was a nation of farmers with no regular troops at all. Proportionately, then, Israel was at a grave disadvantage.

(iii) *Their superior equipment.* Quite apart from the horses and chariots they possessed, which were comparable in effect with the tanks familiar to us in twentieth century warfare, the Philistines had far superior personal weapons, due to their foresight in gaining a monopoly in the trade of blacksmiths throughout the whole region (verses 19–22). Thus the Israelites faced a much bigger and better equipped army; how could they hope to win? Many of them despaired totally of victory (verses 6f.), understandably enough. It was Saul's fear of wholesale desertions that led him to take precipitate action; as it was, his army seems to have dwindled considerably, if one compares verse 2 with verse 15.

It is well known that Joseph Stalin once asked contemptuously, "The Pope! How many divisions has *he* got?" He made a serious mistake in thus underestimating the force of religious opinion, as even the most atheistic sociologist would acknowledge. Israel had an inner cohesion which gave her a strength which would ultimately bring about the defeat of the

Philistines; but in the present emergency, it took a real act of faith to believe in an immediate victory. Nevertheless victory was to be the outcome—not because of Israel's inner unity but because God was not on the side of the big battalions.

WHO RULED ISRAEL?

1 Samuel 13:8–15(a)

> [8]He waited seven days, the time appointed by Samuel; but Samuel did not come to Gilgal, and the people were scattering from him. [9]So Saul said, "Bring the burnt offering here to me, and the peace offerings." And he offered the burnt offering. [10]As soon as he had finished offering the burnt offering, behold, Samuel came; and Saul went out to meet him and salute him. [11]Samuel said, "What have you done?" And Saul said, "When I saw that the people were scattering from me, and that you did not come within the days appointed, and that the Philistines had mustered at Michmash, [12]I said, 'Now the Philistines will come down upon me at Gilgal, and I have not entreated the favour of the Lord'; so I forced myself, and offered the burnt offering." [13]And Samuel said to Saul, "You have done foolishly; you have not kept the commandment of the Lord your God, which he commanded you; for now the Lord would have established your kingdom over Israel for ever. [14]But now your kingdom shall not continue; the Lord has sought out a man after his own heart; and the Lord has appointed him to be prince over his people, because you have not kept what the Lord commanded you." [15]And Samuel arose, and went up from Gilgal to Gibe-ah of Benjamin.

In these hard-pressed circumstances, then, Saul was ready to give battle—but not before sacrifice had been offered to God. We too are familiar with the concept of national days of prayer, for instance, but as in chapter 4, we have to remember that in early Israel they were convinced that their wars were waged not only with God's guidance and protection, but indeed under his banner and for his purposes; he marched with them. The soldiers kept themselves in a holy state (see 21:4f.). So it was vital that proper sacrifices should be offered. If not, God's anger could be expected, and the troops were certain to be demoralized at the outset.

Samuel's instructions, given in 10:8, now became a matter of overriding importance. The text does not make it quite clear whether Samuel arrived slightly later than he had indicated, or whether he came along at the very last moment within the seven days he had stipulated. In any case, it is obvious that Saul was by then so anxious to hold his small army together and to embark on hostilities that he was unwilling to wait any longer for Samuel, and he took it upon himself to offer up the sacrifices. The result was an immediate argument between Israel's two leaders: Saul had been guilty of three faults:

(i) *Lack of faith.* In effect, he was trusting in the size of his army, small as it was; and perhaps too he was trusting in military strategy, planning in some way to wrest the initiative from the Philistine invaders. Yet Israel's only hope was in God.

(ii) *Abusing his office.* Saul was not a priest, and had no right as king to officiate in sacrificial rituals; in handing over the political leadership of Israel, Samuel had been careful to hold on to full spiritual and religious authority. Saul evidently believed that as king he could, at least in an emergency, seize and undertake any role he chose. There was a very important issue at stake here.

(iii) *Disobedience.* The objection to Saul's action which Samuel expressed was neither lack of faith nor abuse of the royal power, though both are implied, but disobedience to God. It is clear that to disobey Samuel was to disobey God, who gave his instructions through the prophet. Once again Saul was reminded that the *real* king of Israel was God, to whom Saul owed the same duty of obedience that his subjects owed to Saul. To do otherwise, said Samuel, was folly (verse 13); it was essential to the well-being of a nation that its rulers should be wise, whether through native ability or by heeding good counsel (whether from God or man). Saul had by a single act demonstrated his folly and thus his unfitness to rule; and without more ado Samuel predicted Saul's loss of the kingdom he had only just won (verse 14). Verse 14 gives the first allusion in 1 Samuel to David, though as yet it is indirect.

We are tempted to feel that Samuel's judgement was premature, and that Saul had some excuse for his conduct. However, much of the remainder of 1 Samuel will show that while Saul was a good soldier he was a poor king. The immediate denunciation of disobedience to God is intended as an object lesson to the nation and its leaders in later epochs. The only hope for Israel ultimately, a small and weak nation in the ancient Near East, was for God to control it absolutely. In the same way the Church, also in itself a weak institution, cannot hope to succeed unless its leadership is fully in touch with God and in harmony with him.

At one level, the question posed by this passage is this: who ruled Israel? At another level, the question is a more personal one: could Saul rule himself, or was he governed by circumstances? The latter is a question relevant to us all, however humble our position in society. How firm are our principles, how reliable are our good intentions, when circumstances or self-interest seem to point in a different direction?

VICTORY FOR ISRAEL

1 Samuel 14:1–23

[1]One day Jonathan the son of Saul said to the young man who bore his armour, "Come, let us go over to the Philistine garrison on yonder side." But he did not tell his father. [2]Saul was staying in the outskirts of Gibe-ah under the pomegranate tree which is at Migron; the people who were with him were about six hundred men, [3]and Ahijah the son of Ahitub, Ichabod's brother, son of Phinehas, son of Eli, the priest of the Lord in Shiloh, wearing an ephod. And the people did not know that Jonathan had gone. [4]In the pass, by which Jonathan sought to go over to the Philistine garrison, there was a rocky crag on the one side and a rocky crag on the other side; the name of the one was Bozez, and the name of the other Seneh. [5]The one crag rose on the north in front of Michmash, and the other on the south in front of Geba.

⁶And Jonathan said to the young man who bore his armour, "Come, let us go over to the garrison of these uncircumcised; it may be that the Lord will work for us; for nothing can hinder the Lord from saving by many or by few." ⁷And his armour-bearer said to him, "Do all that your mind inclines to; behold, I am with you, as is your mind so is mine." ⁸Then said Jonathan, "Behold, we will cross over to the men, and we will show ourselves to them. ⁹If they say to us, 'Wait until we come to you,' then we will stand still in our place, and we will not go up to them. ¹⁰But if they say, 'Come up to us,' then we will go up; for the Lord has given them into our hand. And this shall be the sign to us." ¹¹So both of them showed themselves to the garrison of the Philistines; and the Philistines said, "Look, Hebrews are coming out of the holes where they have hid themselves." ¹²And the men of the garrison hailed Jonathan and his armour-bearer, and said, "Come up to us, and we will show you a thing." And Jonathan said to his armour-bearer, "Come up after me; for the Lord has given them into the hand of Israel." ¹³Then Jonathan climbed up on his hands and feet, and his armour-bearer after him. And they fell before Jonathan, and his armour-bearer killed them after him; ¹⁴and that first slaughter, which Jonathan and his armour-bearer made, was of about twenty men within as it were half a furrow's length in an acre of land. ¹⁵And there was a panic in the camp, in the field, and among all the people; the garrison and even the raiders trembled; the earth quaked; and it became a very great panic.

¹⁶And the watchmen of Saul in Gibe-ah of Benjamin looked; and behold, the multitude was surging hither and thither. ¹⁷Then Saul said to the people who were with him, "Number and see who has gone from us." And when they had numbered, behold, Jonathan and his armour-bearer were not there. ¹⁸And Saul said to Ahijah, "Bring hither the ark of God." For the ark of God went at that time with the people of Israel. ¹⁹And while Saul was talking to the priest, the tumult in the camp of the Philistines increased more and more; and Saul said to the priest, "Withdraw your hand." ²⁰Then Saul and all the people who were with him rallied and went into the battle; and behold, every man's sword was against his fellow, and there was very great confusion. ²¹Now the Hebrews who had been with the Philistines before that time and who had gone up with them into the camp, even they also turned to be with the Israelites who were with Saul and Jonathan. ²²Likewise, when all the men of Israel who had hid themselves in the hill country of Ephraim heard that the Philistines were fleeing, they too followed hard after them in the

battle. 23So the Lord delivered Israel that day; and the battle passed
beyond Beth-aven.

Despite all the adverse circumstances, the first major
engagement between Saul and the Philistines resulted in an
Israelite victory. After Saul's misconduct in the matter of the
sacrifice, the narrator no doubt saw it as significant that Saul's
victory was really due to Jonathan; or rather, it was due to God,
who used Jonathan as his agent of victory. Saul is depicted
partly as out of touch and a puzzled man (verses 16f.) and partly
as indecisive or impetuous (verses 18f.), though by no means
without courage and determination (verse 20). Jonathan,
however, showed the sort of faith in God which his father had
lacked (verse 6). It seems as if he and his armour-bearer found a
very narrow point on the path through the ravine where they
were able to pick off a Philistine detachment one by one; the
rest of the Philistines then panicked, and panic turned into rout
at an earth-tremor (verse 15), a sure sign (they believed) that
God was fighting alongside Israel. The Philistine contempt and
sarcasm (verses 11f.) were grossly misplaced. The description of
them as *uncircumcised* was partly a matter of simple fact;
circumcision was normal practice not only among the Israelites
but many other ancient peoples, so that the Philistines seem to
have been noteworthy for not conforming to the custom.
However, the description came to have religious significance;
perhaps the English word "heathen" best conveys the effect of
the Hebrew word. Such godless infidels could not hope to
defeat the armies of the God of Israel.

Such a theology of warfare is impossible for us today. Even in
the Old Testament, indeed, no wars of Israel after the time of
David were classed as "holy" wars, waged under the banner of
Yahweh. It is as if God's sanction of warfare did not extend
beyond the rescue of an oppressed people in Egypt under Moses
and their rise to full independent nationhood under David. The
New Testament depicts the Christian struggle as a spiritual and
moral fight, not a national one: "We are not fighting against
human beings but against the wicked spiritual forces in the

heavenly world" (Eph. 6:12, *Good News Bible*). No New Testament writer issued a call to the Christian Church to embark on revolution against the oppressions of the Roman Empire. As Hans Küng has written, "No strategy of violence, but only one of non-violence, can be deduced from the example of Jesus Christ." But in the time of Saul and David, God's purposes for the world through Israel could only be brought to fruition if Israel were rescued from Philistine domination and permitted to develop into independent nationhood. Warfare was the only way. Warfare may at times, though very rarely, be the lesser of two evils.

A puzzling verse in this passage is verse 18: did Saul call for the sacred ark of the covenant, and if so why? According to the ancient Greek translation (the Septuagint), he called for the "ephod", not the ark, and many scholars think this is correct; the two nouns are rather similar in Hebrew and could have been confused by a scribe. The ephod was a priestly device by which the will of God could be discovered (see the comments on 14:41 in the next section); if Saul wanted to consult the ephod, he must have been puzzled by the situation and wanted to know what action he ought to take, but then made up his own mind rapidly (verses 19f.). The ark, on the other hand, was used to lead the armies into battle (cp. 4:3–11); but 7:2 rather suggests that the ark was never moved from Kiriath-jearim during many years. If this was an exceptional situation, then, Saul presumably intended to march in solemn and stately fashion into battle; but realizing the situation, he wisely wasted no time but at once set about the pursuit of the routed enemy.

Verse 23 sums up the significance of the battle. The pressure on central Israel was relieved, with good effects on Israelite morale and unity (verses 21f.). (The word *Hebrews* was apparently the Philistines' usual way of referring to Israelites.) Much warfare still lay in the future, but in this first battle of Saul's protracted struggle *the Lord delivered Israel*. It was not Saul who brought the victory; nor was it an enormous and irresistible Israelite army. A timid few can achieve miracles if God is with them, as Jonathan was aware (verse 6). So too the pitiful and frightened handful of disciples of Jesus went on to "turn the world upside down" (Acts 17:6).

SAUL IS OVERRULED

1 Samuel 14:24–46

24And the men of Israel were distressed that day; for Saul laid an oath on the people, saying, "Cursed be the man who eats food until it is evening and I am avenged on my enemies." So none of the people tasted food. 25And all the people came into the forest; and there was honey on the ground. 26And when the people entered the forest, behold, the honey was dropping, but no man put his hand to his mouth; for the people feared the oath. 27But Jonathan had not heard his father charge the people with the oath; so he put forth the tip of the staff that was in his hand, and dipped it in the honeycomb, and put his hand to his mouth; and his eyes became bright. 28Then one of the people said, "Your father strictly charged the people with an oath, saying, 'Cursed be the man who eats food this day.'" And the people were faint. 29Then Jonathan said, "My father has troubled the land; see how my eyes have become bright, because I tasted a little of this honey. 30How much better if the people had eaten freely today of the spoil of their enemies which they found; for now the slaughter among the Philistines has not been great."

31They struck down the Philistines that day from Michmash to Aijalon. And the people were very faint; 32the people flew upon the spoil, and took sheep and oxen and calves, and slew them on the ground; and the people ate them with the blood. 33Then they told Saul, "Behold, the people are sinning against the Lord, by eating with the blood." And he said, "You have dealt treacherously; roll a great stone to me here." 34And Saul said, "Disperse yourselves among the people, and say to them, 'Let every man bring his ox or his sheep, and slay them here, and eat; and do not sin against the Lord by eating with the blood.'" So every one of the people brought his ox with him that night, and slew them there. 35And Saul built an altar to the Lord; it was the first altar that he built to the Lord.

36Then Saul said, "Let us go down after the Philistines by night and despoil them until the morning light; let us not leave a man of them." And they said, "Do whatever seems good to you." But the priest said, "Let us draw near hither to God." 37And Saul inquired of

God, "Shall I go down after the Philistines? Wilt thou give them into the hand of Israel?" But he did not answer him that day. [38]And Saul said, "Come hither, all you leaders of the people; and know and see how this sin has arisen today. [39]For as the Lord lives who saves Israel, though it be in Jonathan my son, he shall surely die." But there was not a man among all the people that answered him. [40]Then he said to all Israel, "You shall be on one side, and I and Jonathan my son will be on the other side." And the people said to Saul, "Do what seems good to you." [41]Therefore Saul said, "O Lord God of Israel, why hast thou not answered thy servant this day? If this guilt is in me or in Jonathan my son, O Lord, God of Israel, give Urim; but if this guilt is in thy people Israel, give Thummim." And Jonathan and Saul were taken, but the people escaped. [42]Then Saul said, "Cast the lot between me and my son Jonathan." And Jonathan was taken.

[43]Then Saul said to Jonathan, "Tell me what you have done." And Jonathan told him, "I tasted a little honey with the tip of the staff that was in my hand; here I am, I will die." [44]And Saul said, "God do so to me and more also; you shall surely die, Jonathan." [45]Then the people said to Saul, "Shall Jonathan die, who has wrought this great victory in Israel? Far from it! As the Lord lives, there shall not one hair of his head fall to the ground; for he has wrought with God this day." So the people ransomed Jonathan, that he did not die. [46]Then Saul went up from pursuing the Philistines; and the Philistines went to their own place.

The victory, we now learn, was less complete than it might have been (see verse 30); and the fault was Saul's. Indeed, the victorious Israelite troops, far from being elated and full of vigour, are described as *distressed* (verse 24), for want of food. It is a commander-in-chief's duty to ensure adequate supplies for his troops, but Saul, who was acting as general as well as king, in effect did the very opposite, by banning his men from eating anything at all. His motives were good, no doubt, but the curse which he pronounced was unnecessary and foolish; the picture here is of a man struggling to do the right thing towards God but in fact out of touch with God and indeed with human nature and human needs as well. This is well illustrated in verses 31–35, where Saul is most careful to ensure that his men broke no religious laws; Israelite law banned the eating of meat with blood in it, cp. Lev. 19:26. Yet it was precisely the desperate hunger which he had caused them which led them into this breach of the law!

In verse 37 we find Saul taking the proper steps to ascertain God's will. It is implied that he called for a priest to use the *ephod*, a special garment which held two objects called respectively *Urim* and *Thummim* (see Exod. 28:30). We do not know what exactly these were nor how the device worked, but it is clear from verse 41 that specific answers could be given—or withheld, as in verse 37. The device is associated with the casting of lots in verse 42. Saul, then, set out to please and obey God first by maintaining his own solemn oath, even at the cost of his son's life, and secondly by ascertaining God's will in the most careful manner. But after all that, his own men defied and defeated him.

We cannot doubt that the narrator, like any modern reader, wholly approved of the fact that Jonathan's life was spared. The whole situation should never have arisen; the irony was that in the previous chapter Saul had disobeyed God of his own volition, but now, when he was determined to obey every religious propriety, he found himself frustrated from doing so. His fitness to rule thus comes into question once again; no man who causes his own subjects to overrule his decisions can be the ideal ruler. Saul is shown to be out of touch not only with God but with the Israelite army too.

Verse 46 may be simply factual, signalling the end of this particular battle; or we may take it as a comment on the whole passage, implying that due to Saul's less-than-sensible actions the Philistines escaped relatively lightly on this occasion. The latter interpretation can be supported by Jonathan's earlier comment, in verse 30. The story is an interesting example of the way in which God overrules in human affairs; Israel won a victory, because God had determined this in advance, but God allowed the victory to be diminished because of Saul's actions. The event, like so many in history, was double-edged.

SAUL'S ACHIEVEMENTS

1 Samuel 14:47-52

47When Saul had taken the kingship over Israel, he fought against all his enemies on every side, against Moab, against the Ammonites, against Edom, against the kings of Zobah, and against the Philistines; wherever he turned he put them to the worse. 48And he did valiantly, and smote the Amalekites, and delivered Israel out of the hands of those who plundered them.

49Now the sons of Saul were Jonathan, Ishvi, and Malchishua; and the names of his two daughters were these: the name of the first-born was Merab, and the name of the younger Michal; 50and the name of Saul's wife was Ahino-am the daughter of Ahima-az. And the name of the commander of his army was Abner the son of Ner, Saul's uncle; 51Kish was the father of Saul, and Ner the father of Abner was the son of Abiel.

52There was hard fighting against the Philistines all the days of Saul; and when Saul saw any strong man, or any valiant man, he attached him to himself.

The biblical writer does not wish the reader to get Saul's abilities and achievements out of perspective; in spite of some personal failings, Saul was certainly no failure as a soldier and general. In battle after battle, we now learn, he was successful, and Israel must have benefited enormously. Verse 47 briefly tells us that his enemies were not only Ammonites (as in chapter 11) and of course Philistines but several other peoples too who had shown hostility to Israel from time to time during the period of the judges. Moab and Edom were small neighbours of Ammon, in southern Transjordan; and Zobah was one of the Aramaean kingdoms further north (see Map 1). The Amalekites introduced in verse 48 were not invaders like the others but nomadic raiders, who inflicted great damage to isolated farms and farmers, especially on the southern borders of Israel. Their sole objective was plunder: we meet them again in chapters 15 and 30.

Verses 49–52 give us some details about Saul's family; his son Ishvi is probably the same as the "Ish-bosheth" of 2 Sam. 2:8ff. The list of names is informative, and the details appear to show the consolidation of Saul's position. With several sons and daughters he did not lack potential successors; nor did he lack capable soldiers who would support him through thick and thin. His own future, and that of his dynasty, seemed assured. Looking at the list of names from a different perspective, we might see all the individuals named here as obstacles standing between David and the throne.

Many of these individuals did in fact come to play a part in the story of David. Ish-bosheth and Abner together obstructed David's rule over the whole of Israel, but only for a limited period. Of the others, two in fact came to support David against Saul—Michal, who married David, and Jonathan, who was his best friend. So appearances were deceptive; Saul's position was not so solidly based as it seemed, and in the course of time. David was able to replace him as king of Israel. Moreover the standing army which was designed to give strength to Saul as well as to Israel was precisely the setting in which David rose to power and influence, as a high-ranking officer. Saul, then, was in full control of the nation of Israel; but he could not foresee the rise of a rival, nor his own family's attitudes to that rival, and above all he could not govern his own fate. Perhaps the moral is to be found in Prov. 27:1: "Do not boast about tomorrow, for you do not know what a day may bring forth."

SAUL AND THE AMALEKITES

1 Samuel 15:1–16

[1]And Samuel said to Saul. "The Lord sent me to anoint you king over his people Israel; now therefore hearken to the words of the Lord. [2]Thus says the Lord of hosts, 'I will punish what Amalek did to Israel in opposing them on the way, when they came up out of Egypt. [3]Now go and smite Amalek, and utterly destroy all that they have; do not spare them, but kill both man and woman, infant and suckling, ox and sheep, camel and ass.'"

⁴So Saul summoned the people, and numbered them in Telaim, two hundred thousand men on foot, and ten thousand men of Judah. ⁵And Saul came to the city of Amalek, and lay in wait in the valley. ⁶And Saul said to the Kenites, "Go, depart, go down from among the Amalekites, lest I destroy you with them; for you showed kindness to all the people of Israel when they came up out of Egypt." So the Kenites departed from among the Amalekites. ⁷And Saul defeated the Amalekites, from Havilah as far as Shur, which is east of Egypt. ⁸And he took Agag the king of the Amalekites alive, and utterly destroyed all the people with the edge of the sword. ⁹But Saul and the people spared Agag, and the best of the sheep and of the oxen and of the fatlings, and the lambs, and all that was good, and would not utterly destroy them; all that was despised and worthless they utterly destroyed.

¹⁰The word of the Lord came to Samuel: ¹¹"I repent that I have made Saul king; for he has turned back from following me, and has not performed my commandments." And Samuel was angry; and he cried to the Lord all night. ¹²And Samuel rose early to meet Saul in the morning; and it was told Samuel, "Saul came to Carmel, and behold, he set up a monument for himself and turned, and passed on, and went down to Gilgal." ¹³And Samuel came to Saul, and Saul said to him, "Blessed be you to the Lord; I have performed the commandment of the Lord." ¹⁴And Samuel said, "What then is this bleating of the sheep in my ears, and the lowing of the oxen which I hear?" ¹⁵Saul said, "They have brought them from the Amalekites; for the people spared the best of the sheep and of the oxen, to sacrifice to the Lord your God; and the rest we have utterly destroyed." ¹⁶Then Samuel said to Saul, "Stop! I will tell you what the Lord said to me this night." And he said to him, "Say on."

A campaign against the Amalekites was to be the occasion of a major clash between king and prophet; Ṣaul and Samuel were permanently estranged as a result of their quarrel (see verse 35). The difficulty for modern readers is that Samuel's instructions to the king strike us as extremely harsh, and we almost instinctively side with Saul in consequence; but it is clear that the biblical writer not only sides with Samuel but insists that Samuel was simply God's spokesman, so that Saul defied not Samuel but God. The chief problem for us concerns a custom that strikes us as barbaric and which we find difficult to understand in religious terms; this was the sacred vow to exterminate a whole people and all their belongings. Here, indeed, it was not a vow but a sacred command (verse 3). Israel was not alone in this practice—which, fortunately, was not all that frequently applied in ancient warfare.

It is only fair to recognize the background: Amalek's whole history, to which verse 2 alludes (making reference to Exod. 17:8-13 and Deut. 25:17ff.), was such that it was apparent that so long as one Amalekite remained alive, no Israelite, however peaceful, was safe in the south of the country. We must also be aware that there was a sort of sacrificial concept about the destruction envisaged; to the Israelite soldier, the Amalekites were not being brutally massacred but in some way being given to God. Nevertheless, as Christians we can only agree that the Israelites had yet much to learn about the character of God, and in humility we should admit that our descendants three thousand years in the future may well consider us very primitive and theologically naive. We can but obey God to the best of our ability and understanding, while always seeking to enlarge that understanding.

This chapter is one which raises wider issues for the modern Christian. It is one of a number of Old Testament passages which envisage warfare in terms of a sacred duty and operation—"holy war", as this phenomenon is commonly known. A key passage is Deut. 20. It is one thing for a nation which finds itself in a state of war to make it a matter of prayer and to seek divine guidance and deliverance, while sincerely attempting to find ways to peace and reconciliation; it is quite another to indulge in violent conflict in a spirit of self-righteousness, and it is sadly true that all too often in history Christians—among others—have justified brutality and naked aggression by the use of such Old Testament passages. Three points need to be made:

(i) The situation envisaged in most relevant chapters is basically defensive, not offensive; as a rule it concerns the right of a community or nation to defend themselves.

(ii) Many such passages are retrospective rather than

programmatic. In other words, Deut. 20 (for instance) is probably looking back on past history and recognizing the immense danger that Canaanite religion had posed to the Israelite faith in the true God. It is not really likely that the intention of such a chapter was to encourage and justify future wars.

(iii) In any case, we must take our guidance from the message of the whole Bible, not from single chapters taken out of historical context. Israel itself seems to have become aware that by no means all its wars were "holy"; and indeed the prophets taught that some invasions suffered by Israel were in a sense "holy war", a punishment sent by God upon his own people. Thus God's real enemy is not some specific nation or people, ancient or modern, but the forces of evil wherever they are to be found. The weapons to be used against these are equally spiritual and non-literal: see Eph. 6:10–17.

In any case, our sympathy for Saul is misplaced. His departure from Samuel's instructions is not fully explained, but it was certainly not inspired by humanitarian motives. Possibly he hoped that the life of the Amalekite king Agag would be ransomed, to the benefit of the royal exchequer. It is at least clear that he acquiesced when his men decided to take the best plunder for themselves, even though he tried to cover up when challenged by Samuel. His statement that the intention was to sacrifice the best livestock (verse 15) was a lie. Whether Saul himself was greedy for plunder is not quite clear, but at any rate he showed no humanitarian interest whatever. Above all, the care he had shown during the Philistine campaign (chapter 14) to obey God's commands to the last letter had now quite evaporated, perhaps in consequence of the mistakes he had made in that campaign.

Saul was probably not so much careless as arrogant, asserting his royal position. There was no good reason for him to overrule Samuel's instructions, but he chose to do so. As king, he would make up his own mind about what should be done. There is in all of us an inclination to resent being told what to do; but those in positions of authority and power are all the more reluctant to acknowledge anyone else's superior authority.

DISOBEDIENCE AND REJECTION

1 Samuel 15:17–35

¹⁷And Samuel said, "Though you are little in your own eyes, are you not the head of the tribes of Israel? The Lord anointed you king over Israel. ¹⁸And the Lord sent you on a mission, and said, 'Go, utterly destroy the sinners, the Amalekites, and fight against them until they are consumed.' ¹⁹Why then did you not obey the voice of the Lord? Why did you swoop on the spoil, and do what was evil in the sight of the Lord?" ²⁰And Saul said to Samuel, "I have obeyed the voice of the Lord, I have gone on the mission on which the Lord sent me, I have brought Agag the king of Amalek, and I have utterly destroyed the Amalekites. ²¹But the people took of the spoil, sheep and oxen, the best of the things devoted to destruction, to sacrifice to the Lord your God in Gilgal." ²²And Samuel said,

"Has the Lord as great delight in burnt offerings and sacrifices,
   as in obeying the voice of the Lord?
Behold, to obey is better than sacrifice,
   and to hearken than the fat of rams.
²³For rebellion is as the sin of divination,
   and stubbornness is as iniquity and idolatry.
Because you have rejected the word of the Lord,
   he has also rejected you from being king."

²⁴And Saul said to Samuel, "I have sinned; for I have transgressed the commandment of the Lord and your words, because I feared the people and obeyed their voice. ²⁵Now therefore, I pray, pardon my sin, and return with me, that I may worship the Lord." ²⁶And Samuel said to Saul, "I will not return with you; for you have rejected the word of the Lord, and the Lord has rejected you from being king over Israel." ²⁷As Samuel turned to go away, Saul laid hold upon the skirt of his robe, and it tore. ²⁸And Samuel said to him, "The Lord has torn the kingdom of Israel from you this day, and has given it to a neighbour of yours, who is better than you. ²⁹And also the Glory of Israel will not lie or repent; for he is not a man, that he should repent." ³⁰Then he said, "I have sinned; yet honour me now before the elders of my people and before Israel, and

return with me, that I may worship the Lord your God." ³¹So
Samuel turned back after Saul; and Saul worshipped the Lord.

³²Then Samuel said, "Bring here to me Agag the king of the
Amalekites." And Agag came to him cheerfully. Agag said, "Surely
the bitterness of death is past." ³³And Samuel said, "As your sword
has made women childless, so shall your mother be childless among
women." And Samuel hewed Agag in pieces before the Lord in
Gilgal.

³⁴Then Samuel went to Ramah; and Saul went up to his house in
Gibe-ah of Saul. ³⁵And Samuel did not see Saul again until the day
of his death, but Samuel grieved over Saul. And the Lord repented
that he had made Saul king over Israel.

The sequel was a fierce denunciation of Saul by the angry
prophet, who no longer recognized Saul as rightful king. By his
own wilful actions Saul had alienated himself not only from
Samuel but from the God who had singled him out to be king.
Saul would remain king, in fact, so long as he lived, but his
doom was sealed from this day on, and another man would gain
the crown (verse 28). As for Agag, he met his death after all;
verse 33 makes it clear that he was no innocent victim of a brutal
campaign.

The most important feature of Samuel's words is the poetic
oracle in verses 22f. Like later prophets too, Samuel contrasted
the inner reality of religion with its outward trappings. While all
too many kings of Israel (though not Saul) were guilty of
idolatry, an equally persistent fault was to maintain an
elaborate sacrificial system in Yahweh's honour, while allowing
or even fostering the wholesale breach of covenant laws. It is all
too human to suppose that, so long as we habitually attend
church and carry out our regular devotions, God will applaud
our piety and turn a blind eye to faults of character and
wrongful actions. The prophetic message is clear and
unequivocal: direct and wholehearted obedience to God's
commands is the only basis of a devout life. It is implied·that
God's commands have already been made known; this was and
is generally the case, even if in some specific situations we may
not always be sure of God's will for us. Obedience will of course

include, not eliminate, the proper outward observance of inward piety.

Verse 22, then, is the key verse of the chapter. It presents a challenge to everybody, great or small: *to obey is better than sacrifice.* Above all, however, it was intended as a challenge to Saul, and to all his successors on the throne of Israel and Judah. Kings are used to demanding obedience, not yielding it, and it goes against the grain for them to acknowledge the superiority of anyone else, even God himself. Besides, in practice obedience to him meant obedience to his prophets; *the word of God* which Saul *rejected* (verse 23) was the command issued to him by Samuel in verse 3. To some extent the history of the Israelite monarchy was a story of tension between king and prophet, in which the king had the political power but the prophet had the religious and moral authority. No amount of public religious observance and ceremony would allow the kings to turn a deaf ear to the prophets with impunity. Probably Saul himself was no hypocrite, but it must have been a temptation to some kings to gain a reputation for piety by lavish religious ceremonial, in order to hide the fact from the people at large that behind the scenes they were wilful, greedy and unjust. To such later kings the story of 1 Sam. 15 presents a solemn warning: disobedience to God resulted in loss of the kingship, sooner or later.

More than once this chapter states that God *repented* of making Saul king. This is the language of human analogy; as verse 29 plainly states, God is in reality no fallible human being who makes mistakes and is obliged to change his mind. Perhaps the best perspective for seeing God's dealings with men, especially in the Old Testament, is under the analogy of a chess game. God allows men such as Saul full freedom of choice and action; but he constantly responds to their moves, and will at appropriate times change his strategy, technique and approach. Saul is in some respects a foil for David; the wrong king shows up in better relief the right king. But Saul was no straw man, no automaton; God gave him the chance to prove himself a worthy king, and the failure was his own. Not till then did God "repent" and take steps to remove the kingship from him.

THE SECRET ANOINTING OF DAVID

1 Samuel 16:1–13

[1]The Lord said to Samuel, "How long will you grieve over Saul, seeing I have rejected him from being king over Israel? Fill your horn with oil, and go; I will send you to Jesse the Bethlehemite, for I have provided for myself a king among his sons." [2]And Samuel said, "How can I go? If Saul hears it, he will kill me." And the Lord said, "Take a heifer with you, and say, 'I have come to sacrifice to the Lord.' [3]And invite Jesse to the sacrifice, and I will show you what you shall do; and you shall anoint for me him whom I name to you." [4]Samuel did what the Lord commanded, and came to Bethlehem. The elders of the city came to meet him trembling, and said, "Do you come peaceably?" [5]And he said, "Peaceably; I have come to sacrifice to the Lord; consecrate yourselves, and come with me to the sacrifice." And he consecrated Jesse and his sons, and invited them to the sacrifice.

[6]When they came, he looked on Eliab and thought, "Surely the Lord's anointed is before him." [7]But the Lord said to Samuel, "Do not look on his appearance or on the height of his stature, because I have rejected him; for the Lord sees not as man sees; man looks on the outward appearance, but the Lord looks on the heart." [8]Then Jesse called Abinadab, and made him pass before Samuel. And he said, "Neither has the Lord chosen this one." [9]Then Jesse made Shammah pass by. And he said, "Neither has the Lord chosen this one." [10]And Jesse made seven of his sons pass before Samuel. And Samuel said to Jesse, "The Lord has not chosen these." [11]And Samuel said to Jesse, "Are all your sons here?" And he said, "There remains yet the youngest, but behold, he is keeping the sheep." And Samuel said to Jesse, "Send and fetch him; for we will not sit down till he comes here." [12]And he sent, and brought him in. Now he was ruddy, and had beautiful eyes, and was handsome. And the Lord said, "Arise, anoint him; for this is he." [13]Then Samuel took the horn of oil, and anointed him in the midst of his brothers; and the Spirit of the Lord came mightily upon David from that day forward. And Samuel rose up, and went to Ramah.

The irrevocable decision that Saul was rejected undermined his authority but by no means curbed his power. For Samuel to anoint another man was to the prophet himself an act of no little courage and to Saul an act of treason, if word of it ever reached him. It was therefore essential to have a cloak of secrecy to cover the operation. It is interesting to recall that Saul too had undergone a secret anointing ceremony (cp. 9:27–10:1), though for quite a different reason. In both cases the symbolic act marked out the man who was to be king; he did not become king immediately.

It is emphasized that the man who would in due course replace Saul was from start to finish God's choice. (i) To begin with, on this occasion there was no rebellious demand by Israelite elders; God might have decided to end the monarchy in Israel as abruptly as it had begun, but instead it was God's free decision to make another man king. (ii) He chose the tribe, too; Saul was of the tribe of Benjamin, but now the true kingship was to move to Judah, the important southern tribe. To an Israelite reader, the mention of Bethlehem made that point clear. (iii) He chose the family: it was to be that of Jesse. (iv) Finally, God chose the individual.

There is great narrative skill in the way that man after man comes before Samuel only to be rejected; and David, like Saul in 10:21f., was not easily found. The skill of the story-telling, however, must not blind us to the point implicit in the drama, namely that the least likely man, in human terms, was God's choice. "Many that are first will be last, and the last first", as Jesus expressed the principle (Mark 10:31). Nevertheless David was a good-looking man, like Saul before him; a winsome personality is an asset if not an essential to a great leader of men. David's eldest brother too had a very attractive appearance, but verse 7 makes the valid point that inward qualities are more important than any outward ones.

David, then, we may infer from verse 7, had both the outward appearance and the inward qualities which would make him a great king. Probably he was Israel's greatest king. His most important qualification for office is reserved till last: *the Spirit of the Lord came mightily upon David* (verse 13). So too had

Saul been equipped for royal position (10:9f. and 11:6). In the Old Testament the function of the Spirit of God is above all to equip a man with the highest possible ability, whether for battle, or royal office, or prophetic office. At this juncture, however, it is not important to say how this gift showed itself in David; what is important is that David received the gift, and held it in readiness for all his future career.

If the Spirit of God in the Old Testament tended to set special men apart from their fellows, in the New Testament we see the Holy Spirit given to *all* Christians. In both cases, however, the indwelling of the Spirit is not a possession to be hugged to oneself with pride but an enabling power for the benefit and service of others. Kingship was not meant as a gift to the individual, to feed his arrogance and vanity, but as a gift to the nation, to whom the king's duty was to act as shepherd. In English usage the term shepherd has more commonly been used as a metaphor for the Christian ministry; the Latin word *pastor* actually means "shepherd". In the whole of the ancient Near East, on the other hand, the word shepherd was very frequently applied to kings; see Ezek. 34 for an extended biblical use of the metaphor. Even outside Israel, then, the king was expected to lead, guide, protect and care for his subjects. Inside Israel David was specially equipped by God to fulfil such a role. The fact that he was already looking after sheep (verse 11) was not only literal but also symbolic. In much the same way, some of the disciples of Jesus were called from being fishermen to become "fishers of men" (cp. Mark 1:17). Even a humble and ordinary occupation may be the most appropriate place of training for a man or woman destined to achieve great things as a Christian leader.

DAVID AND SAUL MEET

1 Samuel 16:14–23

[14]Now the Spirit of the Lord departed from Saul, and an evil spirit from the Lord tormented him. [15]And Saul's servants said to him,

"Behold now, an evil spirit from God is tormenting you. [16]Let our lord now command your servants, who are before you, to seek out a man who is skilful in playing the lyre; and when the evil spirit from God is upon you, he will play it, and you will be well." [17]So Saul said to his servants, "Provide for me a man who can play well, and bring him to me." [18]One of the young men answered, "Behold, I have seen a son of Jesse the Bethlehemite, who is skilful in playing, a man of valour, a man of war, prudent in speech, and a man of good presence; and the Lord is with him." [19]Therefore Saul sent messengers to Jesse, and said, "Send me David your son, who is with the sheep." [20]And Jesse took an ass laden with bread, and a skin of wine and a kid, and sent them by David his son to Saul. [21]And David came to Saul, and entered his service. And Saul loved him greatly, and he became his armour-bearer. [22]And Saul sent to Jesse, saying, "Let David remain in my service, for he has found favour in my sight." [23]And whenever the evil spirit from God was upon Saul, David took the lyre and played it with his hand; so Saul was refreshed, and was well, and the evil spirit departed from him.

It is no coincidence that David's experience of receiving the Spirit of God is at once followed by Saul's loss of it. Saul's rejection by God necessarily meant that the special powers God had previously given to him were now withdrawn. Worse, he began to suffer from some affliction of the mind, which we should today describe in psychological terms; we cannot diagnose his condition accurately three thousand years later, but some of the symptoms—such as morbid suspicions and violent impulses—are mentioned in later narratives. The biblical writer for his part recognized that the same God who gives one man special powers and abilities permits another man (or in this case even the same man) to suffer from problems which enfeeble him. We are careful nowadays not to attribute every illness to the direct action of God (so too Jesus taught, cp. John 9:1ff.); yet God is sovereign, and he may well use illnesses to achieve his purposes. In this case, it was Saul's unhappy condition which first brought about David's arrival at the royal court—as a musician. But from the first other abilities were recognized in him, not least his potential as a soldier (see verse 18).

David's musical abilities, which later made him famous as the Psalmist, were an exceptional talent in a king; but all the other qualities noted by Saul's courtier in verse 18 were royal requisites. Saul had earlier displayed several of them, though perhaps he had never been particularly *prudent in speech*. The most important quality of all, however, was no intrinsic one, and was one no longer enjoyed by Saul: *the Lord was with him*. This means two things. First, it means an *inner experience*, the awareness of God's presence. Without such an experience no man can successfully lead God's people; but with such an awareness, a man is filled with confidence and courage. Secondly, the writer means that *other people* became aware that God was with David. The inner experience was translated into something visible to others. This too was important. The qualities of leadership must be apparent to other people or they are useless.

Even Saul, we discover, could not resist the winsome personality of his new courtier (verse 21). This point is important, since it shows that Saul's later hatred of David was pathological. The true leader can disarm even his rivals. Of course, at this early stage in their relationship Saul was blissfully unaware that David would become a rival. When he was still unprejudiced against David, then, Saul thought highly of him and was glad to receive help and service from him.

This story of how David first met Saul and how he came to the royal court makes two points. The first is that David did not engineer it. David was no ruthlessly ambitious man, determined to rise up the social ladder—any more than Saul himself had been (cp. chapter 9). David's hands were clean. The second point is that God overruled to bring David to court, through the sheer chance (as it seemed) that one of Saul's courtiers knew something about him and brought him to Saul's attention. So it was God, not David, who was responsible for the young man's first steps towards the throne.

GOLIATH'S CHALLENGE . .

1 Samuel 17:1-11

¹Now the Philistines gathered their armies for battle; and they were gathered at Socoh, which belongs to Judah, and encamped between Socoh and Azekah, in Ephes-dammim. ²And Saul and the men of Israel were gathered, and encamped in the valley of Elah, and drew up in line of battle against the Philistines. ³And the Philistines stood on the mountain on the one side, and Israel stood on the mountain on the other side, with a valley between them. ⁴And there came out from the camp of the Philistines a champion named Goliath, of Gath, whose height was six cubits and a span. ⁵He had a helmet of bronze on his head, and he was armed with a coat of mail, and the weight of the coat was five thousand shekels of bronze. ⁶And he had greaves of bronze upon his legs, and a javelin of bronze slung between his shoulders. ⁷And the shaft of his spear was like a weaver's beam, and his spear's head weighed six hundred shekels of iron; and his shield-bearer went before him. ⁸He stood and shouted to the ranks of Israel, "Why have you come out to draw up for battle? Am I not a Philistine, and are you not servants of Saul? Choose a man for yourselves, and let him come down to me. ⁹If he is able to fight with me and kill me, then we will be your servants; but if I prevail against him and kill him, then you shall be our servants and serve us." ¹⁰And the Philistine said, "I defy the ranks of Israel this day; give me a man, that we may fight together." ¹¹When Saul and all Israel heard these words of the Philistine, they were dismayed and greatly afraid.

What did it mean, in practical terms, that *the Spirit of the Lord departed from Saul* (16:14)? Another battle situation provides a quick and clear illustration. The Philistines again sent an invading army on to Israelite territory, and Saul was by now able to employ a regular army of his own to counter the Philistine manoeuvre (verses 1f.); but this time there was a new and frightening development, in that the enemy had a warrior of giant dimensions who threw out a challenge to which the Israelites were totally unable to respond. Nowadays warfare is of a very different character, and we are quite unfamiliar with such practices as single combat and representative combat. In Israel's world, however, warfare followed various codes of convention; and it would have been utterly humiliating for Israel to ignore or decline Goliath's challenge. Yet they could find nobody with the courage to confront the Philistine champion, and so a sort of stalemate ensued for about six weeks (verse 16).

It was a humiliating stalemate for Israel. One is inclined to wonder why Jonathan, whose bravery had been conspicuous at Michmash (cp. chapter 14), did not volunteer; or why Abner, the commander-in-chief, made no move to find a brawny Israelite soldier who might at least give Goliath some sort of challenge. The narrator, however, is not concerned with either Jonathan or Abner; his interest centres on the fact that Saul (who was himself a very tall man, cp. 9:2) was terrified—and all Israel with him (verse 11). Saul, then, had lost his earlier qualities of courage and leadership in battle, and as a result the whole army, Jonathan and Abner included, was demoralized. This was the practical result of Saul's loss of God's presence and God's Spirit, and it becomes clear that both were vital to the leadership of the nation, and indeed vital to the nation's welfare.

While Saul is an exceptional case, there is a general moral to be learned, namely that yesterday's leader is not necessarily today's leader. Christian leadership cannot depend on past successes, but must rest on continuing faith and on the constant renewal of the gifts of God. Indeed, the only leader who does not ultimately fail is "Jesus the pioneer and perfecter of our faith" who is "the same yesterday and today and for ever" (Heb. 12:2; 13:8).

... AND DAVID'S RESPONSE

1 Samuel 17:12–40

[12]Now David was the son of an Ephrathite of Bethlehem in Judah, named Jesse, who had eight sons. In the days of Saul the man was already old and advanced in years. [13]The three eldest sons of Jesse

had followed Saul to the battle; and the names of his three sons who went to the battle were Eliab the first-born, and next to him Abinadab, and the third Shammah. [14]David was the youngest; the three eldest followed Saul, [15]but David went back and forth from Saul to feed his father's sheep at Bethlehem. [16]For forty days the Philistine came forward and took his stand, morning and evening.

[17]And Jesse said to David his son, "Take for your brothers an ephah of this parched grain, and these ten loaves, and carry them quickly to the camp to your brothers; [18]also take these ten cheeses to the commander of their thousand. See how your brothers fare, and bring some token from them."

[19]Now Saul, and they, and all the men of Israel, were in the valley of Elah, fighting with the Philistines. [20]And David rose early in the morning, and left the sheep with a keeper, and took the provisions, and went, as Jesse had commanded him; and he came to the encampment as the host was going forth to the battle line, shouting the war cry. [21]And Israel and the Philistines drew up for battle, army against army. [22]And David left the things in charge of the keeper of the baggage, and ran to the ranks, and went and greeted his brothers. [23]As he talked with them, behold, the champion, the Philistine of Gath, Goliath by name, came up out of the ranks of the Philistines, and spoke the same words as before. And David heard him.

[24]All the men of Israel, when they saw the man, fled from him, and were much afraid. [25]And the men of Israel said, "Have you seen this man who has come up? Surely he has come up to defy Israel; and the man who kills him, the king will enrich with great riches, and will give him his daughter, and make his father's house free in Israel." [26]And David said to the men who stood by him, "What shall be done for the man who kills this Philistine, and takes away the reproach from Israel? For who is this uncircumcised Philistine, that he should defy the armies of the living God?" [27]And the people answered him in the same way, "So shall it be done to the man who kills him."

[28]Now Eliab his eldest brother heard when he spoke to the men; and Eliab's anger was kindled against David, and he said, "Why have you come down? And with whom have you left those few sheep in the wilderness? I know your presumption, and the evil of your heart; for you have come down to see the battle." [29]And David said, "What have I done now? Was it not but a word?" [30]And he turned away from him toward another, and spoke in the same way; and the people answered him again as before.

³¹When the words which David spoke were heard, they repeated them before Saul; and he sent for him. ³²And David said to Saul, "Let no man's heart fail because of him; your servant will go and fight with this Philistine." ³³And Saul said to David, "You are not able to go against this Philistine to fight with him; for you are but a youth, and he has been a man of war from his youth." ³⁴But David said to Saul, "Your servant used to keep sheep for his father; and when there came a lion, or a bear, and took a lamb from the flock, ³⁵I went after him and smote him and delivered it out of his mouth; and if he arose against me, I caught him by his beard, and smote him and killed him. ³⁶Your servant has killed both lions and bears; and this uncircumcised Philistine shall be like one of them, seeing he has defied the armies of the living God." ³⁷And David said, "The Lord who delivered me from the paw of the lion and from the paw of the bear, will deliver me from the hand of this Philistine." And Saul said to David, "Go, and the Lord be with you!" ³⁸Then Saul clothed David with his armour; he put a helmet of bronze on his head, and clothed him with a coat of mail. ³⁹And David girded his sword over his armour, and he tried in vain to go, for he was not used to them. Then David said to Saul, "I cannot go with these; for I am not used to them." And David put them off. ⁴⁰Then he took his staff in his hand, and chose five smooth stones from the brook, and put them in his shepherd's bag or wallet; his sling was in his hand, and he drew near to the Philistine.

This section of the chapter introduces David and his family as if for the first time; it contains no hint that Saul had met him before (apart from verse 15) and says nothing of any previous experience as a soldier. See verses 33–36, and contrast 16:18, 21. The only reasonable explanation is that at this point the biblical author has made use of a different source document, which presumably began its story of David with this account of his fight against Goliath. The author himself must have added verse 15, by way of explanation. It is possible that the correct sequence of events was that David was first a musician at court, then defeated Goliath, then became Saul's armour-bearer, and finally gained higher rank in Saul's army.

The document here utilized by the biblical author, then, omitted David's earlier history. By so doing, it heightened the dramatic effect of the story: David is the unknown man who saved the day for Israel, the shepherd who defeated an experienced soldier, the young lad who laid low a giant, and (18:18) the country boy who married the princess. It is unfortunate that in our rather sceptical times such a black-and-white picture strikes some readers as too good to be true, but it would be quite wrong to dismiss the story as a legend. An exploit such as this is needed to account for David's prodigious rise from obscurity to fame, acquiring a reputation which caused Saul to be jealous of him.

The heightening of the drama is from one point of view simply good story-telling; it is no wonder that the tale of David and Goliath is one of the best known and best loved Bible stories. There is more to it than just the narrator's art, however: several morals and theological points are made in the course of the narrative.

(i) The Philistine was defying God when he defied Israel— taunting God, in fact (verse 26). Such godless arrogance was bound to meet divine punishment eventually; and this recognition at once gave David a source of faith and courage.

(ii) David was already well able to protect his father's flocks from predators (verses 34f.). The present situation was no different in kind: the nation of Israel was the flock of God (a familiar biblical picture, cp. Ezek. 34 and John 10:14ff.) and Goliath was no more than a predator—very dangerous, of course, but no more so than wild animals. It is symbolically appropriate that David felled Goliath with a shepherd's weapons.

(iii) David did not underestimate the danger, but he saw it in the perspective of God's purposes and of God's previous goodness to him (verse 37).

(iv) There is probably symbolic meaning in David's rejection of Saul's armour: David's rise to the throne would be due entirely to God, and not at all to any benefits Saul might bestow on him.

(v) In the whole episode there is a lesson that God overruled to bring on to the scene the right man at the right time. It was not mere chance that put three of David's brothers on the battlefield, and that induced their father Jesse to send David with provisions for them. David's rise to prominence was foreordained, and so was Israel's deliverance by David from the Philistine threat.

DAVID'S VICTORY

1 Samuel 17:41–58

⁴¹And the Philistine came on and drew near to David, with his shield-bearer in front of him. ⁴²And when the Philistine looked, and saw David, he disdained him; for he was but a youth, ruddy and comely in appearance. ⁴³And the Philistine said to David, "Am I a dog, that you come to me with sticks?" And the Philistine cursed David by his gods. ⁴⁴The Philistine said to David, "Come to me, and I will give your flesh to the birds of the air and to the beasts of the field." ⁴⁵Then David said to the Philistine, "You come to me with a sword and with a spear and with a javelin; but I come to you in the name of the Lord of hosts, the God of the armies of Israel, whom you have defied. ⁴⁶This day the Lord will deliver you into my hand, and I will strike you down, and cut off your head; and I will give the dead bodies of the host of the Philistines this day to the birds of the air and to the wild beasts of the earth; that all the earth may know that there is a God in Israel, ⁴⁷and that all this assembly may know that the Lord saves not with sword and spear; for the battle is the Lord's and he will give you into our hand."

⁴⁸When the Philistine arose and came and drew near to meet David, David ran quickly toward the battle line to meet the Philistine. ⁴⁹And David put his hand in his bag and took out a stone, and slung it, and struck the Philistine on his forehead; the stone sank into his forehead, and he fell on his face to the ground.

⁵⁰So David prevailed over the Philistine with a sling and with a stone, and struck the Philistine, and killed him; there was no sword in the hand of David. ⁵¹Then David ran and stood over the Philistine, and took his sword and drew it out of its sheath, and killed him, and cut off his head with it. When the Philistines saw that

their champion was dead, they fled. ⁵²And the men of Israel and Judah rose with a shout and pursued the Philistines as far as Gath and the gates of Ekron, so that the wounded Philistines fell on the way from Sha-araim as far as Gath and Ekron. ⁵³And the Israelites came back from chasing the Philistines, and they plundered their camp. ⁵⁴And David took the head of the Philistine and brought it to Jerusalem; but he put his armour in his tent.

⁵⁵When Saul saw David go forth against the Philistine, he said to Abner, the commander of the army, "Abner, whose son is this youth?" And Abner said, "As your soul lives, O king, I cannot tell." ⁵⁶And the king said, "Inquire whose son the stripling is." ⁵⁷And as David returned from the slaughter of the Philistine, Abner took him, and brought him before Saul with the head of the Philistine in his hand. ⁵⁸And Saul said to him, "Whose son are you, young man?" And David answered, "I am the son of your servant Jesse the Bethlehemite."

When at last the two protagonists clashed, the contest was over in a moment; as all the world knows, it was David who won. The earliest readers too were completely familiar with the details before they read the story, so the narrative spends very little time on the actual contest; three verses are sufficient for that (verses 49ff.). The sequel was very important for Israel; the victory begun by the death of Goliath thrust the Philistines back into their own territory. Gath and Ekron (verse 52) were two of their five chief cities, lying on the coastal plain (see Map 2). A contrast may well be intended with 14:23, 46, where Saul's victory was not nearly so far-reaching; and also with 29:11, where the Philistines came right back into Israelite country, but only after David had been forced out of Saul's armies. At his very first battle, therefore, David achieved more than Saul ever did.

The battle details are given tersely and concisely. Considerably more space is given to the verbal battle (verses 41–47) which preceded the physical encounter. Goliath's words, expressing his contempt and indignation at the unlikely champion the Israelites had at last produced, are natural enough in the circumstances; but they were wrong in two respects. Once again, his arrogance and his self-confidence are very evident—the sort of pride that goes before a fall. Secondly, he spoke in the name of his gods (verse 43), which confirmed in David's eyes that this was not a fight between man and man but between the true God and false gods. David's response, accordingly, challenged precisely these points: his adversary's trust was totally misplaced, reposing as it did in his own prowess and fearsome weapons. David, by contrast, put his whole trust in the God of Israel; though it is important to note that this did not mean that he would fail to use his own weapons and the skill he had acquired in their use. As Cromwell is reputed to have said, "Put your trust in God . . . and keep your powder dry." There was an important lesson here for later Israel, confronted by "giant" nations such as Babylon; national courage comes from trust in the Almighty, though this must be coupled with diplomatic, political, and even military skills.

The final paragraph of the chapter again stresses how relatively unknown David was. The purpose of Saul's questions about him is not absolutely clear to us, but it was probably connected with his earlier promises to anyone who would defeat Goliath (verse 25); it became important to learn as much about David's background as possible, now that he was to become a prominent court figure and the king's son-in-law. The reader may be intended to detect the first stirrings of jealousy in Saul's mind as he realized that David had shown the courage that he himself had lacked, and that the whole army must be aware of it.

From the point of view of personalities, the story of David and Goliath marks a stage in the rise of David and the decline of Saul. From a national point of view, it is yet another instance of God's activity in looking after his people and meeting their needs. Both aspects are equally important; it was part of God's care for Israel that he should at the same time rescue them from Philistine domination and also provide the best leadership for them. David was already proving himself a true shepherd, saving his "flock" from the attacks of such "wild beasts" as the Philistine armies.

SUCCESS AND ENVY

1 Samuel 18:1–16

¹When he had finished speaking to Saul, the soul of Jonathan was knit to the soul of David, and Jonathan loved him as his own soul. ²And Saul took him that day, and would not let him return to his father's house. ³Then Jonathan made a covenant with David, because he loved him as his own soul. ⁴And Jonathan stripped himself of the robe that was upon him, and gave it to David, and his armour, and even his sword and his bow and his girdle. ⁵And David went out and was successful wherever Saul sent him; so that Saul set him over the men of war. And this was good in the sight of all the people and also in the sight of Saul's servants.

⁶As they were coming home, when David returned from slaying the Philistine, the women came out of all the cities of Israel, singing and dancing, to meet King Saul, with timbrels, with songs of joy, and with instruments of music. ⁷And the women sang to one another as they made merry,
"Saul has slain his thousands,
    and David his ten thousands."
⁸And Saul was very angry, and this saying displeased him; he said, "They have ascribed to David ten thousands, and to me they have ascribed thousands; and what more can he have but the kingdom?" ⁹And Saul eyed David from that day on.

¹⁰And on the morrow an evil spirit from God rushed upon Saul, and he raved within his house, while David was playing the lyre, as he did day by day. Saul had his spear in his hand; ¹¹and Saul cast the spear, for he thought, "I will pin David to the wall." But David evaded him twice.

¹²Saul was afraid of David, because the Lord was with him but had departed from Saul. ¹³So Saul removed him from his presence, and made him a commander of a thousand; and he went out and came in before the people. ¹⁴And David had success in all his undertakings; for the Lord was with him. ¹⁵And when Saul saw that he had great success, he stood in awe of him. ¹⁶But all Israel and Judah loved David; for he went out and came in before them.

In the rise of David we have a picture presented to us of the ideal, though not faultless, ruler. The events of chapter 17 have already demonstrated his unhesitating trust in God and his keen awareness of God's loving purposes for Israel, at a time when nobody else had this insight; his skill and leadership in battle is also prominent in chapter 17, and chapter 18 now puts it beyond doubt that David's military abilities were real and lasting: his defeat of Goliath was no flash in the pan.

This passage adds to these qualifications for leadership yet another one—a lovable character that won the hearts of everybody who knew him or knew of him. Verse 16 indicates that it was not just his own tribe, Judah, but the whole nation which admired his military leadership ("to go in and out" means to campaign). Probably the reference in this verse is primarily to the soldiers of Israel and Judah, while in verses 6f. it is noted how popular he was with the ordinary people, such as the womenfolk who did not of course march into battle. In verse 5 it is observed that there was no jealousy of him even at Saul's court; *Saul's servants* here are the leading men of the kingdom, his courtiers, who might well have been suspicious or resentful of one who could easily have been viewed as an upstart.

Most notable of all was the attitude of Jonathan, the crown prince. If anyone might have felt threatened by David's rise it was Jonathan, but he too fell under David's spell, unreservedly. Their friendship has become proverbial; nothing would ever shake the solemn covenant into which they entered. Here, however, the emphasis is not on Jonathan's loyalty, as yet untested, but on David's compelling charm. The crown prince himself welcomed the man who would one day displace him; it was symbolic that Jonathan himself clothed David in royal robes and insignia.

The only hostility to David came from Saul, whose loss of control is emphasized (verses 10ff.). He was not himself when on an impulse he attacked David. At the root of Saul's hostility lay envy. The women's song was not at all intended by them as a slight towards Saul. The Hebrew term *ten thousands* is not a precise figure, and "myriads" might be a better translation here; all that was meant was that Saul and David between them had accounted for very large numbers of the enemy. But it is easy to see why Saul resented the suggestion that David was at least his equal.

Altogether, then, David won over the whole populace, and overawed even the king (verse 15). In today's phraseology, he had immense charisma and was a born leader: but the biblical writer prefers to say that *the Lord was with him* (verse 14). Leadership, like any human talent, is God-given; and, as Saul well knew, it was a talent that could be taken away (verse 12). No talent can be taken for granted.

Envy and jealousy are all too powerful human emotions which can arise whenever someone is confronted with another person of greater abilities, possessions or reputation. The danger is perhaps all the greater when a younger person begins to rival or to overshadow an established leader. Saul gave way to such emotions; the outstanding biblical example of a man who had the humility to give way graciously is John the Baptist, cp. John 1:26f., 3:30. John was able to maintain a great reputation; Saul deteriorated to the point of failure and ignominy.

DAVID'S EXPLOITS

1 Samuel 18:17–30

17Then Saul said to David, "Here is my elder daughter Merab; I will give her to you for a wife; only be valiant for me and fight the Lord's battles." For Saul thought, "Let not my hand be upon him, but let the hand of the Philistines be upon him." 18And David said to Saul, "Who am I, and who are my kinsfolk, my father's family in Israel, that I should be son-in-law to the king?" 19But at the time when Merab, Saul's daughter, should have been given to David, she was given to Adri-el the Meholathite for a wife.

20Now Saul's daughter Michal loved David; and they told Saul, and the thing pleased him. 21Saul thought, "Let me give her to him, that she may be a snare for him, and that the hand of the Philistines may be against him." Therefore Saul said to David a second time, "You shall now be my son-in-law." 22And Saul commanded his servants, "Speak to David in private and say, 'Behold, the king has delight in you, and all his servants love you; now then become the king's son-in-law.'" 23And Saul's servants spoke those words in the ears of David. And David said, "Does it seem to you a little thing to become the king's son-in-law, seeing that I am a poor man and of no repute?" 24And the servants of Saul told him, "Thus and so did David speak." 25Then Saul said, "Thus shall you say to David, 'The king desires no marriage present except a hundred foreskins of the Philistines, that he may be avenged of the king's enemies.'" Now Saul thought to make David fall by the hand of the Philistines. 26And when his servants told David these words, it pleased David well to be the king's son-in-law. Before the time had expired, 27David arose and went, along with his men, and killed two hundred of the Philistines; and David brought their foreskins, which were given in full number to the king, that he might become the king's son-in-law. And Saul gave him his daughter Michal for a wife. 28But when Saul saw and knew that the Lord was with David, and that all Israel loved him, 29Saul was still more afraid of David. So Saul was David's enemy continually.

30Then the princes of the Philistines came out to battle, and as often as they came out David had more success than all the servants of Saul; so that his name was highly esteemed.

The same basic themes as in verses 1–16 continue through the chapter: David's attractive and winning personality, David's military prowess, and Saul's enmity towards him. All three motifs are seen to develop with the passage of time.

(i) The affection and devotion which David inspired in the whole nation are indicated in verse 28 (where the RSV translation with "all Israel" follows the Greek Septuagint rather than the Hebrew text). More specifically, Saul's own daughter Michal loved him, as verse 20 tells us (and also the Hebrew text of verse 28). The little episode recounted in verses 17ff. meant that although Saul had at first decided to encourage David's marriage to Merab, his elder daughter, presumably in order to honour the promise mentioned in 17:25, he later changed his mind, not wishing to give David the added glamour and power-base of a royal marriage. But his hopes of excluding David from the royal family were dashed by Michal's love for him, so the king changed his mind once more—perhaps a sign of his disturbed personality. Apart from its effects on Saul, Michal's love for David proved once again that nobody, not even inside the royal family, was proof against David's attractiveness.

(ii) David's further prowess in battle with the Philistines was directly connected with his marriage into the royal family. It was customary in Israel for a bridegroom to pay what is known as a "bride-price" to his prospective father-in-law, and a large payment, usually of precious metal or of livestock, would of course be appropriate in order to gain a royal bride. David's family was not wealthy (see verses 18 and 23), so Saul asked instead for the gory present of a hundred Philistine foreskins. The idea is reminiscent of scalping practices in the Indian wars in the United States of America; in this case the grisly trophies would not only prove that a hundred men had been killed but would also show that they were indeed Philistines (since other peoples in the region would have lost their foreskins by the practice of circumcision). At a time when the fighting with the Philistines probably consisted of border skirmishes rather than pitched battles, it would have been no quick and easy task to amass this *marriage present*; but David achieved twice what was asked of him! Thus Saul's hope that David would take one battle risk too many was thwarted. David survived, and emerged with an enhanced reputation as a soldier second to none (verse 30). At that time leadership of the nation required great military abilities; and David had them.

(iii) Saul's hostility, which had started in an impulsive fashion (verses 10f.), now became a constant factor in his relationship with the younger man (verse 29). There was no immediate total breach between them, and Saul's feelings ebbed and flowed, but from now on the overriding theme of the story of the two men was to be the fact of Saul's fear of David. We can sympathize to the extent that Saul rightly sensed that David would one day become king; but the narrative, here and in later chapters, makes it clear that David never took any direct action against Saul; and it was in no way to his discredit that he gained universal acceptance and admiration.

God's control over affairs could be seen in the fact that even Saul's hostile actions resulted in greater success and greater reputation for David. Events consistently proved that "the Lord was with David", cp. 16:18; 18:14.

SAUL'S HOSTILITY

1 Samuel 19:1-17

¹And Saul spoke to Jonathan his son **and** to all his servants, that they should kill David. But Jonathan, Saul's son, delighted much in David. ²And Jonathan told David, "Saul my father seeks to kill you; therefore take heed to yourself in the morning, stay in a secret place and hide yourself; ³and I will go out and stand beside my father in the field where you are, and I will speak to my father about you; and if I learn anything I will tell you." ⁴And Jonathan spoke well of David to Saul his father, and said to him, "Let not the king sin against his servant David; because he has not sinned against you, and because his deeds have been of good service to you; ⁵for he took his life in his hand and he slew the Philistine, and the Lord wrought a great victory for all Israel. You saw it, and rejoiced; why then will you sin against innocent blood by killing David without cause?" ⁶And Saul hearkened to the voice of Jonathan; Saul swore, "As the Lord lives, he shall not be put to death." ⁷And Jonathan called David, and Jonathan showed him all these things. And Jonathan brought David to Saul, and he was in his presence as before.

⁸And there was war again; and David went out and fought with the Philistines, and made a great slaughter among them, so that they fled before him. ⁹Then an evil spirit from the Lord came upon Saul, as he sat in his house with the spear in his hand; and David was playing the lyre. ¹⁰And Saul sought to pin David to the wall with the spear; but he eluded Saul, so that he struck the spear into the wall. And David fled, and escaped.

¹¹That night Saul sent messengers to David's house to watch him, that he might kill him in the morning. But Michal, David's wife, told him, "If you do not save your life tonight, tomorrow you will be killed." ¹²So Michal let David down through the window; and he fled away and escaped. ¹³ Michal took an image and laid it on the bed and put a pillow of goats' hair at its head, and covered it with the

clothes. ¹⁴And when Saul sent messengers to take David, she said, "He is sick." ¹⁵Then Saul sent the messengers to see David, saying, "Bring him up to me in the bed, that I may kill him." ¹⁶And when the messengers came in, behold, the image was in the bed, with the pillow of goats' hair at its head. ¹⁷Saul said to Michal, "Why have you deceived me thus, and let my enemy go, so that he has escaped?" And Michal answered Saul, "He said to me, 'Let me go; why should I kill you?'"

This passage tells of three episodes which illustrate Saul's hostility to David, and which also show how it came about that David was forced to leave the royal court. The story told in verses 8ff. is very like that in 18:10f. It may be that the same incident is being retold, perhaps because the author was using a different source document here, but it is by no means impossible that Saul succumbed to the same evil impulse more than once. Evidently Saul always had a spear at his side or in his hand; this spear figures in several later narratives. The temptation to use it must have been great at times. On this occasion it was sheer jealousy of David's military achievements which provoked the king.

In the first incident (verses 1-7) Saul's method was quite different: this was no sudden impulse but a cold-blooded plot to murder David, which involved several of his courtiers. In some ways this was a much more dangerous situation, since David could do little to protect himself against a stab in the back from any courtier who wanted to ingratiate himself with the king. It was Jonathan's loyalty and willingness to take firm action which saved David this time. There is dramatic irony in the fact that it was Jonathan, whom David would displace, who saved David's life. Note how Jonathan, and through him the biblical writer, emphasizes David's innocence of any disloyalty (verse 5).

If Saul acted by himself in verses 8ff., and with the secret collaboration of just a few courtiers in verses 1-7, we find him taking more overt action against David in verses 11-17. This time it was not Saul's son but his daughter, David's wife Michal, who saved the king-to-be. It took deceit and lies to achieve her aim, and the *image* of verse 13 rather suggests that she worshipped other gods beside Yahweh; but the narrator makes no moral comment on all this. An extreme situation demands extreme measures: the point is that David's life hung by a thread.

Two points emerge from this sorry tale. First, who can doubt that it was really God who preserved David's life? It was foreordained that David should be king of Israel, and no move of Saul's would be allowed to thwart the divine plan. Second, it is significant that the two persons who acted as God's agents to rescue David were Saul's own children, Jonathan and Michal. Their willingness to do so not only confirms the fact that David won all hearts but also testifies to David's innocence of any act of treason or sedition. If David had given Saul any genuine reason to attack him, he could not have expected Jonathan in particular to side with him against the king. David's departure from the court (verse 18), again, was no act of desertion; he could do nothing else.

DAVID'S FIRST ESCAPE FROM THE COURT

1 Samuel 19:18-24

18Now David fled and escaped, and he came to Samuel at Ramah, and told him all that Saul had done to him. And he and Samuel went and dwelt at Naioth. 19And it was told Saul, "Behold, David is at Naioth in Ramah." 20Then Saul sent messengers to take David; and when they saw the company of the prophets prophesying, and Samuel standing as head over them, the Spirit of God came upon the messengers of Saul, and they also prophesied. 21When it was told Saul, he sent other messengers, and they also prophesied. And Saul sent messengers again the third time, and they also prophesied. 22Then he himself went to Ramah, and came to the great well that is in Secu; and he asked, "Where are Samuel and David?" And one said, "Behold, they are at Naioth in Ramah." 23And he went from there to Naioth in Ramah; and the Spirit of God came upon him also, and as he went he prophesied, until he came to Naioth in Ramah. 24And he too stripped off his clothes, and he too prophesied before Samuel, and lay naked all that day and all that night. Hence it is said, "Is Saul also among the prophets?"

Whatever David's future might be, the stark political reality at this time was that within Israel's territory he was very much at Saul's mercy; Saul was king of a united Israel and his will was law. The abuse of power is one underlying aspect of the story of Saul and David, and is too an important theme in a study of actual leadership and ideal leadership. Israel's kings had, for good or ill, the power of life and death over their subjects—at least, if they could lay their hands on them!

It was natural enough for David to go first to Ramah, to consult Samuel. Samuel was not only a prophet who might advise David but also the previous leader of Israel whose political influence might possibly have afforded him some aid; however, in the event we find Samuel offering David neither counsel nor protection. As far as the latter goes, indeed, it is doubtful if Samuel now had anything except moral influence to exert in Israel.

Yet in a strange sense Samuel was able to bring David temporary relief from pursuit. This fourth episode in a chapter of narrow escapes reveals God himself as David's rescuer when all human aid failed. The method of deliverance seems very strange to us, though it was all of a piece with Saul's earlier history (cp. 10:9–12). In this context *prophesying* denotes an ecstatic state (the NEB uses the word "rapture" for it) in which those participating, probably with music and dancing, to some extent lost control over their actions. Certainly first Saul's men and eventually the king himself lost *all* control of their actions. No criticism whatever is implied of Samuel and the company of prophets which he superintended; but it is plain that Saul's actions were the object of scorn, as he lost all dignity.

It is generally true that it is possible for good and worthy religious experiences to turn gradually into something far less desirable—religious mania, bigotry, imbalance, etc. Experience must never be allowed to replace or displace a sincere desire to understand and to obey God's will, revealed to us in the Scriptures. "The fruit of the Spirit is love, joy, peace, patience, kindness, goodness, faithfulness, gentleness, self-control" (Gal. 5:22f.); and where these are conspicuous by their absence, all claims to possess the Spirit of God may justifiably be viewed with caution. As Jesus himself said, "You will know them by their fruits" (Matt. 7:16).

In Saul's case, it is easy to interpret his experience at Naioth as just part of his growing psychological disturbance; but it must not be forgotten not only that he had incurred God's anger previously but also that in all his attacks on David he was totally out of touch with God's will and heedless of it. These chapters never suggest that Saul was a helpless victim of circumstances, a mere plaything of the Almighty. He went to Naioth of his own free choice, in pursuit of an innocent man; if God there took away his self-control, it was not to harm Saul but to rescue David.

DAVID AND JONATHAN

1 Samuel 20:1–23

¹Then David fled from Naioth in Ramah, and came and said before Jonathan, "What have I done? What is my guilt? And what is my sin before your father, that he seeks my life?" ²And he said to him, "Far from it! You shall not die. Behold, my father does nothing either great or small without disclosing it to me; and why should my father hide this from me? It is not so." ³But David replied, "Your father knows well that I have found favour in your eyes; and he thinks, 'Let not Jonathan know this, lest he be grieved.' But truly, as the Lord lives and as your soul lives, there is but a step between me and death." ⁴Then said Jonathan to David, "Whatever you say, I will do for you." ⁵David said to Jonathan, "Behold, tomorrow is the new moon, and I should not fail to sit at table with the king; but let me go, that I may hide myself in the field till the third day at evening. ⁶If your father misses me at all, then say, 'David earnestly asked leave of me to run to Bethlehem his city; for there is a yearly sacrifice there for all the family.' ⁷If he says, 'Good!' it will be well with your servant; but if he is angry, then know that evil is determined by him.

⁸Therefore deal kindly with your servant, for you have brought your servant into a sacred covenant with you. But if there is guilt in me, slay me yourself; for why should you bring me to your father?" ⁹And Jonathan said, "Far be it from you! If I knew that it was determined by my father that evil should come upon you, would I not tell you?" ¹⁰Then said David to Jonathan, "Who will tell me if your father answers you roughly?" ¹¹And Jonathan said to David, "Come, let us go out into the field." So they both went out into the field.

¹²And Jonathan said to David, "The Lord, the God of Israel, be witness! When I have sounded my father, about this time tomorrow, or the third day, behold, if he is well disposed toward David, shall I not then send and disclose it to you? ¹³But should it please my father to do you harm, the Lord do so to Jonathan, and more also, if I do not disclose it to you, and send you away, that you may go in safety. May the Lord be with you, as he has been with my father. ¹⁴If I am still alive, show me the loyal love of the Lord, that I may not die; ¹⁵and do not cut off your loyalty from my house for ever. When the Lord cuts off every one of the enemies of David from the face of the earth, ¹⁶let not the name of Jonathan be cut off from the house of David. And may the Lord take vengeance on David's enemies." ¹⁷And Jonathan made David swear again by his love for him; for he loved him as he loved his own soul.

¹⁸Then Jonathan said to him, "Tomorrow is the new moon; and you will be missed, because your seat will be empty. ¹⁹And on the third day you will be greatly missed; then go to the place where you hid yourself when the matter was in hand, and remain beside yonder stone heap. ²⁰And I will shoot three arrows to the side of it, as though I shot at a mark. ²¹And behold, I will send the lad, saying, 'Go, find the arrows.' If I say to the lad, 'Look, the arrows are on this side of you, take them,' then you are to come, for, as the Lord lives, it is safe for you and there is no danger. ²²But if I say to the youth, 'Look, the arrows are beyond you,' then go; for the Lord has sent you away. ²³And as for the matter of which you and I have spoken, behold, the Lord is between you and me for ever."

After Saul's display of naked and murderous hostility to David in chapter 19, it comes as a surprise to find that Jonathan was unaware of the situation (verse 2), apparently thinking that the reconciliation he had effected (19:1–7) had been permanent. It is understandable, to be sure, that Saul might have hidden both his feelings and his actions from Jonathan in view of his son's deep attachment to David.

Much more surprising, on the other hand, is the repeated suggestion that after all that had happened David was expected to resume his seat at the royal table. The problem is perhaps to be explained by recourse once again to the author's use of separate source documents; or it may be that the events of these chapters are not recorded in strict chronological order. Otherwise we must assume a considerable interval in the middle of verse 1; one could speculate that Saul's experience at Naioth prompted a change of attitude which allowed David to return to court. (The first half of verse 1 could easily be attached to the previous chapter; chapter divisions were not introduced into the Old Testament until the Middle Ages.)

At any rate, the situation here described is evidently a turning-point in David's career; reasonably enough, he must find out once and for all what Saul's intentions towards him really were, and very naturally it is to Jonathan that he turned. Once again, the power that Saul wielded is implicit in the whole story; even Jonathan, crown prince though he was, had to be careful. The plan he concocted with David, in order to pass word to him, had two intentions. One, of course, was to allow David to avoid being seen, because of the danger to him. The other was to relieve Jonathan too of danger, namely the danger of being accused of treason and of conspiracy with an outlaw. Saul's power is also the background to the degree of deceit forced upon both David and Jonathan; once again the Bible does not rebuke their lies but uses the lies to illustrate and emphasize the peril in which they were placed.

The narrative centres round the loyal friendship between the two young men. It was not a friendship of mere sentiment and impulse but one of deep and lasting obligations. They had at the outset (18:3) made a "covenant", a solemn agreement governing their undertakings and obligations to each other. This degree of formality was perhaps due to the strange political relationship in which they found themselves; when we recall that both men, for different reasons, expected to be king one day, it is astonishing that they were not deadly enemies. At this stage it would have been easy for Jonathan to renege and have David eliminated as a rival; while at a later date David could have acted to destroy Jonathan's whole family. Both men, however, were bound by their promises.

Friendships are not normally cemented in a solicitor's office, so to speak; but true friendship always envisages lasting obligations, loyalty, and if need be personal self-sacrifice. Any friendship which is broken as soon as difficulties arise is not worthy of the name. "A friend loves at all times", says the proverb (Prov. 17:17), and Jonathan proved it.

Friendships are one of the most enriching of life's experiences: how poor is the man or woman who is friendless! Friends enrich life because they *give*, without counting the cost. Jonathan was a man who gave to David more than he received; and in doing so he showed how different he was from the typical king described in 8:11–17, whose sole function was to *take*. Life has its givers and its takers; Jonathan was supremely a giver—and David, though destined to become a king, persistently declined to take anything away from Saul. He patiently waited for God to give him the crown of Israel.

THE TEST OF FRIENDSHIP

1 Samuel 20:24–42

24So David hid himself in the field; and when the new moon came, the king sat down to eat food. 25The king sat upon his seat, as at other times, upon the seat by the wall; Jonathan sat opposite, and Abner sat by Saul's side, but David's place was empty.

26Yet Saul did not say anything that day; for he thought, "Something has befallen him; he is not clean, surely he is not clean." 27But on the second day, the morrow after the new moon, David's place was empty. And Saul said to Jonathan his son, "Why has not the son of Jesse come to the meal either yesterday or today?" 28Jonathan answered Saul, "David earnestly asked leave of me to go to Bethlehem; 29he said, 'Let me go; for our family holds a sacrifice in the city, and my brother has commanded me to be there. So now, if I have found favour in your eyes, let me get away, and see my brothers.' For this reason he has not come to the king's table."

³⁰Then Saul's anger was kindled against Jonathan, and he said to him, "You son of a perverse, rebellious woman, do I not know that you have chosen the son of Jesse to your own shame, and to the shame of your mother's nakedness? ³¹For as long as the son of Jesse lives upon the earth, neither you nor your kingdom shall be established. Therefore send and fetch him to me, for he shall surely die." ³²Then Jonathan answered Saul his father, "Why should he be put to death? What has he done?" ³³But Saul cast his spear at him to smite him; so Jonathan knew that his father was determined to put David to death. ³⁴And Jonathan rose from the table in fierce anger and ate no food the second day of the month, for he was grieved for David, because his father had disgraced him.

³⁵In the morning Jonathan went out into the field to the appointment with David, and with him a little lad. ³⁶And he said to his lad, "Run and find the arrows which I shoot." As the lad ran, he shot an arrow beyond him. ³⁷And when the lad came to the place of the arrow which Jonathan had shot, Jonathan called after the lad and said, "Is not the arrow beyond you?" ³⁸And Jonathan called after the lad, "Hurry, make haste, stay not." So Jonathan's lad gathered up the arrows, and came to his master. ³⁹But the lad knew nothing; only Jonathan and David knew the matter. ⁴⁰And Jonathan gave his weapons to his lad, and said to him, "Go and carry them to the city." ⁴¹And as soon as the lad had gone, David rose from beside the stone heap and fell on his face to the ground, and bowed three times; and they kissed one another, and wept with one another, until David recovered himself. ⁴²Then Jonathan said to David, "Go in peace, forasmuch as we have sworn both of us in the name of the Lord saying, 'The Lord shall be between me and you, and between my descendants and your descendants, for ever.'" And he rose and departed; and Jonathan went into the city.

The course of the story reveals something of Israelite court etiquette. On special occasions (such as the new moon, verse 24) courtiers were expected to dine with the king without fail, unless either there were good religious reasons for absence or else special permission had been given. Contact with a dead body, for instance, would render a man unfit, technically "unclean", and Saul at first assumed that such was the reason

for David's absence (verse 26). Special permission to absent
oneself, on the other hand, would be granted only by the king
himself or by the crown prince, who probably acted as palace
chamberlain. We may reasonably assume that Jonathan had
authority to give David such permission, and also that the
explanation given in verses 28f. was plausible—not that it was
true—and should have been acceptable to Saul.

Saul's immediate anger told Jonathan all he needed to know:
to keep a man at court was normally a sign of high honour, but
sometimes a king used the "honour" as a device to keep
somebody suspected of disloyalty under close observation.
Plainly, then, Saul's motives had recently been suspicion of
David, not honour to him. The harsh words and plain speaking,
too, revealed the depth and sincerity of Saul's feelings in the
matter. His hatred of David was by now deep-seated, no longer
just an occasional impulse. Saul's irrational mind is to be seen
in the fact that one moment he was complaining that Jonathan
was endangering his own kingdom, the next he all but killed
Jonathan himself!

Jonathan's utter loyalty towards David was expressed in
words and deeds, and provides a model of true friendship. In
the first place, he never doubted David for a moment; nothing
Saul might say would convince him that David deserved the
king's hostility. Then he was prepared to challenge what was
said against David, even at the risk of the king's anger—and, as
it turned out, at some risk to his own person. Jonathan was to
remain fully loyal to his father as well, but where Saul was
wrong, Jonathan showed no hesitation. He was also willing to
stand up for David's reputation publicly; if Saul's words
publicly disgraced David, Jonathan's refusal to stay at the royal
table that day was an equally public sign that he dissociated
himself from the king's attitude to his friend.

The irony of it is that what Saul said in verse 31 was in fact
true. While the biblical writer goes to considerable pains to
insist that David was never seditious, never disloyal to Saul, it
was still the fact that David would one day become king,
whereas Jonathan never would. However, Jonathan's loss of

the throne was in no way caused by David; from one point of view it was God's will to deprive Jonathan of royal position, and from another it was the Philistines who deprived him, since they killed him in battle on the same day as his father (cp. chapter 31). Jonathan was therefore perfectly right to deny the implications of Saul's remarks in verse 31.

Jonathan's final sign of loyal friendship, then, was to fulfil the sad task of getting word to David of his danger. He began by carrying out carefully the plans they had made; but in the end he changed the plan slightly, because otherwise the two friends would never have met. This was the end of their happy years of comradeship, and it was only fitting that they should meet briefly to express their affection and to say farewell. Jonathan's last words to David (verse 42), confirming what had been said earlier (verses 14ff.), hold the implication that he himself, unlike his father, was quite content for David to become king in due course. The biblical writer wants to establish beyond any reader's doubt that nobody, not even Jonathan, tried to obstruct David's rise to kingly position, with the single exception of Saul, who was a man of disturbed mind, fighting against God's will.

DAVID AT NOB

1 Samuel 21:1–10

¹Then came David to Nob to Ahimelech the priest; and Ahimelech came to meet David trembling, and said to him, "Why are you alone, and no one with you?" ²And David said to Ahimelech the priest, "The king has charged me with a matter, and said to me, 'Let no one know anything of the matter about which I send you, and with which I have charged you.' I have made an appointment with the young men for such and such a place. ³Now then, what have you at hand? Give me five loaves of bread, or whatever is here." ⁴And the priest answered David, "I have no common bread at hand, but there is holy bread; if only the young men have kept themselves from women." ⁵And David answered the priest, "Of a truth women have been kept from us as always when I go on an expedition; the vessels

of the young men are holy, even when it is a common journey; how much more today will their vessels be holy?" 6So the priest gave him the holy bread; for there was no bread there but the bread of the Presence, which is removed from before the Lord, to be replaced by hot bread on the day it is taken away.

7Now a certain man of the servants of Saul was there that day, detained before the Lord; his name was Doeg the Edomite, the chief of Saul's herdsmen.

8And David said to Ahimelech, "And have you not here a spear or a sword at hand? For I have brought neither my sword nor my weapons with me, because the king's business required haste." 9And the priest said, "The sword of Goliath the Philistine, whom you killed in the valley of Elah, behold, it is here wrapped in a cloth behind the ephod; if you will take that, take it, for there is none but that here." And David said, "There is none like that; give it to me."

10And David rose and fled that day from Saul, and went to Achish the king of Gath.

From now on David was a fugitive and an outlaw. At first he was very much on his own, and the two episodes in this chapter illustrate in different ways the extent of his difficulties. All the political and military strength lay in Saul's hands and there seemed little hope that David could escape for long. This first episode, at Nob, shows that not even at a sanctuary was there any asylum. David did not expect it or ask for it, and Ahimelech's fear (verse 1) tells its own tale. Had David been accused of homicide, under Israelite law and procedure he could have asked for protection (cp. Exod. 21:13), but as an outlaw it seemed that every man's hand was against him. By stressing all this the biblical author draws attention to two things. The first is that David was certainly no rebel; if at a later stage he gathered a band of men around him, at the point when he was harried from Saul's court he was entirely without support and supporters of any kind. His only friend was Jonathan, and he had no option but to remain at court (20:42). David instigated no rebellion whatever.

Secondly, the author means the reader to understand that God protected David, from beginning to end of his long period

on the run from Saul. God had destined him for the kingship
and no extremity would thwart God's plans.

David, for his part, would not have been human if he had not
been afraid. While at times the Old Testament describes God as
performing miracles to rescue his servants, as a rule God's plans
demand human co-operation. It was right and proper for David
to take what steps he could for his own preservation. Yet
undoubtedly the author intends the reader to find some fault
with David's behaviour at Nob, because David himself admitted some degree of failure (cp. 22:21f.). We may fairly fault him
on three counts:

(i) *Deceit.* At the start of the chapter David told Ahimelech a
lie, giving enough detail to allay the priest's suspicions.

(ii) *Selfishness.* In his concern for his own safety, he gave no
thought at all to the danger in which he was putting Ahimelech.
He recognized Doeg, and suspected that he would report to
Saul, but he still implicated the innocent priest.

(iii) *Lack of faith in God.* His self-centred deceit was quite
unnecessary, a sign that he did not look to God for help at this
critical juncture. His attitude at Nob stands in marked contrast
to his serene faith when confronting Goliath (chapter 17). Faith
is something to be exercised on a daily basis; yesterday's faith
by no means guarantees today's trust and fidelity.

David, then, was no plaster saint—far from it. Yet it is by no
means the main purpose of this passage to highlight his failings.
It is instructive that the only comment on this episode made by
our Lord himself was to justify David's use of sacred bread in
view of his desperate need for food (Mark 2:25f.). One must
never judge a man without taking account of his circumstances;
it is far too easy to sit in judgement on others from the security
of one's armchair. To portray the extremity of David's plight,
then, is the main purpose of the narrative.

Nob, where this incident took place, has not been mentioned
before. From the biblical data, it seems to have been very close
to Jerusalem, which was still in non-Israelite hands. Ahimelech
belonged to the family of Eli, so it seems that after the disasters
recorded in chapter 4 the survivors of this priestly family left

Shiloh and went south to Nob to continue their ministry to Israel. It is possible that the Shiloh sanctuary had been destroyed or desecrated by the Philistines. Shiloh was not intended to be the centre of Israelite worship; nor for that matter was Nob. The disasters that befell these two sanctuaries may well have paved the way for Jerusalem to become the repository of the ark of the covenant and the home of the Temple.

DAVID AT GATH

1 Samuel 21:11-15

> [11]And the servants of Achish said to him, "Is not this David the king of the land? Did they not sing to one another of him in dances,
>   'Saul has slain his thousands,
>   and David his ten thousands'?"
> [12]And David took these words to heart, and was much afraid of Achish the king of Gath. [13]So he changed his behaviour before them and feigned himself mad in their hands, and made marks on the doors of the gate, and let his spittle run down his beard. [14]Then said Achish to his servants, "Lo, you see the man is mad; why then have you brought him to me? [15]Do I lack madmen, that you have brought this fellow to play the madman in my presence? Shall this fellow come into my house?"

David's next step took him outside the borders of Israel. It is natural enough for outlaws to go into exile in some friendly or at any rate neutral territory. The difficulty was that David had already gained an enormous reputation as an Israelite soldier, especially against the Philistines, and the situation which developed at Gath, a major Philistine city, is not really surprising. It is evident that the song which had been adopted by Israelite women after David's victory over Goliath (cp. 18:7) was also only too well known to the Philistines—we may guess that they had heard it as a taunt-song on numerous occasions. Music knows no frontiers, it is said! On the other hand, the Philistine courtiers were not well informed when they claimed that David was *the king of the land*; their comment is however an interesting sidelight on Saul's dislike of the implications of the popular song.

Later on David returned to Gath, we are told in chapter 27, but by then he had many soldiers behind him, a fact which altered the circumstances considerably. It is clearly implied here that his life was in imminent danger; he certainly had reason to think it was, at any rate. Once again, therefore, he took refuge in deceit, pretending to be a madman. There were two motives behind this action. In the first place, the Philistines could be expected to relax once they knew that the man who had done them such damage in past battles was now insane; what harm could he do them in the future? Secondly, insanity was often believed in the ancient world to be an affliction of the gods, and it was customary to treat madmen as taboo if not holy, people who should not be harmed in any way. David's ruse was therefore quite clever and proved effective.

Orientals are to this day very impressed by examples of adroitness and trickery, and probably the earliest readers would have enjoyed this story, which not only proved David's astuteness but also a certain gullibility on the part of Achish. In all the episodes involving Achish, in fact, one gets the impression that he was too ingenuous and trusting for his own good. So it is quite likely that the narrator told this story partly to glorify David; a leader of men must be astute, quick to sum up a dangerous situation and quick to respond to it. The deceit practised by David is therefore treated as morally neutral, it would seem. It was one thing for David to deceive a priest of his own nation like Ahimelech; it was quite another for him to outwit a foreign king and an enemy of Israel.

We must on the other hand recognize that the New Testament teachings about truth and integrity place a higher standard before us. We are at liberty to apply this standard to David too, in which case the lesson is once again that David was driven to extremes by the danger in which he found himself through no fault of his own; and that his life hung by a thread once more. God allowed him to take the dangerous and foolish step of fleeing to the Philistines; God took care of him there and brought him safely back to Israelite soil.

Another lesson is that fear (verse 12) was the cause of David's deceit, both of Ahimelech and of Achish. Fear, like pride, is a destructive human trait, which can lead to a variety of wrongful actions. It is a basic human reaction to frightening circumstances, of course, but the Christian can overcome it by the depth of his trust in God, as many a Christian martyr has demonstrated.

DAVID'S SUPPORTERS

1 Samuel 22:1–10

[1]David departed from there and escaped to the cave of Adullam; and when his brothers and all his father's house heard it, they went down there to him. [2]And every one who was in distress, and every one who was in debt, and every one who was discontented, gathered to him; and he became captain over them. And there were with him about four hundred men.

[3]And David went from there to Mizpeh of Moab; and he said to the king of Moab, "Pray let my father and my mother stay with you, till I know what God will do for me." [4]And he left them with the king of Moab, and they stayed with him all the time that David was in the stronghold. [5]Then the prophet Gad said to David, "Do not remain in the stronghold; depart, and go into the land of Judah." So David departed, and went into the forest of Hereth.

[6]Now Saul heard that David was discovered, and the men who were with him. Saul was sitting at Gibe-ah, under the tamarisk tree on the height, with his spear in his hand, and all his servants were standing about him. [7]And Saul said to his servants who stood about him, "Hear now, you Benjaminites; will the son of Jesse give every one of you fields and vineyards, will he make you all commanders of thousands and commanders of hundreds, [8]that all of you have conspired against me? No one discloses to me when my son makes a league with the son of Jesse, none of you is sorry for me or discloses to me that my son has stirred up my servant against me, to lie in wait, as at this day." [9]Then answered Doeg the Edomite, who stood by the servants of Saul, "I saw the son of Jesse coming to Nob, to Ahimelech the son of Ahitub, [10]and he inquired of the Lord for him,

and gave him provisions, and gave him the sword of Goliath the Philistine."

David now moved to his native Judah, where he hoped that several factors might turn out to his advantage. His knowledge of the terrain could easily help him to elude his pursuers, and his fellow-tribesmen might be expected to give him some protection, perhaps being willing to hide him or to give him information about Saul's movements, or at least to turn a blind eye to his own movements. Events were to prove that too many hands were against him, but at least Judah was worth trying.

The developments outlined in verses 1f. were rather to be expected. Human nature alone would have made many of his own family and clan wish to support him; the family was a very vital and important unit in Israelite society. In any case, they were no doubt in considerable danger of Saul's deciding to attack them simply because they were related to David. As soon as his fellow-clansmen joined him, however, he became a natural focus for any dissidents in Judah and further afield. We are given no details of Saul's administration, but since he was the first king we may well assume that it was rather makeshift and far from perfect; many of those who came to David's headquarters no doubt had good reason to be *discontented*. In view of the large number of followers who joined him at Adullam, it is not surprising that David, with all his military experience, became their *captain*. This amounted to something of a military uprising, though for defensive, not offensive, purposes. David may have hoped to be allowed a small segment of Judah as an independent holding, similar to the later arrangement at Ziklag in Philistine territory (cp. 27:5f.).

Verses 3ff. again show that David was becoming much more important than a mere fugitive from justice. His parents, who in view of their age could not share the hardships of a roving life in the wilderness areas of Judah, moved to Moab, where they had relatives (as we learn from the book of Ruth); but they did so by special permission of the Moabite king, no less. David, then, was already beginning to embark on political negotiations and manoeuvres. The mention of the prophet Gad is equally significant; lone individuals did not have their own prophets. David is beginning to look like a king in some respects, though a king in exile. There is a contrast implied, too: Saul had lost all prophetic support, but David already has a prophet to advise him.

The loneliness of Saul's position is next highlighted, as the scene of the action returns to his court (verses 6–10). Here is the king, with all his very real power and with a full retinue of courtiers, and yet he feels isolated and at odds with them all. He was sure that Jonathan had actively conspired against him with David, and he accused the rest of a conspiracy of silence, if nothing worse. He had no hesitation in interpreting the news of David's small force of men as a rebellion in the making, and he evidently feared that David might be attempting to bribe his courtiers. His opening words constitute a rather pathetic appeal to them, in which he stressed that they were his own fellow-tribesmen, Benjaminites, and could expect no favours from a Judaean like David.

Here, then, is a sorry picture of a king deeply suspicious of his entire court. It is no ideal ruler who is unable to command, or believes he cannot, the loyalty of his own relatives and chosen men. Saul is seen as less and less of a king as the story proceeds.

The only man to respond to these unfair accusations was Doeg, no doubt hoping to gain a reward. The narrator gives us no direct assessment of Doeg the Edomite, but since in many periods of Israel's history the Israelites disliked the Edomites intensely, we may fairly assume that the writer expected the reader to be prejudiced against Doeg from the start. As far as facts go, he told the truth, but it was not the whole truth by any means; as a result Saul was embittered against Ahimelech before ever he had the chance to question him. Doeg's portrayal of Ahimelech gave substance to Saul's suspicions that there was rebellion afoot. His words are a prime example of the way in which malicious and self-seeking people will tell those in authority what they wish to hear rather than give an accurate and balanced account.

THE MASSACRE OF THE PRIESTS

1 Samuel 22:11–23

[11]Then the king sent to summon Ahimelech the priest, the son of Ahitub, and all his father's house, the priests who were at Nob; and all of them came to the king. [12]And Saul said, "Hear now, son of Ahitub." And he answered, "Here I am, my lord." [13]And Saul said to him, "Why have you conspired against me, you and the son of Jesse, in that you have given him bread and a sword, and have inquired of God for him, so that he has risen against me, to lie in wait, as at this day?" [14]Then Ahimelech answered the king, "And who among all your servants is so faithful as David, who is the king's son-in-law, and captain over your bodyguard, and honoured in your house? [15]Is today the first time that I have inquired of God for him? No! Let not the king impute anything to his servant or to all the house of my father; for your servant has known nothing of all this, much or little." [16]And the king said, "You shall surely die, Ahimelech, you and all your father's house." [17]And the king said to the guard who stood about him, "Turn and kill the priests of the Lord; because their hand also is with David, and they knew that he fled, and did not disclose it to me." But the servants of the king would not put forth their hand to fall upon the priests of the Lord. [18]Then the king said to Doeg, "You turn and fall upon the priests." And Doeg the Edomite turned and fell upon the priests, and he killed on that day eighty-five persons who wore the linen ephod. [19]And Nob, the city of the priests, he put to the sword; both men and women, children and sucklings, oxen, asses and sheep, he put to the sword.

[20]But one of the sons of Ahimelech the son of Ahitub, named Abiathar, escaped and fled after David. [21]And Abiathar told David that Saul had killed the priests of the Lord. [22]And David said to Abiathar, "I knew on that day, when Doeg the Edomite was there, that he would surely tell Saul. I have occasioned the death of all the persons of your father's house. [23]Stay with me, fear not; for he that seeks my life seeks your life; with me you shall be in safe-keeping."

The story of the tragedy at Nob offers a pen-portrait of four different men, and gives us no little insight into human nature. The man with the power, the man who gave orders for the massacre, was of course King Saul, but certain roles in the affair were played by David (as we have already seen), Doeg, and Ahimelech too. We may consider them in reverse order.

(i) *Ahimelech* had been a frightened man when David visited Nob (21:1), but when he found himself on trial for his life he proved to be a man of courage, integrity and honour. We could fault him only for his lack of tact. Lies might possibly have served him better—who knows?—but he admitted all the *actions* of which he stood accused, denying only the *motives*. A lesser man would have attacked David violently for his duplicity, but Ahimelech chose rather to challenge the king's whole attitude to David; perhaps he realized how desperate David had been. Here was a man, then, who put truth before everything else; and, as others have found, the cause of truth can give great moral courage in a crisis.

(ii) *Doeg* now showed himself in his true colours, a man without pity or compunction. Where Saul's other courtiers were understandably very unwilling to attack Ahimelech and the other priests, Doeg showed no hesitation. His single-minded devotion was not to duty nor to Saul, however, but to himself and his own interests. We do not hear more of him, but no doubt he was duly rewarded by Saul for all that he had done.

(iii) *David*, who had unwittingly begun the whole chapter of events which culminated in the massacre, was helpless to prevent it or to intervene. However, he did all that could be done in the circumstances. In the first place, he freely admitted his fault and accepted the blame; a lesser man would have put all the blame on Saul. Secondly, he gave a solemn undertaking to protect the lone survivor, Abiathar (verse 23). It is significant that when Abiathar fled from Nob he went to David's camp; in other words, he recognized that David had intended no harm to the priesthood, and was confident that David would look after him.

(iv) *Saul*, it goes without saying, was guilty of the grossest brutality and wanton bloodshed—destroying a whole town and its inhabitants because of a conspiracy that did not exist except in his own mind. Undoubtedly the whole story shows the extent to which his personality had disintegrated: the man who had formerly saved Israel from its enemies was now himself the worst enemy of Israel's religious establishment. We do not know whether the Philistines had harmed Shiloh, or if so, to what extent; we do know, in bloody detail, what happened to Nob. Saul's unfitness to rule is self-evident; the crown must pass to another man.

While Saul's actions were due to his morbid state of mind, they do nevertheless illustrate vividly the dangers of absolute power, and what is required in an ideal ruler. A king must be able to recognize the truth when he hears it (as Solomon did, cp 1 Kings 3:16–28). He must act with due restraint and control of his powers. He must promote justice; and if injustice has to be punished, he must not pronounce vindictive and brutal verdicts. Here Saul failed on every count.

Finally, the departure of Abiathar from Saul's kingdom to David's camp was in itself symbolic. David now had both a prophet and a priest in his retinue, whereas Saul now had neither; Samuel had rejected Saul, and Saul showed the supreme folly of rejecting the priesthood. There may have been priests at other sanctuaries who gave him some support, for all we know to the contrary, but Saul's actions at Nob must have alienated many of his citizens, certainly the more devout among them.

DAVID AND KEILAH

1 Samuel 23:1-14

¹Now they told David, "Behold, the Philistines are fighting against Keilah, and are robbing the threshing floors." ²Therefore David inquired of the Lord, "Shall I go and attack these Philistines?" And the Lord said to David, "Go and attack the Philistines and save Keilah." ³But David's men said to him, "Behold, we are afraid here in Judah; how much more then if we go to Keilah against the armies of the Philistines?" ⁴Then David inquired of the Lord again. And the Lord answered him, "Arise, go down to Keilah; for I will give the

Philistines into your hand." [5]And David and his men went to Keilah, and fought with the Philistines, and brought away their cattle, and made a great slaughter among them. So David delivered the inhabitants of Keilah.

[6]When Abiathar the son of Ahimelech fled to David to Keilah, he came down with an ephod in his hand. [7]Now it was told Saul that David had come to Keilah. And Saul said, "God has given him into my hand; for he has shut himself in by entering a town that has gates and bars." [8]And Saul summoned all the people to war, to go down to Keilah, to besiege David and his men. [9]David knew that Saul was plotting evil against him; and he said to Abiathar the priest, "Bring the ephod here." [10]Then said David, "O Lord, the God of Israel, thy servant has surely heard that Saul seeks to come to Keilah, to destroy the city on my account. [11]Will the men of Keilah surrender me into his hand? Will Saul come down, as thy servant has heard? O Lord, the God of Israel, I beseech thee, tell thy servant." And the Lord said, "He will come down." [12]Then said David, "Will the men of Keilah surrender me and my men into the hand of Saul?" And the Lord said, "They will surrender you." [13]Then David and his men, who were about six hundred, arose and departed from Keilah, and they went wherever they could go. When Saul was told that David had escaped from Keilah, he gave up the expedition. [14]And David remained in the strongholds in the wilderness, in the hill country of the Wilderness of Ziph. And Saul sought him every day, but God did not give him into his hand.

Saul remained very much in command of the situation and the events at Keilah proved that there were Israelites, even in David's native Judah, who were prepared to support the king loyally. Indeed, it must have been very difficult for a country town like Keilah to do anything but show loyalty to Saul: if a sacred town like Nob had been sacked simply on suspicion of showing sympathy to David, what hope was there of Keilah's escaping Saul's anger and vengeance if it refused to surrender the outlaw to him?

The Keilah episode illustrates David's whole dilemma during this period—a dilemma he was unable to solve, so that eventually he was forced to leave the country (chapter 27). While it gave David a measure of strength and protection to have a growing body of supporters (by now six hundred strong, verse 13), it also created major problems. A lone individual can hope to escape notice and to find just about enough food to keep alive in the more barren and uninhabited parts of southern Judah; but six hundred men could not be hidden for long, and they could not live off the land for long either. They had to keep on the move, both for safety and for provisions.

David, then, had insoluble problems to face; but he was not without resources. He had the services of both Gad the prophet and now Abiathar the priest to advise him; in other words, he could consult God himself, and he did not fail to do so. Saul had power but was bereft of guidance; in the long run he was bound to lose.

If David was guided by God to go to Keilah, however, why was the move a failure? The answer is that it was not really a failure. It is true that the people of Keilah proved unwilling to shelter David, but that was only part of the story; indeed, if they had tried to shelter him, Saul would have besieged the town (note his words in verse 7) and captured David when he broke into it. The more important aspect of the incident at Keilah was that David befriended and aided the town of his own free will and left again without exacting any payment or causing them any harm. Even if they were unable to show it, the citizens must have felt some gratitude; and thus David built up goodwill for the future. It would have been fatal to his cause if he had alienated his own fellow-tribesmen in Judah; he could not afford a second Nob. If the story of what happened at Keilah got around, it would have helped to counteract any ill reputation which the massacre at Nob had gained for David.

David demonstrated at Keilah that he put his fellow-citizens' interests before his own, and also that he was still an Israelite champion against the Philistines. With such a small force at his disposal, he could not have opposed a Philistine invading army—Saul must be left to cope with threats of that magnitude—but at Keilah the Philistines were not invading but simply mounting armed raids, to plunder and harass the Judaean people there.

Still under God's guidance, David got away again from Keilah just in time. He continued to elude Saul (verse 14), in spite of relentless pursuit, for the simple reason that God had no intention of letting Saul capture him.

A NARROW ESCAPE FOR DAVID

1 Samuel 23:15-29

[15]And David was afraid because Saul had come out to seek his life. David was in the Wilderness of Ziph at Horesh. [16]And Jonathan, Saul's son, rose, and went to David at Horesh, and strengthened his hand in God. [17]And he said to him, "Fear not; for the hand of Saul my father shall not find you; you shall be king over Israel, and I shall be next to you; Saul my father also knows this." [18]And the two of them made a covenant before the Lord; David remained at Horesh, and Jonathan went home.

[19]Then the Ziphites went up to Saul at Gibe-ah, saying, "Does not David hide among us in the strongholds at Horesh, on the hill of Hachilah, which is south of Jeshimon? [20]Now come down, O king, according to all your heart's desire to come down; and our part shall be to surrender him into the king's hand." [21]And Saul said, "May you be blessed by the Lord; for you have had compassion on me. [22]Go, make yet more sure; know and see the place where his haunt is, and who has seen him there; for it is told me that he is very cunning. [23]See therefore, and take note of all the lurking places where he hides, and come back to me with sure information. Then I will go with you; and if he is in the land, I will search him out among all the thousands of Judah." [24]And they arose, and went to Ziph ahead of Saul.

Now David and his men were in the wilderness of Maon, in the Arabah to the south of Jeshimon. [25]And Saul and his men went to seek him. And David was told; therefore he went down to the rock which is in the wilderness of Maon. And when Saul heard that, he pursued after David in the wilderness of Maon. [26]Saul went on one side of the mountain, and David and his men on the other side of the mountain; and David was making haste to get away from Saul, as Saul and his men were closing in upon David and his men to capture them, [27]when a messenger came to Saul, saying, "Make haste and come; for the Philistines have made a raid upon the land." [28]So Saul returned from pursuing after David, and went against the Philistines; therefore that place was called the Rock of Escape.

²⁹And David went up from there, and dwelt in the strongholds of En-gedi.

In this passage David moved eastwards from Keilah, till at Engedi (verse 29) he could go no further east; Engedi is on the shores of the Dead Sea (see Map 2). He was now in wild and rather barren country, with just a few towns here and there, one of them Ziph; and the story shows how precarious his position was, if ever the local population turned against him—as the people of Ziph did. No credit attaches to them for this betrayal; on the other hand we should probably not condemn them either. They could hardly appreciate that David was destined to be king, and they were doing no more than help the lawful authority to capture an outlaw. At least they could not be accused of putting tribal loyalties before national ones.

Jonathan and Saul present interesting contrasts in this passage. There is irony, and perhaps intentional humour as well, in the fact that while Saul and his whole army were unable to lay their hands on David, Jonathan had no difficulty, apparently, in contacting and conversing with his friend. In practical terms, one may guess that Jonathan was trusted by David, and allowed to "find" him. This is the last story about Jonathan in the book—the next we hear of him is his death, 31:2—and in this last conversation with David he abdicated his own claim to the throne; Saul, meanwhile, was trying to assert his grasp of the throne by eliminating his rival. Lastly, while Saul's actions were causing David alarm and fear, Jonathan's role was to encourage David; he came for no other reason.

The biblical writer uses this brief story about Jonathan to confirm to the reader the fact that nothing could prevent David from becoming king. It also emphasizes that David was no usurper; Jonathan himself, had he lived, would have willingly acknowledged David as king. Such an emphasis will have been important, to counteract a certain amount of propaganda against David, which seems to have circulated after David gained the throne.

The narrative about Saul's near-capture of David teaches the same lesson; however close he came to capturing David, Saul could not in the last resort thwart God's plans for him. On this occasion he would have succeeded but for the Philistines, we are told; so God used the Philistines to rescue David!

The political situation had developed into a rather complex three-cornered struggle: Saul viewed both David and the Philistines as his enemies, and no doubt the Philistines viewed both David and Saul as their enemies. David, for his part, treated the Philistines as enemies, but he had no desire to be Saul's adversary, and did his best to evade him, not to fight him; David wanted to do nothing that would alienate his own fellow-countrymen. It was in these circumstances that the Philistine raid took place (verse 27), forcing Saul to recognize that they were his chief adversary and to abandon for the time being his pursuit of David.

This event is a good illustration of the complexity and ambiguity of history: both those Israelites who were raided by the Philistines and also Saul and his soldiers will have failed to see the hand of God in the Philistine attack. It requires an act of faith to believe that God is overruling in human affairs; and very often his purpose can only be seen in retrospect. Not till David had become king will the Israelites as a whole have been able to interpret this Philistine raid in the same way that the biblical writer has done.

The event is also a good example of a typical biblical miracle. Many miracles were not supernatural events as such—a Philistine raid was, unhappily, an everyday affair—but the miracle lay in the timing of them. If the Philistines had attacked one day afterwards, David would have been captured and no doubt summarily executed by Saul. The raid happened just at the right time for David. Such an escape will have caused him deep gratitude to God and also strengthened his faith in God. To Saul, however, the same event was a sign, if he had the insight to recognize it, that God was not on his side in his relentless hostility to David. It is more likely, however, that he put all the blame on the Philistines for David's escape and made no attempt to see God's purpose in the sequence of events. He had mistakenly supposed that he could discern God's hand in David's entry into Keilah (verse 7). Saul, like the rest of us, was prone to wishful thinking, and it is typical of human nature to see God's hand where and when we choose to do so and to ignore it on other occasions.

A NARROW ESCAPE FOR SAUL

1 Samuel 24:1–22

[1]When Saul returned from following the Philistines, he was told, "Behold, David is in the wilderness of En-gedi." [2]Then Saul took three thousand chosen men out of all Israel, and went to seek David and his men in front of the Wildgoats' Rocks. [3]And he came to the sheepfolds by the way, where there was a cave; and Saul went in to relieve himself. Now David and his men were sitting in the innermost parts of the cave. [4]And the men of David said to him, "Here is the day of which the Lord said to you, 'Behold, I will give your enemy into your hand, and you shall do to him as it shall seem good to you.'" Then David arose and stealthily cut off the skirt of Saul's robe. [5]And afterward David's heart smote him, because he had cut off Saul's skirt. [6]He said to his men, "The Lord forbid that I should do this thing to my lord, the Lord's anointed, to put forth my hand against him, seeing he is the Lord's anointed." [7]So David persuaded his men with these words, and did not permit them to attack Saul. And Saul rose up and left the cave, and went upon his way.

[8]Afterward David also arose, and went out of the cave, and called after Saul, "My lord the king!" And when Saul looked behind him, David bowed with his face to the earth, and did obeisance. [9]And David said to Saul, "Why do you listen to the words of men who say, 'Behold, David seeks your hurt'? [10]Lo, this day your eyes have seen how the Lord gave you today into my hand in the cave; and some bade me kill you, but I spared you. I said, 'I will not put forth my hand against my lord; for he is the Lord's anointed.' [11]See, my father, see the skirt of your robe in my hand; for by the fact that I cut off the skirt of your robe, and did not kill you, you may know and see that there is no wrong or treason in my hands. I have not sinned against you, though you hunt my life to take it. [12]May the Lord

judge between me and you, may the Lord avenge me upon you; but my hand shall not be against you. [13]As the proverb of the ancients says, 'Out of the wicked comes forth wickedness'; but my hand shall not be against you. [14]After whom has the king of Israel come out? After whom do you pursue? After a dead dog! After a flea! [15]May the Lord therefore be judge, and give sentence between me and you, and see to it, and plead my cause, and deliver me from your hand."

[16]When David had finished speaking these words to Saul, Saul said, "Is this your voice, my son David?" And Saul lifted up his voice and wept. [17]He said to David, "You are more righteous than I; for you have repaid me good, whereas I have repaid you evil. [18]And you have declared this day how you have dealt well with me, in that you did not kill me when the Lord put me into your hands. [19]For if a man finds his enemy, will he let him go away safe? So may the Lord reward you with good for what you have done to me this day. [20]And now, behold, I know that you shall surely be king, and that the kingdom of Israel shall be established in your hand. [21]Swear to me therefore by the Lord that you will not cut off my descendants after me, and that you will not destroy my name out of my father's house." [22]And David swore this to Saul. Then Saul went home; but David and his men went up to the stronghold.

It was dramatic irony, to begin with, that David's narrow escape in the wilderness of Maon should be immediately followed by Saul's narrow excape near Engedi. More, it was a clear sign for those with eyes to see it that God was on David's side. There was this major difference: Saul had never had David in his hands, but now David was actually in a position to kill Saul. Saul would never have let such a chance slip; David could and did. It is true that Saul was then persuaded to abandon his pursuit of David (temporarily!), but that occurred only after the shock of finding that he owed David his life, and after David's challenging words to him. Basically we have a portrait of contrasting temperaments, Saul suspicious and vindictive but yet impulsive, David more deliberate, more magnanimous, and free from personal malice.

It is not made wholly clear why David cut off a piece of Saul's robe, nor why his conscience then troubled him. One possibility is that the loss of a piece of his robe would make the king look ridiculous. Another explanation is that David suddenly saw it as a symbolic action, like the episode in 15:27f.: to take a piece of the royal robe could be interpreted as a desire to steal from Saul the royal position. This explanation makes excellent sense in the context, because David went on to emphasize Saul's royal status (verse 6), while Saul presently admitted that David would indeed one day be king (verse 20). Royal status and the right of a king to his life are important themes of the chapter.

The brief argument between David and his men is of special interest. Both he and they believed that God had arranged matters so that Saul was at their mercy (verse 4); the disagreement was about what God wished them to do with Saul. David's men stressed that he was their *enemy*, so deserved to be killed; David must have been very tempted to listen to such arguments, but instead he chose to emphasize that Saul was *the Lord's anointed*, in other words the man whom God himself had given the special and privileged status of *king*. Both parties were of course right—Saul was both the king and David's personal enemy. Human nature all too often puts personal considerations first, but David showed not only mercy but also political insight in sparing Saul's life. The argument also highlights once again the ambiguity of history: God had put Saul at their mercy, but that allowed two very different options for action.

For David to confront Saul was the height of courage, needless to say, though he put himself in God's hands (verse 15). His argument was a clever and persuasive one. The fact that he had not attacked Saul now, when the piece of Saul's robe proved that he could easily have killed him, was in turn proof that he was not and never had been Saul's enemy. The *proverb* in verse 13 must mean that wicked people are unable to change their nature; if David really had been a rebel against Saul, he could not have resisted the chance to kill the king. His final argument in verse 14 was a tactful one, stressing his own insignificance and unimportance.

Saul's admission in verse 20 that David, far from being insignificant, would one day be king, is a surprising one. It is meant to show to the reader not only that Saul had his lucid, even clairvoyant, moments, but also that in a sense he gave his approval to David's succession to the throne. But Saul was not to be trusted for long; there was no suggestion that David ought to return to the royal court. The two men went their separate ways (verses 22).

DAVID'S ANGER WITH NABAL

1 Samuel 25:1–22

[1]Now Samuel died; and all Israel assembled and mourned for him, and they buried him in his house at Ramah.

Then David rose and went down to the wilderness of Paran. [2]And there was a man in Maon, whose business was in Carmel. The man was very rich; he had three thousand sheep and a thousand goats. He was shearing his sheep in Carmel. [3]Now the name of the man was Nabal, and the name of his wife Abigail. The woman was of good understanding and beautiful, but the man was churlish and ill-behaved; he was a Calebite. [4]David heard in the wilderness that Nabal was shearing his sheep. [5]So David sent ten young men; and David said to the young men, "Go up to Carmel, and go to Nabal, and greet him in my name. [6]And thus you shall salute him: 'Peace be to you, and peace be to your house, and peace be to all that you have. [7]I hear that you have shearers; now your shepherds have been with us, and we did them no harm, and they missed nothing, all the time they were in Carmel. [8]Ask your young men, and they will tell you. Therefore let my young men find favour in your eyes; for we come on a feast day. Pray, give whatever you have at hand to your servants and to your son David.'"

[9]When David's young men came, they said all this to Nabal in the name of David; and then they waited. [10]And Nabal answered David's servants, "Who is David? Who is the son of Jesse? There are many servants nowadays who are breaking away from their masters. [11]Shall I take my bread and my water and my meat that I have killed for my shearers, and give it to men who come from I do not know where?" [12]So David's young men turned away, and came back and told him all this. [13]And David said to his men, "Every man gird on his sword!" And every man of them girded on his sword; David also

girded on his sword; and about four hundred men went up after David, while two hundred remained with the baggage.

[14]But one of the young men told Abigail, Nabal's wife, "Behold, David sent messengers out of the wilderness to salute our master; and he railed at them. [15]Yet the men were very good to us, and we suffered no harm, and we did not miss anything when we were in the fields, as long as we went with them; [16]they were a wall to us both by night and by day, all the while we were with them keeping the sheep. [17]Now therefore know this and consider what you should do; for evil is determined against our master and against all his house, and he is so ill-natured that one cannot speak to him."

[18]Then Abigail made haste, and took two hundred loaves, and two skins of wine, and five sheep ready dressed, and five measures of parched grain, and a hundred clusters of raisins, and two hundred cakes of figs, and laid them on asses. [19]And she said to her young men, "Go on before me; behold, I come after you." But she did not tell her husband Nabal. [20]And as she rode on the ass, and came down under cover of the mountain, behold, David and his men came down toward her; and she met them. [21]Now David had said, "Surely in vain have I guarded all that this fellow has in the wilderness, so that nothing was missed of all that belonged to him; and he has returned me evil for good. [22]God do so to David and more also, if by morning I leave so much as one male of all who belong to him."

The death of Samuel (verse 1) marked the end of an era; it is doubtful if the news of it had any effect on David's movements in the south of Judah. *Paran* was far to the south, and the name should perhaps be corrected to "Maon", to provide a link with verse 2. The ancient Greek translation known as the Septuagint has the name Maon. (See Map 2).

The chapter as a whole is concerned with a rich farmer called Nabal and his wife Abigail, and with their relations with David. The beginning of the story shows very vividly the sort of dilemma in which David found himself, as he endeavoured to get adequate provision for his large band of men. Some modern writers have accused David of working a "protection racket", and compare his actions with those of criminals who extort money from shopkeepers on the pretext of "protecting" them, in reality threatening to damage the shops if the money is not

paid. It is true that David's men did provide unsolicited
protection for Nabal's shepherds and herdsmen, and that when
Nabal refused to give David's men any provisions David set out
to attack him (verses 21f.). However, there the similarities end.
David was an outlaw but no criminal, and the people of Judah
were his own folk, so the protection he offered them—from
raiders like Amalekites and Philistines, or from occasional wild
animals—was freely given in the hope of a generous response in
terms of food, not cash. Demands with menaces would have
been quite fatal to his cause, in fact, alienating the only people
who might offer any help. It is clear from the story that the
Nabal episode was far from typical. It is emphasized that Nabal
was exceptionally rude and hostile, and it is implied that even so
David's angry decision to attack him was hasty and ill-advised.

It is important to assess Nabal's actions in the light of the
culture of the time. Hospitality was and is an accepted
obligation in the East; Jesus too had sharp words for a man
whose hospitality was mean and grudging, cp. Luke 7:44–47.
Besides, sheep-shearing time was rather like our harvest
festivals, a time when generosity and giving were the order of
the day, as at Christmas time in Christian countries and
communities. Nabal, then, was defying all the normal
conventions. We cannot even find an excuse for him on the
ground that he was a loyal supporter of Saul, in spite of his
sneer at David in verse 10. He was no political foe of David; he
was simply a Scrooge. He was also a stubborn and ill-natured
man, whom nobody could reason with (verse 17).

Even so, David's impetuous action in giving orders to kill
Nabal and his entire family was not only morally wrong but
would also have been disastrous for David's cause. As it was,
his fellow-Judaeans were rather neutral towards him, as the
reactions of Keilah and Ziph (chapter 23) have already shown.
One violent attack by David on a well-known Judaean citizen
would almost certainly have cost him the throne, and might
well have led to his instant betrayal to Saul. So prudence as well
as morality suggested that David should have swallowed the
insults. Anger, however justifiable, nearly always leads to

overreaction. The Sermon on the Mount reminds us sharply that anger and murder are but a step apart (Matt. 5:21f.).

The only hope of averting the danger lay with Abigail, whose generous provision (verse 18) would at once do something to remedy her husband's refusal to provide anything at all.

ABIGAIL'S WISDOM AND ITS RESULTS

1 Samuel 25:23-44

[23]When Abigail saw David, she made haste, and alighted from the ass, and fell before David on her face, and bowed to the ground. [24]She fell at his feet and said, "Upon me alone, my lord, be the guilt; pray let your handmaid speak in your ears, and hear the words of your handmaid. [25]Let not my lord regard this ill-natured fellow, Nabal; for as his name is, so is he; Nabal is his name, and folly is with him; but I your handmaid did not see the young men of my lord, whom you sent. [26]Now then, my lord, as the Lord lives, and as your soul lives, seeing the Lord has restrained you from bloodguilt, and from taking vengeance with your own hand, now then let your enemies and those who seek to do evil to my lord be as Nabal. [27]And now let this present which your servant has brought to my lord be given to the young men who follow my lord. [28]Pray forgive the trespass of your handmaid; for the Lord will certainly make my lord a sure house, because my lord is fighting the battles of the Lord; and evil shall not be found in you so long as you live. [29]If men rise up to pursue you and to seek your life, the life of my lord shall be bound in the bundle of the living in the care of the Lord your God; and the lives of your enemies he shall sling out as from the hollow of a sling. [30]And when the Lord has done to my lord according to all the good that he has spoken concerning you, and has appointed you prince over Israel, [31]my lord shall have no cause of grief, or pangs of conscience for having shed blood without cause or for my lord taking vengeance himself. And when the Lord has dealt well with my lord, then remember your handmaid."

[32]And David said to Abigail, "Blessed be the Lord, the God of Israel, who sent you this day to meet me! [33]Blessed be your discretion, and blessed be you, who have kept me this day from bloodguilt and from avenging myself with my own hand! [34]For as

surely as the Lord the God of Israel lives, who has restrained me from hurting you, unless you had made haste and come to meet me, truly by morning there had not been left to Nabal so much as one male." [35]Then David received from her hand what she had brought him; and he said to her, "Go up in peace to your house; see, I have hearkened to your voice, and I have granted your petition."

[36]And Abigail came to Nabal; and, lo, he was holding a feast in his house, like the feast of a king. And Nabal's heart was merry within him, for he was very drunk; so she told him nothing at all until the morning light. [37]And in the morning, when the wine had gone out of Nabal, his wife told him these things, and his heart died within him, and he became as a stone. [38]And about ten days later the Lord smote Nabal; and he died.

[39]When David heard that Nabal was dead, he said, "Blessed be the Lord who has avenged the insult I received at the hand of Nabal, and has kept back his servant from evil; the Lord has returned the evil-doing of Nabal upon his own head." Then David sent and wooed Abigail, to make her his wife. [40]And when the servants of David came to Abigail at Carmel, they said to her, "David has sent us to you to take you to him as his wife." [41]And she rose and bowed with her face to the ground, and said, "Behold, your handmaid is a servant to wash the feet of the servants of my lord." [42]And Abigail made haste and rose and mounted on an ass, and her five maidens attended her; she went after the messengers of David, and became his wife.

[43]David also took Ahino-am of Jezreel; and both of them became his wives. [44]Saul had given Michal his daughter, David's wife, to Palti the son of Laish, who was of Gallim.

Abigail's approach to David was a model of tact. She treated him like a king and assured him of her belief that he would become king. The way she dismissed her husband's actions as unimportant was particularly skilful. Probably with intended humour she made a pun on the name Nabal, one meaning of which was "fool", as if to say, "What on earth could you expect of a man like that?" (verse 25). By this means she disarmed David, and proceeded to divert his attention to herself—and himself.

Abigail's representation of David as king has been described as prophetic. The narrator in fact presents a process. First the prophet Samuel had recognized David as future king; after some time Jonathan had recognized the fact, and then even Saul himself. Now an intelligent citizen in Judah glimpses this truth about God's plans. Later on, after Saul's death, Judah as a whole would accept David as king; it would take some time longer for the whole nation to do the same.

An important aspect of kingship is discussed in Abigail's speech. As we have seen, David was on the point of brutally and vindictively destroying an enemy, Nabal. Abigail gives two good reasons why no king or future king should act in this fashion.

(i) *He has no need to do so.* God himself can be trusted to deal with enemies of the leaders he has chosen and appointed (verse 29). So long as David was fighting God's battles (verse 28), rather than pursuing his own squabbles, all would be well. Here was a lesson for any future king of Israel, not to dissipate his energies (as indeed Saul was doing) in personal vendettas within his own realm but to maintain his whole nation's welfare against any external foes.

(ii) *To do so would destroy his peace of mind.* Remorse and pangs of conscience would inevitably follow a deed of vindictive revenge (verse 31). A leader must not lose his personal integrity in this way. High-handed actions of such a kind are a sure sign of the corruption power is apt to bring in its train, and leaders of God's people must be on their guard against every temptation to abuse their power.

The story switches back to Nabal in verses 36ff., and we learn that his death rapidly followed his escape from David's vengeance; this was no coincidence, but a proof of the truth of Abigail's words to David that God deals with the enemies of his chosen men. No doubt there was a physical cause for Nabal's death, a disease such as a stroke or heart attack, but the biblical writer sees God's hand in life and death alike.

Abigail's beauty and wisdom made her a fitting queen-to-be, and David married her (verses 39–42). Saul had been cruel enough to marry off Michal to another man, but David found compensation in two other marriages, with Abigail and with Ahinoam. It does not seem to have been expected that kings should content themselves with a single wife; even a relatively minor citizen like Samuel's father had had two wives (cp. 1:2). There is therefore no implied criticism of David in this detail. Rather, it tends to show how God looked after David's interests. Abigail was a rich widow, we know, and we may surmise that Ahinoam was no less well-to-do. By such marriages David was probably able to afford to maintain his six hundred men with less difficulty than had been the case till now. Perhaps, too, these marriages helped David to forge closer links with the people of Judah. Till quite recent times "diplomatic" marriages were an important method of establishing and strengthening bonds and alliances between families, clans, tribes and nations.

SAUL'S SECOND ESCAPE

1 Samuel 26:1-25

¹Then the Ziphites came to Saul at Gibe-ah, saying, "Is not David hiding himself on the hill of Hachilah, which is on the east of Jeshimon?" ²So Saul arose and went down to the wilderness of Ziph, with three thousand chosen men of Israel, to seek David in the wilderness of Ziph. ³And Saul encamped on the hill of Hachilah, which is beside the road on the east of Jeshimon. But David remained in the wilderness; and when he saw that Saul came after him into the wilderness, ⁴David sent out spies, and learned of a certainty that Saul had come. ⁵Then David rose and came to the place where Saul had encamped; and David saw the place where Saul lay, with Abner the son of Ner, the commander of his army; Saul was lying within the encampment, while the army was encamped around him.

⁶Then David said to Ahimelech the Hittite, and to Joab's brother Abishai the son of Zeruiah, "Who will go down with me into the camp to Saul?" And Abishai said, "I will go down with you." ⁷So David and Abishai went to the army by night; and there lay Saul sleeping within the encampment, with his spear stuck in the ground at his head; and Abner and the army lay around him. ⁸Then said

Abishai to David, "God has given your enemy into your hand this day; now therefore let me pin him to the earth with one stroke of the spear, and I will not strike him twice." ⁹But David said to Abishai, "Do not destroy him; for who can put forth his hand against the Lord's anointed, and be guiltless?" ¹⁰And David said, "As the Lord lives, the Lord will smite him; or his day shall come to die; or he shall go down into battle and perish. ¹¹The Lord forbid that I should put forth my hand against the Lord's anointed; but take now the spear that is at his head, and the jar of water, and let us go." ¹²So David took the spear and the jar of water from Saul's head; and they went away. No man saw it, or knew it, nor did any awake; for they were all asleep, because a deep sleep from the Lord had fallen upon them.

¹³Then David went over to the other side, and stood afar off on the top of the mountain, with a great space between them; ¹⁴and David called to the army, and to Abner the son of Ner, saying, "Will you not answer, Abner?" Then Abner answered, "Who are you that calls to the king?" ¹⁵And David said to Abner, "Are you not a man? Who is like you in Israel? Why then have you not kept watch over your lord the king? For one of the people came in to destroy the king your lord. ¹⁶This thing that you have done is not good. As the Lord lives, you deserve to die, because you have not kept watch over your lord, the Lord's anointed. And now see where the king's spear is, and the jar of water that was at his head."

¹⁷Saul recognised David's voice, and said, "Is this your voice, my son David?" And David said, "It is my voice, my lord, O king." ¹⁸And he said, "Why does my lord pursue after his servant? For what have I done? What guilt is on my hands? ¹⁹Now therefore let my lord the king hear the words of his servant. If it is the Lord who has stirred you up against me, may he accept an offering; but if it is men, may they be cursed before the Lord, for they have driven me out this day that I should have no share in the heritage of the Lord, saying, 'Go, serve other gods.' ²⁰Now therefore, let not my blood fall to the earth away from the presence of the Lord; for the king of Israel has come out to seek my life, like one who hunts a partridge in the mountains."

²¹Then Saul said, "I have done wrong; return, my son David, for I will no more do you harm, because my life was precious in your eyes this day; behold, I have played the fool, and have erred exceedingly." ²²And David made answer, "Here is the spear, O king! Let one of the young men come over and fetch it. ²³The Lord

rewards every man for his righteousness and his faithfulness; for the
Lord gave you into my hand today, and I would not put forth my
hand against the Lord's anointed. [24]Behold, as your life was precious
this day in my sight, so may my life be precious in the sight of the
Lord, and may he deliver me out of all tribulation." [25]Then Saul said
to David, "Blessed be you, my son David! You will do many things
and will succeed in them." So David went his way, and Saul returned
to his place.

Although the details are quite different, this chapter tells a story
remarkably similar to that contained in chapter 24. Once again
David is pursued by Saul but manages to turn the tables,
gaining a golden opportunity to kill the king. Once again he is
urged by his own men to seize the opportunity, but refuses to
do so; once again he lets Saul know what has happened, and
once again Saul apologizes to David for his wrongful pursuit of
him. As a result it is often stated that chapters 24 and 26 are
simply different versions of the same incident, but other
scholars feel that the differences in detail are too numerous to
support such a conclusion. It is at any rate clear that the biblical
writer was convinced that David twice spared Saul's life, and he
told both stories in full detail in order to emphasize the lessons
which could be drawn from the double event.

(i) The first lesson was undoubtedly that God was giving
David his protection; no matter how big Saul's army was, his
pursuit of David was doomed to failure. Saul, on the other
hand, found that God had withdrawn his protection from him.
If he was vulnerable to the little army of David how much more
vulnerable he must be to the Philistine armies—and so events
soon proved (chapter 31). The narrator even tells us that Saul's
whole army was unable to stay awake (verse 12)! Not even a
soldier of Abner's reputation was capable of protecting the
king.

(ii) A second important theme is that David was completely
innocent of harming Saul or even of wishing him harm. This
repeated emphasis in the books of Samuel must date from a
time when enemies of David inside Israel were trying to blacken
his character, claiming that he had been guilty of treachery and

treason towards King Saul. A more general lesson is that good leaders in the making do not attack their predecessors; a clear conscience towards them is just as important as a clear conscience towards ordinary citizens (cp. 25:31). Similarly, today's leaders ought not to be jealous of tomorrow's leaders.

(iii) Once again it is stressed that no man has the right to attack a leader chosen and anointed by God, however wrong or ill-advised his actions. The New Testament too supports law and order; cp. Rom. 13:1.

The most distinctive section of this story, when compared with chapter 24, is the speech of David to Saul in verses 18ff. By now David had come to realize that this cat-and-mouse game between him and Saul could not continue indefinitely, and—as we shall see in chapter 27—he was on the point of leaving Israelite territory. It is plain from verses 18ff. that he viewed such a move as a very serious and unhappy prospect. The attitude of Israelites to their homeland went beyond ordinary loyalty and patriotism; it had a powerful religious dimension, for Israel was the "Promised Land", the land long promised by God to their ancestors and in due course given to them. To leave it was to abandon God's best gift to them; and also, as David stated, to lose contact with the public worship of their God, for there were no temples nor altars to him outside the borders of Israel. By these words David, and the story-teller, made it plain that David's impending departure to Philistine territory was forced upon him and was absolutely contrary to his own wishes.

Verse 19 poses the question, was it David's fault or someone else's that he was to be driven into exile? (Possibly there were other people who had poisoned Saul's mind against David, but probably David really meant Saul himself.) If Saul had insisted that the fault was David's, then David was ready to listen to the accusation, and if guilty he would willingly offer up sacrifices to seek divine forgiveness; but of course once again Saul had to confess that he was the one in the wrong (verse 21). Thus David's reputation was cleared even before he went over to the Philistines.

We should be inclined to use the word propaganda nowadays

to describe material of this sort, to the extent that its purpose was to clear David's name. However, there is no need for cynicism; it is important for a leader of God's people that his reputation should be as blameless as his conscience.

DAVID IN EXILE

1 Samuel 27:1–28:2

[1]And David said in his heart, "I shall now perish one day by the hand of Saul; there is nothing better for me than that I should escape to the land of the Philistines; then Saul will despair of seeking me any longer within the borders of Israel, and I shall escape out of his hand." [2]So David arose and went over, he and the six hundred men who were with him, to Achish the son of Maoch, king of Gath. [3]And David dwelt with Achish at Gath, he and his men, every man with his household, and David with his two wives, Ahino-am of Jezreel, and Abigail of Carmel, Nabal's widow. [4]And when it was told Saul that David had fled to Gath, he sought for him no more.

[5]Then David said to Achish, "If I have found favour in your eyes, let a place be given me in one of the country towns, that I may dwell there; for why should your servant dwell in the royal city with you?" [6]So that day Achish gave him Ziklag; therefore Ziklag has belonged to the kings of Judah to this day. [7]And the number of the days that David dwelt in the country of the Philistines was a year and four months.

[8]Now David and his men went up, and made raids upon the Geshurites, the Girzites, and the Amalekites; for these were the inhabitants of the land from of old, as far as Shur, to the land of Egypt. [9]And David smote the land, and left neither man nor woman alive, but took away the sheep, the oxen, the asses, the camels, and the garments, and came back to Achish. [10]When Achish asked, "Against whom have you made a raid today?" David would say, "Against the Negeb of Judah," or "Against the Negeb of the Jerahmeelites," or, "Against the Negeb of the Kenites." [11]And David saved neither man nor woman alive, to bring tidings to Gath, thinking, "Lest they should tell about us, and say, 'So David has done.'" Such was his custom all the while he dwelt in the country of the Philistines. [12]And Achish trusted David, thinking, "He has made

himself utterly abhorred by his people Israel; therefore he shall be my servant always."

¹In those days the Philistines gathered their forces for war, to fight against Israel. And Achish said to David, "Understand that you and your men are to go out with me in the army." ²David said to Achish, "Very well, you shall know what your servant can do." And Achish said to David, "Very well, I will make you my bodyguard for life."

Once again, Saul's impulse to be reconciled with David proved very short-lived, and the day came when the younger man felt that he could not continue his outlaw existence any longer. Even if he had had sufficient trust in God to be sure that he would survive (which is doubtful, in view of verse 1), both he and his men must have grown weary of the constant harassment and nervous tension, the constant movement from one place to another, and the daily problems of finding sufficient food. His reluctant decision to lead his men, together with their families, into Philistine territory is wholly intelligible.

In view of his earlier reception in Gath (see 21:10–15), it nevertheless took considerable courage to return there now. One factor was that the Philistines were sure to have heard by now of Saul's bitter hostility to him and military manoeuvres in pursuit of him, so that they would no longer view him in the same light, as an Israelite champion against themselves. The most important change in the situation, however, was that now he did not go to Gath unaccompanied but as the leader of a tried and tested small army. No doubt the Philistines could have overpowered it had they wished, but the use of mercenary troops was quite frequent in and around Palestine, and since the Philistines were relatively short of manpower, at least in comparison with Israel, it would have suited them very well to make use of David's men as mercenaries. If the idea had not occurred to them, we may be sure that David would have put it into their minds. Probably, indeed, the town of Ziklag was leased to David in return for specified military services.

It is certain that Achish, the king of Gath, instructed David to make attacks on Israelites, for two reasons. In the first place, the Israelites were the Philistines' major enemy, of course.

Secondly, Achish realized that as soon as David did attack his own people, he would lose for ever the possibility of changing sides. However, David tricked him for the second time. He pretended to be making raids on the various areas of Judah mentioned in verse 10, but in reality the victims of his campaigns were Amalekites and others, nomads who were prone to attack any of the settled population, Israelites and Philistines alike. In this way he actively helped his own fellow Judaeans.

To achieve this deception, he had to ensure that no Amalekite prisoner-of-war ever fell into Philistine hands; so all prisoners had to be killed. This act of deliberate butchery is very distasteful to modern readers, but in view of the total enmity between Israel and Amalek it is no surprise that the writer spared no tears over the death of any Amalekites. In any case, the writer's chief purpose is to show the lengths to which David was driven. It is hard to see how David could have avoided attacking his own people by any other means.

His very success in deceiving Achish led David into even deeper difficulties, because the Philistine king became so sure that he could trust David that he incorporated the small Israelite force into his own army (28:1). A major conflict with Saul's armies was now impending, and the signs were that David would be forced to fight alongside the Philistines against his own people. His ready reply to Achish, *"Very well, you shall know what your servant can do"*, was putting a brave face on what must have been a cruel dilemma. Thus David's deception led to even worse problems: "O, what a tangled web we weave, when first we practise to deceive."

Perhaps the biblical writer means the reader to draw the lesson that David should have consulted priest or prophet before marching into Philistine territory to offer Achish his services; at any rate, by now the reader can be sure that in the end God will arrange events to David's benefit, whatever mistakes and deceptions the future king made. Even so, considerable suspense is built up, as the narrative switches from David and his problems back to Saul—and his problems.

THE EXTENT OF SAUL'S DIFFICULTIES

1 Samuel 28:3-7

> ³Now Samuel had died, and all Israel had mourned for him and buried him in Ramah, his own city. And Saul had put the mediums and the wizards out of the land. ⁴The Philistines assembled, and came and encamped at Shunem; and Saul gathered all Israel, and they encamped at Gilboa. ⁵When Saul saw the army of the Philistines, he was afraid, and his heart trembled greatly. ⁶And when Saul inquired of the Lord, the Lord did not answer him, either by dreams, or by Urim, or by prophets. ⁷Then Saul said to his servants, "Seek out for me a woman who is a medium, that I may go to her and inquire of her." And his servants said to him, "Behold, there is a medium at Endor."

The Philistines first assembled their armies at Aphek **(29:1)** and then marched northwards to the Valley of Jezreel and encamped at Shunem (28:4), which was well and truly inside Israelite territory, and so Saul was forced to meet their challenge. See Map 2; the geographical details show clearly that the events recorded in chapter 29 happened before those of 28:3–25. The narrator has rearranged his material for literary reasons, switching attention from David to Saul, back to David, and finally back to Saul, in the course of the final chapters of 1 Samuel.

Verses 3–7 set the scene for what occurred at Endor. Saul's problems were grave.

(i) This Philistine invasion was, it seems clear, their most powerful thrust into Israel since Saul had become king. The size of their armies was itself frightening, and their strategy was clever, too. Till now nearly all the battles between Israelites and Philistines had taken place in hilly or mountainous areas, and both sides had become aware that the Philistines' superior weapons, especially their chariots, were of little value except on level ground. So on this occasion they took care to stay on level ground, in the broad Valley of Jezreel. This is the only area in

Palestine where it is possible to reach the River Jordan from the Mediterranean coastal plain without having to cross mountains. Saul could not ignore such a thrust; to begin with, their invasion threatened to cut Israel in half. He must have realized that a frontal assault on them, there on ground of their own choosing, was likely to prove disastrous; but what else could he do?

(ii) He could get no guidance from God. Verse 6 tells us that he made every effort to obtain such guidance, but it was denied him. By now the biblical writer and the reader alike can only feel some sympathy for him. He was not at all an irreligious man, but for too long he had gone his own way; his earlier wilfulness and disobedience now bore their fruit. He had determined to act as an absolute monarch, refusing to do what the prophet Samuel instructed him; and it goes without saying that his relentless pursuit of David had been against God's will. Very well, if he had chosen to bow to nobody's advice, now he would get no advice when he wanted and desperately needed it. Like many another individual in history, he thought he could command God and have dealings with him on his own terms. Now he discovered his mistake.

Verse 6 lists three regular means by which God's will was conveyed in ancient Israel—personal, priestly and prophetic.

(a) God might speak to man through dreams, as in the case of Joseph in particular, cp. Gen. 37:5–9; 40:1–41:36. But no helpful dream now came Saul's way.

(b) Secondly, there was the Urim and Thummim, a device which seems in a sense to have been mechanical in its workings: see the commentary on 14:24–46. Saul had his priests who could use it, just as David had Abiathar's help (cp. 23:6–12), but as we have seen before, this device could fail to give any answer, and this was Saul's problem now.

(c) We do not know what prophets if any Saul had access to; David had the services of Gad (cp. 22:5). Prophets heard the inner voice of God, but they were simply his spokesmen, and now they received no message to pass on to the king.

It is the measure of Saul's despair that he turned in such

circumstances to a medium. Such practitioners were firmly banned under Israelite law, and he himself had in the past done much to maintain this law (verse 3), but now he could find no other means of obtaining the guidance he sought.

The Bible takes an uncompromising stand against mediums; it is strange, in view of this, that spiritualism today can claim to be a form of Christianity. It is simply impossible for anyone to be sure what genuine information, if any, can be gained by resorting to seances and mediums; too often the supposed information is false, whether we attribute it to the trickery of the medium or to the actions of evil spirits. So any so-called guidance obtained by this means is highly suspect. It is definitely not the way to learn anything about God's will. Horton Davies has written, "At heart Spiritism is not trust in God: it is born of distrust in Him. It is an attempt to substitute experimental certainty for faith. It is the monstrous design to subject God to the indignity of a test tube examination." 1 Sam. 28 is no basis for resorting to mediums, even though on this exceptional occasion God did condescend to speak to the enquirer.

THE VOICE OF SAMUEL

1 Samuel 28:8–25

[8]So Saul disguised himself and put on other garments, and went, he and two men with him; and they came to the woman by night. And he said, "Divine for me by a spirit, and bring up for me whomever I shall name to you." [9]The woman said to him, "Surely you know what Saul has done, how he has cut off the mediums and the wizards from the land. Why then are you laying a snare for my life to bring about my death?" [10]But Saul swore to her by the Lord, "As the Lord lives, no punishment shall come upon you for this thing." [11]Then the woman said, "Whom shall I bring up for you?" He said, "Bring up Samuel for me." [12]When the woman saw Samuel, she cried out with a loud voice; and the woman said to Saul, "Why have you deceived me? You are Saul." [13]The king said to her, "Have no fear; what do you see?" And the woman said to Saul, "I see a god coming up out of

the earth." [14]He said to her, "What is his appearance?" And she said, "An old man is coming up; and he is wrapped in a robe." And Saul knew that it was Samuel, and he bowed with his face to the ground, and did obeisance.

[15]Then Samuel said to Saul, "Why have you disturbed me by bringing me up?" Saul answered, "I am in great distress; for the Philistines are warring against me, and God has turned away from me and answers me no more, either by prophets or by dreams; therefore I have summoned you to tell me what I shall do." [16]And Samuel said, "Why then do you ask me, since the Lord has turned from you and become your enemy? [17]The Lord has done to you as he spoke by me; for the Lord has torn the kingdom out of your hand, and given it to your neighbour, David. [18]Because you did not obey the voice of the Lord, and did not carry out his fierce wrath against Amalek, therefore the Lord has done this thing to you this day. [19]Moreover the Lord will give Israel also with you into the hand of the Philistines; and tomorrow you and your sons shall be with me; the Lord will give the army of Israel also into the hand of the Philistines."

[20]Then Saul fell at once full length upon the ground, filled with fear because of the words of Samuel; and there was no strength in him, for he had eaten nothing all day and all night. [21]And the woman came to Saul, and when she saw that he was terrified, she said to him, "Behold, your handmaid has hearkened to you; I have taken my life in my hand, and have hearkened to what you have said to me. [22]Now therefore, you also hearken to your handmaid; let me set a morsel of bread before you; and eat, that you may have strength when you go on your way." [23]He refused, and said, "I will not eat." But his servants, together with the woman, urged him; and he hearkened to their words. So he arose from the earth, and sat upon the bed. [24]Now the woman had a fatted calf in the house, and she quickly killed it, and she took flour, and kneaded it and baked unleavened bread of it, [25]and she put it before Saul and his servants; and they ate. Then they rose and went away that night.

Saul, then, consulted a medium, first disguising himself in an attempt to deceive the woman, who would certainly know his reputation as an enemy of such people. There are one or two puzzling features about verses 8–14. For a start, it is not clear how and why the woman came to recognize Saul, but this detail is not very important. More important is the question whether the writer wishes us to believe that mediums really did have the power to communicate with the dead. Perhaps he did; or he may mean to imply that God after all condescended to grant Saul's wishes, in spite of his recourse to a medium. It is possible that the story suggests that the woman was herself surprised at the sight of Samuel. It may well be significant that, although she conjured up Samuel in the first place, she was then set on one side; Samuel conversed directly with Saul, who could see and hear him without difficulty. At any rate, this story in no way supports spiritualist practices; Saul's previous hostility to mediums and diviners is endorsed by implication, and the narrative is intended to emphasize how desperate and helpless he was. Another central emphasis is that God spoke not through mediums but through prophets like Samuel, men who spoke nothing but the truth, fearlessly. However, in Old Testament times God provided a constant succession of his spokesmen, and it was never necessary for him to resuscitate a dead prophet; if he chose to bring Samuel from the dead on this one special occasion, that was a sign of his grace, not of his approval of superstitious practices.

In death as in life, Samuel told Saul the straight and unvarnished truth. His words (verses 16-19) bear two of the marks of the true prophet:

(i) He foretold the future in precise detail (verse 19).

(ii) He denounced wrong actions, explaining exactly why Saul had incurred the anger and rejection of God.

It is still the prophetic task of the Church to point the finger unerringly at actions and attitudes which God must condemn, and to indicate at least something of the future by spelling out the inevitable results if these actions and attitudes remain unchanged.

Very often the prophet also appealed for a change of attitude, but in this case it was far too late. Saul had long ago set out on his course of action, and now nothing could avert tomorrow's tragedy. Not only would he himself be *with* Samuel, in other words a dead man, but his sons and many Israelite soldiers too were to lose their lives. Again we are reminded of a king's responsibilities to his people; if he leads them badly, they will inevitably suffer. The transfer of power from the rejected king (Saul) to the chosen king (David) could not take place without great hardship for the nation.

One particular point to note is that Saul asked Samuel what he ought to do, but to that question there was still no reply; instead he was told what was going to happen. He wanted a plan of campaign to avoid disaster; instead he received confirmation that disaster was certain. No plan of campaign was of the slightest use. Saul's prostration and anguish were natural enough, though he was able, with difficulty and after much persuasion, to pull himself together sufficiently to go through the motions of leadership for the last few hours of his life.

Many men and women have been desperate to know the future; indeed, it is only human nature to speculate, to study trends, and to listen to forecasts and predictions. But when we study this story, we are reminded that it is often better not to know the future: "God holds the key of all unknown—and I am glad" is an excellent motto for the Christian. The right attitude in seeking divine guidance is to seek God's help as to what to do, and to investigate what actions would glorify him, not to ask to read the future. To that extent Saul was right; his fault was that he had not asked early enough or persistently enough, and now it was too late.

DAVID'S DISMISSAL

1 Samuel 29:1-11

[1]Now the Philistines gathered all their forces at Aphek; and the Israelites were encamped by the fountain which is in Jezreel. [2]As the lords of the Philistines were passing on by hundreds and by thousands, and David and his men were passing on in the rear with Achish, [3]the commanders of the Philistines said, "What are these Hebrews doing here?" And Achish said to the commanders of the

Philistines, "Is not this David, the servant of Saul, king of Israel, who has been with me now for days and years, and since he deserted to me I have found no fault in him to this day." 4But the commanders of the Philistines were angry with him; and the commanders of the Philistines said to him, "Send the man back, that he may return to the place to which you have assigned him; he shall not go down with us to battle, lest in the battle he become an adversary to us. For how could this fellow reconcile himself to his lord? Would it not be with the heads of the men here? 5Is not this David, of whom they sing to one another in dances,

'Saul has slain his thousands,
and David his ten thousands'?"

6Then Achish called David and said to him, "As the Lord lives, you have been honest, and to me it seems right that you should march out and in with me in the campaign; for I have found nothing wrong in you from the day of your coming to me to this day. Nevertheless the lords do not approve of you. 7So go back now; and go peaceably, that you may not displease the lords of the Philistines." 8And David said to Achish, "But what have I done? What have you found in your servant from the day I entered your service until now, that I may not go and fight against the enemies of my lord the king?" 9And Achish made answer to David, "I know that you are as blameless in my sight as an angel of God; nevertheless the commanders of the Philistines have said, 'He shall not go up with us to the battle.' 10Now then rise early in the morning with the servants of your lord who came with you; and start early in the morning, and depart as soon as you have light." 11So David set out with his men early in the morning, to return to the land of the Philistines. But the Philistines went up to Jezreel.

Saul's dilemma was over; now he had nothing to look forward to except death and disaster. David's problems were also resolved before the battle began—indeed, before the Philistine troops moved on from their mustering point at Aphek. David was never anywhere near the battlefield. Perhaps one motive behind this chapter is to make precisely this point, in order to counter any malicious propaganda which claimed that he had in fact fought against his own countrymen and helped the Philistines to destroy Saul's army. The chief motive, however, is a frequent one in these chapters: to demonstrate that God faithfully looked after David's welfare, time and time again. If David's move into Philistine territory had been a wrong one, God did not abandon him there; far from it. Another underlying theme is that God is just as active and powerful in foreign lands as in Israel itself; just as the ark of the covenant had demonstrated God's power in Philistine territory (chapters 5f.), so now David so to speak took God's power with him into the same foreign country.

We live in a world where relatively few people believe in a whole variety of gods. In the West, most people believe in one God or none at all. It is not easy, therefore, for us to appreciate fully the attractiveness of polytheism in the ancient world. It was the "natural" creed, even for many Israelites, and those faithful Israelites who worshipped only their one God (Yahweh by name) were the odd men out in their world. Because of this fact, the biblical writers often felt the need to stress the power and influence of their God and to show how he controlled all aspects of the world, both inside and outside Israel itself. One major criticism of polytheistic belief is that those who hold it can see no overall pattern or purpose in life or in history: everything becomes disjointed and meaningless. Many people nowadays, without being polytheists, are just as prone to this sort of outlook. It is all too easy nowadays to view God as one power, and to attribute almost godlike powers to such things as economic forces, science, poverty, and so on; and then to become fatalistic and apathetic. One needs to *see* a purpose in order to *feel* a sense of purpose in one's own life and activities. God is just as active in economics, physics, agriculture, and all human activities as he is in the religious sphere.

This story shows how godless men can have insight and wisdom and still be overruled by God. Achish, who trusted David so implicitly, was a dupe, fooled by David; and yet it was his fellow-kings who—in all their shrewdness—rescued David from the cruel necessity of fighting against his own people. Thus they gave him the chance to retain his popularity in Israel, and so to become king of Israel—and so eventually to have the power to defeat the Philistines once and for all! If only the

Philistine kings could have foreseen what would happen, they would have been inclined to agree with Achish's plan—not because David could be trusted, but precisely because he could not be trusted.

David protested vigorously against his dismissal (verse 8). One can only suppose that he was still trying to impress on King Achish that by now he was the sworn enemy of Israel; this was carrying the deception considerably further than was necessary. Deception had become the whole basis of his way of life while in Philistia; but the situation would soon be radically altered by the death and defeat of Saul. God could rescue his chosen leader from moral difficulties and failures just as easily as from physical dangers. God's primary role, in Old and New Testaments alike, is as Saviour; he offers all men his salvation, which is something received not just once-for-all in the experience of conversion but on a daily basis in all the moral problems of life.

DAVID AND THE AMALEKITES

1 Samuel 30:1–31

¹Now when David and his men came to Ziklag on the third day, the Amalekites had made a raid upon the Negeb and upon Ziklag. They had overcome Ziklag, and burned it with fire, ²and taken captive the women and all who were in it, both small and great; they killed no one, but carried them off, and went their way. ³And when David and his men came to the city, they found it burned with fire, and their wives and sons and daughters taken captive. ⁴Then David and the people who were with him raised their voices and wept, until they had no more strength to weep. ⁵David's two wives also had been taken captive, Ahino-am of Jezreel, and Abigail the widow of Nabal of Carmel. ⁶And David was greatly distressed; for the people spoke of stoning him, because all the people were bitter in soul, each for his sons and daughters. But David strengthened himself in the Lord his God.

⁷And David said to Abiathar the priest, the son of Ahimelech, "Bring me the ephod." So Abiathar brought the ephod to David. ⁸And David inquired of the Lord, "Shall I pursue after this band?

Shall I overtake them?" He answered him, "Pursue; for you shall surely overtake and shall surely rescue." [9]So David set out, and the six hundred men who were with him, and they came to the brook Besor, where those stayed who were left behind. [10]But David went on with the pursuit, he and four hundred men; two hundred stayed behind, who were too exhausted to cross the brook Besor.

[11]They found an Egyptian in the open country, and brought him to David; and they gave him bread and he ate, they gave him water to drink, [12]and they gave him a piece of a cake of figs and two clusters of raisins. And when he had eaten, his spirit revived; for he had not eaten bread or drunk water for three days and three nights. [13]And David said to him, "To whom do you belong? And where are you from?" He said, "I am a young man of Egypt, servant to an Amalekite; and my master left me behind because I fell sick three days ago. [14]We had made a raid upon the Negeb of the Cherethites and upon that which belongs to Judah and upon the Negeb of Caleb; and we burned Ziklag with fire." [15]And David said to him, "Will you take me down to this band?" And he said, "Swear to me by God, that you will not kill me, or deliver me into the hands of my master, and I will take you down to this band."

[16]And when he had taken him down, behold, they were spread abroad over all the land, eating and drinking and dancing, because of all the great spoil they had taken from the land of the Philistines and from the land of Judah. [17]And David smote them from twilight until the evening of the next day; and not a man of them escaped, except four hundred young men, who mounted camels and fled. [18]David recovered all that the Amalekites had taken; and David rescued his two wives. [19]Nothing was missing, whether small or great, sons or daughters, spoil or anything that had been taken; David brought back all. [20]David also captured all the flocks and herds; and the people drove those cattle before him, and said, "This is David's spoil."

[21]Then David came to the two hundred men, who had been too exhausted to follow David, and who had been left at the brook Besor; and they went out to meet David and to meet the people who were with him; and when David drew near to the people he saluted them. [22]Then all the wicked and base fellows among the men who had gone with David said, "Because they did not go with us, we will not give them any of the spoil which we have recovered, except that each man may lead away his wife and children, and depart." [23]But David said, "You shall not do so, my brothers, with what the Lord

has given us; he has preserved us and given into our hand the band that came against us. ²⁴Who would listen to you in this matter? For as his share is who goes down into the battle, so shall his share be who stays by the baggage; they shall share alike." ²⁵And from that day forward he made it a statute and an ordinance for Israel to this day.

²⁶When David came to Ziklag, he sent part of the spoil to his friends, the elders of Judah, saying, "Here is a present for you from the spoil of the enemies of the Lord"; ²⁷it was for those in Bethel, in Ramoth of the Negeb, in Jattir, ²⁸in Aroer, in Siphmoth, in Eshtemoa, ²⁹in Racal, in the cities of the Jerahmeelites, in the cities of the Kenites, ³⁰in Hormah, in Borashan, in Athach, ³¹in Hebron, for all the places where David and his men had roamed.

We are still kept in suspense about the battle between Saul and the Philistines, because the writer chooses to follow the fortunes of David instead. Turned away with his men from the Philistine armies, he naturally made his way back to his headquarters at Ziklag, only to find the town burnt down and abandoned. This chapter shows how the Amalekites were the enemies of all the settled peoples of the whole region, Israelites and Philistines alike. No doubt the fact that both the Israelite and the Philistine armies had marched far to the north, in order to fight each other, gave the Amalekites a rare opportunity for a major raid on an undefended area. Obviously David was taken completely by surprise by this event; equally, the Amalekites did not expect him and his troops to return south so swiftly, and so David was able to catch them unawares in turn. He had killed all Amalekite prisoners in the past (cp. 27:11), but they were not out for revenge but for profit, and did not kill any of their captives, who could be ransomed at a high cost or else sold as slaves.

Once again we are to see God's controlling hand in the whole affair. God had saved David from being forced to attack his own fellow-Israelites, and his return to Ziklag was in the very nick of time. Even then, the Amalekite raiders would no doubt have been almost impossible to locate in the sparsely inhabited Negeb districts (semi-wilderness areas), if David and his men had not chanced to come across the Egyptian who was able to give them precise information (verses 11–15). We are not meant to view all this as mere chance; it is stressed that David consulted the priest Abiathar and through him received clear guidance from God (verses 7f.): so David was given the guidance for his campaign which Saul had been denied.

This chapter illustrates how fickle human nature is. In their initial distress at losing their entire families, David's soldiers came close to murdering him on the spot. Then in delighted relief at rescuing their wives and children unharmed and retrieving all their property, they handed over all the spoils freely to David—a remarkable change of attitude in a short space of time. The attitude of the Jerusalem crowds to Jesus on Palm Sunday and a few days later provides another glaring example of the way men and women, especially in a crowd, become prisoners of the passions of the moment. This picture shows another side of leadership; a man can only lead to the extent that he is allowed to do so. Ultimately leadership can only be by consent—at least, the consent of a sufficient number of people to support the person at the top. Leaders often need to exercise the power of persuasion; but in this case David could not have turned disaster into triumph by mere persuasion. Strong and effective action was needed, and thanks to God's help, he was able to provide it.

There were two important sequels to the victorious campaign against the Amalekites:

(i) Verses 21–25: in a sense, this was David's first military victory as king—for by now that was virtually his position among his own troops. He would go on to win many other victories in the years that followed, and it was important to establish at the outset how he meant to handle the spoils of battle. These were to be distributed, he insisted, with scrupulous fairness. Each task within the army was of equal merit and importance. It is clear that David's firm stand on this issue commended itself to the great majority of his followers; only the greedy few held a different opinion.

Leadership must show itself in fairness to all, firmly applied, without bowing to sectional interests. To cement the unity of any community, from a nation to a local church, it is important for the leaders to make every member feel useful and valuable. Paul's metaphor of the church as a body makes the point very effectively: see 1 Cor. 12:14–26.

(ii) Verses 26–31: there were sufficient spoils not only to pay the troops but also to repay past benefits. Many victorious kings have used surplus plunder to enrich themselves and to build grandiose palaces; David used these first spoils to show his gratitude to the citizens of those areas and towns in Judah where he and his men had wandered when being pursued by Saul. This is the sort of loyalty that good leaders show, and David was not slow to show it. The gesture would very soon stand him in good stead, since it helped to cement good relationships between him and Judah, and enabled him to be accepted as king in Judah. It would be wrong and cynical to suggest that this was his motive, rather than generosity and gratitude; David could not foresee Saul's death, nor could he know at this point that Judah would break away from the rest of Israel. The general point made by the writer is that throughout his years as a fugitive and an exile David brought nothing but good to his fellow-tribesmen in Judah, even at his own expense.

THE BATTLE OF GILBOA

1 Samuel 31:1–13

[1]Now the Philistines fought against Israel; and the men of Israel fled before the Philistines, and fell slain on Mount Gilboa. [2]And the Philistines overtook Saul and his sons; and the Philistines slew Jonathan and Abinadab and Malchishua, the sons of Saul. [3]The battle pressed hard upon Saul, and the archers found him; and he was badly wounded by the archers. [4]Then Saul said to his armour-bearer, "Draw your sword, and thrust me through with it, lest these uncircumcised come and thrust me through, and make sport of me." But his armour-bearer would not; for he feared greatly. Therefore

Saul took his own sword, and fell upon it. ⁵And when his armour-bearer saw that Saul was dead, he also fell upon his sword, and died with him. ⁶Thus Saul died, and his three sons, and his armour-bearer, and all his men, on the same day together. ⁷And when the men of Israel who were on the other side of the valley and those beyond the Jordan saw that the men of Israel had fled and that Saul and his sons were dead, they forsook their cities and fled; and the Philistines came and dwelt in them.

⁸On the morrow, when the Philistines came to strip the slain, they found Saul and his three sons fallen on Mount Gilboa. ⁹And they cut off his head, and stripped off his armour, and sent messengers throughout the land of the Philistines, to carry the good news to their idols and to the people. ¹⁰They put his armour in the temple of Ashtaroth; and they fastened his body to the wall of Beth-shan. ¹¹But when the inhabitants of Jabesh-gilead heard what the Philistines had done to Saul, ¹²all the valiant men arose, and went all night, and took the body of Saul and the bodies of his sons from the wall of Beth-shan; and they came to Jabesh and burnt them there. ¹³And they took their bones and buried them under the tamarisk tree in Jabesh, and fasted seven days.

David's military success in the far south of the country was in stark contrast to the scene at the battle of Gilboa, far to the north, where Saul and his army suffered a crushing defeat, and Saul died along with three of his sons, Jonathan among them. We are told all this with remarkably few details. We do not know which side started the battle, nor what the attempted strategy was; Saul's men, in retreat, hoped that the slopes of Mount Gilboa would hamper the enemy's advance, but even that proved a vain hope. The fact was that Saul's defeat and death were determined beforehand, so the battle tactics were of little account in the narrator's eyes. Saul, then, was at the end humiliated, but certainly not disgraced. He showed dignity and courage at the last, and the writer casts no final rebuke at him, in spite of his suicide. As David had more than once acknowledged, Saul had been selected by God as king of Israel, and that was no mean position. Even the public indignities inflicted on his corpse by the gloating Philistines did not last very long, because of the courageous action of one group of

Israelite citizens. They came from Jabesh-gilead, east of the River Jordan, a town which Saul had rescued at the very start of his reign (cp. chapter 11); evidently this city had remembered to be grateful over many years. Saul's vicious action against the town of Nob (chapter 22) and his relentless hostility to David tend to make us forget that many in Israel had had much cause to be grateful to Saul, who had soundly defeated several minor enemies and had kept the Philistines at bay for a generation.

It is not easy to come to a balanced assessment of Saul and his reign, partly because the Bible concentrates on his relationships with Samuel and David and tells us very little about the other aspects of Saul, as man and king. David had a high regard for him as a soldier (cp. 2 Sam. 1:17-27), and the people of Jabesh-gilead were prepared to risk their lives just to rescue his corpse. On the other hand, his final defeat had very serious effects on the Israelites; some of these effects are indicated in verse 7. No doubt he had created an administrative structure and a standing army which probably survived him; but the army itself suffered heavy losses at this battle and the survivors scattered to their homes. On the whole, the Philistine victory at Mount Gilboa seems to have put Israel back in the position in which it had found itself before the monarchy began. There was a lesson in this for Israel: monarchy itself would not save Israel. The essential thing was for the Israelites to have the *right* king. The reader knows by now that this was to be David; but we must remember that few in Israel were aware of this fact as yet; indeed, they had to find it out for themselves.

In some ways, Saul's greatest legacy was that he had shown what a good king might achieve; he had set possibilities and targets in front of the Israelite people. But when all is said and done, he failed. His failure was not due to military or political lack of ability, nor to Israelite weakness, but to his own refusal to be obedient to the will of God. However talented and courageous a man may be, he will fail the test of history unless he recognizes and acknowledges the Lord of history. This principle applies as much to the ordinary citizen as it does to men in prominent positions.

THE NEWS REACHES DAVID

2 Samuel 1:1-16

¹After the death of Saul, when David had returned from the slaughter of the Amalekites, David remained two days in Ziklag; ²and on the third day, behold, a man came from Saul's camp, with his clothes rent and earth upon his head. And when he came to David, he fell to the ground and did obeisance. ³David said to him, "Where do you come from?" And he said to him, "I have escaped from the camp of Israel." ⁴And David said to him, "How did it go? Tell me." And he answered, "The people have fled from the battle, and many of the people also have fallen and are dead; and Saul and his son Jonathan are also dead." ⁵Then David said to the young man who told him, "How do you know that Saul and his son Jonathan are dead?" ⁶And the young man who told him said, "By chance I happened to be on Mount Gilboa; and there was Saul leaning upon his spear; and lo, the chariots and the horsemen were close upon him. ⁷And when he looked behind him, he saw me, and called to me. And I answered, 'Here I am.' ⁸And he said to me, 'Who are you?' I answered him, 'I am an Amalekite.' ⁹And he said to me, 'Stand beside me and slay me; for anguish has seized me, and yet my life still lingers.' ¹⁰So I stood beside him, and slew him, because I was sure that he could not live after he had fallen; and I took the crown which was on his head and the armlet which was on his arm, and I have brought them here to my lord."

¹¹Then David took hold of his clothes, and rent them; and so did all the men who were with him; ¹²and they mourned and wept and fasted until evening for Saul and for Jonathan his son and for the people of the Lord and for the house of Israel, because they had fallen by the sword. ¹³And David said to the young man who told him, "Where do you come from?" And he answered, "I am the son of a sojourner, an Amalekite." ¹⁴David said to him, "How is it you were not afraid to put forth your hand to destroy the Lord's anointed?" ¹⁵Then David called one of the young men and said, "Go, fall upon him." And he smote him so that he died. ¹⁶And David said to him, "Your blood be upon your head; for your own mouth has testified against you, saying, 'I have slain the Lord's anointed.'"

The narrative continues without any break. The division of Samuel into two books is artificial; it was not until the Old Testament was translated into Greek that the division was made. 1 Sam. 31:7 has briefly indicated what effects the outcome of the battle of Gilboa had on Israelites in the north of the country; we are now told how the story reached the south of the land, where David was, and how he reacted to the news. Of course the Philistine victory was bad news for any and every Israelite, but a lesser man than David would have gloated over the death of Saul, so long his bitter enemy; and a more ambitious man than David would have been equally pleased about the death of Jonathan, since he would naturally have succeeded his father had he lived. Once again we are told that David was not Saul's enemy, not even in his private thoughts.

The man who brought him the news was an Amalekite, one of the hated race who had recently raided Ziklag, David's headquarters (cp. 1 Sam. 30). However, he was obviously not a member of the raiding party, and may even have been a soldier in Saul's army. David did not comment on his nationality but on his own claims. His story that he had "helped" Saul to commit suicide seems to have been untrue, in view of the details given in 1 Sam. 31:4f.; it seems certain that he imagined that David would be delighted to receive the news of Saul's death, and no less pleased to get possession of the royal crown. The Amalekite messenger's action is of special interest; even though he probably knew that Saul had a surviving son (Ish-bosheth by name, cp. 2:8ff.), he deliberately brought the crown to David, which shows that he was convinced that David would be the next king of Israel. This gesture might well have been very gratifying to a lesser man than David, but David was not influenced by such flattery, and he took an attitude to the messenger's story which came as a great shock to the man.

We might tend to feel that the Amalekite was very unlucky. To begin with, his story was untrue, and he had not killed Saul; but those who tell lies for the purpose of gain can hardly complain when what they say is taken seriously. But even if his story were true, to administer the *coup de grâce* to a dying man could be interpreted as an act of mercy—especially when the Philistines would otherwise have tortured and tormented the wounded king.

David was not in the least concerned with the ethics of euthanasia or suicide; his one and only consideration was that this messenger claimed to have killed the king of Israel, the crime of regicide. He himself—though admittedly in very different circumstances—had refused even to lift a finger against the king, simply because of his sacred status as *the Lord's anointed* (cp. 1 Sam. 24:6; 26:9ff.). Only God himself had the right to determine when and how the man whom he had anointed should die; whatever his motives, the Amalekite had been guilty of murder and treason, and had usurped the prerogative of God himself. Nothing less than the death penalty was appropriate for such a deed. Once again, then, it is stressed that David put the highest value on royal status.

The Amalekite treated David as the new king; David responded by acting as a judge. In fact, the two offices went together; the king was the chief judge, perhaps the only judge, in the land. More and more, therefore, David was having to take the role of king. All that remained was for the proper formal recognition of him as king by his subjects-to-be. Step by step, God's will for David was becoming clearer to the nation.

DAVID'S ELEGY

2 Samuel 1:17–27

[17]And David lamented with this lamentation over Saul and Jonathan his son, [18]and he said it should be taught to the people of Judah; behold, it is written in the Book of Jashar. He said:
[19]"Thy glory, O Israel, is slain upon thy high places!
        How are the mighty fallen!
[20]Tell it not in Gath,
        publish it not in the streets of Ashkelon;
    lest the daughters of the Philistines rejoice,
        lest the daughters of the uncircumcised exult.

²¹"Ye mountains of Gilboa,
    let there be no dew or rain upon you,
    nor upsurging of the deep!
For there the shield of the mighty was defiled,
    the shield of Saul, not anointed with oil.

²²"From the blood of the slain,
    from the fat of the mighty,
the bow of Jonathan turned not back,
    and the sword of Saul returned not empty.

²³"Saul and Jonathan, beloved and lovely!
    In life and in death they were not divided;
they were swifter than eagles,
    they were stronger than lions.

²⁴"Ye daughters of Israel, weep over Saul,
    who clothed you daintily in scarlet,
    who put ornaments of gold upon your apparel.

²⁵"How are the mighty fallen
    in the midst of the battle!

"Jonathan lies slain upon thy high places.
²⁶ I am distressed for you, my brother Jonathan;
very pleasant have you been to me;
    your love to me was wonderful,
    passing the love of women.

²⁷"How are the mighty fallen,
    and the weapons of war perished!"

David's reaction to the messenger was swift and relentless; his reaction to the name of Saul was quite different, showing nothing but praise and admiration for the dead king. He felt no hatred of the man who had pursued him so single-mindedly, nor did he brush him aside like a bad memory. On the contrary, he composed an elegy, a poem to be learned and repeated by the people of Israel, so that the name of Saul, with that of Jonathan, should never be forgotten. The Hebrew text of verse 18 is difficult and uncertain, but it seems that David not only incorporated this poem in a book but also took steps to ensure that it became well-known, by frequent repetition. This happened only in *Judah*, because David's authority extended no further for some years after Saul's death; but it was particularly appropriate for Judah to be reminded of its debt to Saul, who was not a Judaean, especially during the years when one of Saul's sons was ruling the rest of Israel and fighting against Judah (as chapter 2 goes on to describe).

The poem expresses the nation's debt to both Saul and Jonathan and David's personal debt to Jonathan's friendship—David was not hypocritical enough to claim that Saul had ever been his close friend. The poem is not always easy to understand; it is important to remember, in the first place, that its language is meant to be poetic, so that it is full of figures of speech of various kinds, and its author never intended it to be taken with literal woodenness. For instance, he did not really suppose that the news of the Philistine victory could or would be kept a secret from the Philistine cities (verse 20), nor did he imagine that the hills of Gilboa, where so many Israelite soldiers had died with Saul, would be denied normal weather conditions (verse 21). Nor was his description of Jonathan's friendship meant to be taken as a criticism of his own wives (verse 26).

David's first description of Saul is as the *glory* of Israel; the Hebrew word really means "beauty" and also "gazelle", so the poem pictures Saul as the beautiful mountain gazelle, with all its grace and sure-footedness. The images of *eagles* and *lions* (verse 23) are more familiar to us. Chiefly David remembered Saul as a soldier: the word *mighty* (verse 19) means a warrior. As a soldier, Saul had been consistently effective (verse 22), especially against the Philistines, and because of this had brought prosperity to Israel (verse 24). The final statement of the poem (verse 27) suggests that Saul and Jonathan had been the very best *weapons* available to the Israelites, and now at one stroke both were gone. Israel was very much the poorer for their passing; no wonder the Philistines were rejoicing (verse 20).

In recalling a man's good points, we can be moved to gratitude or emulation, or perhaps both. There was still much to be done to defeat the Philistines, but Saul had at least pointed the way and shown by courage and dedication to the task that it could be done. To recall such good points is much more sensible than remembering a man's failings and failures, which may, it is true, prove a useful warning to others, but all too often lead to self-righteousness and complacency.

Except for verse 26, Jonathan's name is less prominent than Saul's. He too was a fine soldier, but it was above all his loyal friendship which David recalled and treasured in his memory. The friendship between David and Jonathan has become proverbial, the very model of what a friendship should be. It was long-lasting and consistent even when they were parted; loyal and selfless; yet it was realistic, and it was not allowed to override other relationships and responsibilities. All this arose out of spontaneous and real comradeship and affection, needless to say.

In this connection, it should perhaps be added that the words of verse 26 have misled certain modern writers into the speculation that David and Jonathan were "lovers", in a homosexual relationship. This is undoubtedly a misunderstanding, which arises partly from the modern English usage of the word "love" and partly from the failure to read verse 26 as a poetic, not a literal, statement. In view of the consistent biblical repudiation of homosexual practices, it is quite certain that this biblical writer never meant his words to signify any such thing; indeed, he would have been horrified to see his words misrepresented in such a fashion. It is vital to our understanding of the Bible that we should read it in its own cultural context.

RIVAL KINGS

2 Samuel 2:1–11

[1]After this David inquired of the Lord, "Shall I go up into any of the cities of Judah?" And the Lord said to him, "Go up." David said, "To which shall I go up?" And he said, "To Hebron." [2]So David

went up there, and his two wives also, Ahino-am of Jezreel, and Abigail the widow of Nabal of Carmel. ³And David brought up his men who were with him, every one with his household; and they dwelt in the towns of Hebron. ⁴And the men of Judah came, and there they anointed David king over the house of Judah.

When they told David, "It was the men of Jabesh-gilead who buried Saul," ⁵David sent messengers to the men of Jabesh-gilead, and said to them, "May you be blessed by the Lord, because you showed this loyalty to Saul your lord, and buried him! ⁶Now may the Lord show steadfast love and faithfulness to you! And I will do good to you because you have done this thing. ⁷Now therefore let your hands be strong, and be valiant; for Saul your lord is dead, and the house of Judah has anointed me king over them."

⁸Now Abner the son of Ner, commander of Saul's army, had taken Ish-bosheth the son of Saul, and brought him over to Mahanaim; ⁹and he made him king over Gilead and the Ashurites and Jezreel and Ephraim and Benjamin and all Israel. ¹⁰Ish-bosheth, Saul's son, was forty years old when he began to reign over Israel, and he reigned two years. But the house of Judah followed David. ¹¹And the time that David was king in Hebron over the house of Judah was seven years and six months.

The ordinary machinery of government broke down with the death of Saul and his crown prince, Jonathan, and it was left to two high-ranking soldiers to fill the political vacuum. One was Abner, who had been Saul's chief general, and the other was David, at one time one of Saul's commanders but now the general of his own small army at Ziklag, on the western frontier of Judah. It is still a frequent occurrence for the army to take control in times of national crisis and emergency.

The actions of the two men were rather different. Abner determined to seize power for himself, but to exercise it indirectly; so he set up a puppet-king, a surviving son of Saul's called Ish-bosheth (verses 8f.). This move evidently had the popular support of the great majority of Israelites, the one big exception being the tribe of Judah. The details given about Ish-bosheth's realm give us some indication of the effects of the recent Philistine victory. Although he was recognized as king over his own tribal territory, Benjamin, he dared not attempt to make Gibeah his capital, as Saul had done; the only safe place for his capital and headquarters was on the east of the Jordan, well away from Philistine bases. So Mahanaim was chosen (see Map 2). It is difficult to guess how much control he really exercised over *Jezreel and Ephraim and Benjamin*, now that the Philistines were powerful again in areas west of the river. At any rate, he was undoubtedly a weak king (thanks to Abner) in a weakened kingdom. Abner's act in making Ish-bosheth king was quite a natural step, but yet it was undertaken for selfish motives, and evidently without any consideration for God's will in the matter; no prophet was consulted.

With David, on the other hand, the very first step was to seek to find out God's will, and only afterwards did he move from Ziklag to Hebron, one of the chief cities of Judah. Hebron was a very suitable capital, but David, unlike Abner, did not seize power; it was the tribe of Judah which took the initiative and crowned David as their king. Ish-bosheth's subjects *accepted* Ish-bosheth as king; David's subjects *chose* David as king. It is interesting to note that although the Bible lays stress on the importance of the divine choice, passages like this recognize the great importance of popular choice. The ideal ruler is one who is both chosen by God and also fully acceptable to his people.

So at last David took the first direct step towards becoming king of all Israel. His message to the townsfolk of Jabesh-gilead (verses 5–7) shows that he was already looking ahead to kingship over the whole country. Jabesh-gilead, the city which had shown such loyalty to Saul (cp. 1 Sam. 31:11ff.), was over in Transjordan, not very far north of Ish-bosheth's capital, but David's message to it ignored the very existence of his rival! David did not ask them to support him against Ish-bosheth; rather, he conveyed the idea that both Judah and Jabesh were on the same side—not against Ish-bosheth but against the Philistines. (It seems as if the Philistines were quite happy to permit David to be king of Judah, no doubt because it suited them to see Israel divided into two warring camps.)

It is not quite clear how long Israel and Judah were divided; verse 11 reports that David was king of Judah for seven years or so, while Ish-bosheth lasted as king of the northern tribes for only two years. It is doubtful if Ish-bosheth's citizens waited fully five years after Ish-bosheth's death before accepting David as king; and it seems equally improbable that David was king of Judah for five years *before* Abner made Ish-bosheth king in Mahanaim. The figures are thus a little puzzling, but at any rate Israel was not to remain divided for very long. All the time it was divided, the Philistines were really the dominant factor; and that was not God's intention for his people.

CIVIL WAR

2 Samuel 2:12–3:1

12Abner the son of Ner, and the servants of Ish-bosheth the son of Saul, went out from Mahanaim to Gibeon. 13And Joab the son of Zeruiah, and the servants of David, went out and met them at the pool of Gibeon; and they sat down, the one on the one side of the pool, and the other on the other side of the pool. 14And Abner said to Joab, "Let the young men arise and play before us." And Joab said, "Let them arise." 15Then they arose and passed over by number, twelve for Benjamin and Ish-bosheth the son of Saul, and twelve of the servants of David. 16And each caught his opponent by the head, and thrust his sword in his opponent's side; so they fell down together. Therefore that place was called Helkath-hazzurim, which is at Gibeon. 17And the battle was very fierce that day; and Abner and the men of Israel were beaten before the servants of David.

18And the three sons of Zeruiah were there, Joab, Abishai, and Asahel. Now Asahel was as swift of foot as a wild gazelle; 19and Asahel pursued Abner, and as he went he turned neither to the right hand nor to the left from following Abner. 20Then Abner looked behind him and said, "Is it you, Asahel?" And he answered, "It is I." 21Abner said to him, "Turn aside to your right hand or to your left, and seize one of the young men, and take his spoil." But Asahel would not turn aside from following him. 22And Abner said again to Asahel, "Turn aside from following me; why should I smite you to the ground? How then could I lift up my face to your brother Joab?" 23But he refused to turn aside; therefore Abner smote him in the belly with the butt of his spear, so that the spear came out at his back; and he fell there, and died where he was. And all who came to the place where Asahel had fallen and died, stood still.

24But Joab and Abishai pursued Abner; and as the sun was going down they came to the hill of Ammah, which lies before Giah on the way to the wilderness of Gibeon. 25And the Benjaminites gathered themselves together behind Abner, and became one band, and took their stand on the top of a hill. 26Then Abner called to Joab, "Shall the sword devour for ever? Do you not know that the end will be bitter? How long will it be before you bid your people turn from the pursuit of their brethren?" 27And Joab said, "As God lives, if you had not spoken, surely the men would have given up the pursuit of their brethren in the morning." 28So Joab blew the trumpet; and all the men stopped, and pursued Israel no more, nor did they fight any more.

29And Abner and his men went all that night through the Arabah; they crossed the Jordan, and marching the whole forenoon they came to Mahanaim. 30Joab returned from the pursuit of Abner; and when he had gathered all the people together, there were missing of David's servants nineteen men besides Asahel. 31But the servants of David had slain of Benjamin three hundred and sixty of Abner's men. 32And they took up Asahel, and buried him in the tomb of his father, which was at Bethlehem. And Joab and his men marched all night, and the day broke upon them at Hebron.

1There was a long war between the house of Saul and the house of David; and David grew stronger and stronger, while the house of Saul became weaker and weaker.

In the circumstances, it was impossible that the two Israelite kingdoms should be neutral towards each other. It is doubtful whether David had any wish to attack Ish-bosheth or his kingdom, but the rest of Israel must have disapproved of Judah's breaking away, and of its refusal to accept Saul's son as king. Probably, then, Abner was the aggressor in the incident related here; but we cannot be sure. The two sides met at Gibeon, which was in Benjamin, very close to the frontier of Judah (see Map 2). At first sight, it looks as if some sort of sporting contest went wrong and led to fighting and bloodshed; but it is virtually certain that the verb *play* in verse 14 here means to engage in representative combat, and most modern

English versions translate the verse accordingly. David and Goliath had engaged in single combat (cp. 1 Sam. 17); this time there were twelve men on each side. If one side had won, probably the moral victory won would have avoided further bloodshed.

Warfare followed fairly strict rules and conventions in the ancient world. In a case of civil war, like this, it was vital to reduce hostilities to a minimum, to avoid a legacy of hatred and bitterness; both sides wanted victory, naturally, but neither side wished to humiliate the other, and both were anxious to avoid blood-feuds and vendettas which might continue for many years. However, on this occasion things did not go as planned, and a considerable number of Benjaminites died (verse 31); the numbers are not large by today's standards, but Benjamin was a small tribe. Some men did not forgive David readily: see 16:5–8. We do not know how many battles and skirmishes took place altogether, but David was consistently successful (3:1). This was yet another sign that God favoured him and had rejected not only Saul but his family as well.

The chief interest in the story concerns the death of one man, Asahel. He was no ordinary Judaean soldier but the brother of David's senior military officer, Joab; and the man who killed him was the chief general on the opposite side, Abner. This event, which Abner did his best to avoid, was soon to have an important sequel; but as for the story itself, the narrator's chief interest is to show how concerned both Abner and Joab were to avoid needless bloodshed. Both of them recognized that the men on the other side were their *brethren* (verses 26f.), their own flesh and blood. This was both true and wise. Abner also wisely showed his concern for future relationships when he tried to persuade Asahel to leave him alone (verse 22); it was not his fault that Asahel would not listen.

In the heat of battle it is far from easy to acknowledge that the other man is one's own fellow-citizen, even in a civil war; much less is it possible in wars against foreigners to recognize that the enemy are our *brethren*—fellow human beings in the sight of God. This recognition needs to be made before the fighting

starts, or it will be too late. Wise leadership shows itself in
seeing possible conflicts before they arise, and in taking every
practicable step to avoid them. In this case we can see that
Abner was being wise too late; it was he who had crowned as
king a man whom God had never chosen, and so provoked a
needless war with Judah, which had already adopted David as
its king. His own people were bound to suffer as a result; and
though he did not know it, he had put his own life in permanent
danger. With Abner, the pursuit of power was to bring personal
disaster.

ISH-BOSHETH'S FAILURE

2 Samuel 3:2–19

2And sons were born to David at Hebron: his first-born was Amnon,
of Ahino-am of Jezreel; 3and his second, Chile-ab, of Abigail the
widow of Nabal of Carmel; and the third, Absalom the son of
Maacah the daughter of Talmai king of Geshur; 4and the fourth,
Adonijah the son of Haggith; and the fifth, Shephatiah the son of
Abital; 5and the sixth, Ithre-am, of Eglah, David's wife. These were
born to David in Hebron.

6While there was war between the house of Saul and the house of
David, Abner was making himself strong in the house of Saul. 7Now
Saul had a concubine, whose name was Rizpah, the daughter of
Aiah; and Ish-bosheth said to Abner, "Why have you gone in to my
father's concubine?" 8Then Abner was very angry over the words of
Ish-bosheth, and said, "Am I a dog's head of Judah? This day I keep
showing loyalty to the house of Saul your father, to his brothers, and
to his friends, and have not given you into the hand of David; and
yet you charge me today with a fault concerning a woman. 9God do
so to Abner, and more also, if I do not accomplish for David what
the Lord has sworn to him, 10to transfer the kingdom from the house
of Saul, and set up the throne of David over Israel and over Judah,
from Dan to Beer-sheba." 11And Ish-bosheth could not answer
Abner another word, because he feared him.

12And Abner sent messengers to David at Hebron, saying, "To
whom does the land belong? Make your covenant with me, and
behold, my hand shall be with you to bring over all Israel to you."

¹³And he said, "Good; I will make a covenant with you; but one thing I require of you; that is, you shall not see my face, unless you first bring Michal, Saul's daughter, when you come to see my face." ¹⁴Then David sent messengers to Ish-bosheth Saul's son, saying, "Give me my wife Michal, whom I betrothed at the price of a hundred foreskins of the Philistines." ¹⁵And Ish-bosheth sent, and took her from her husband Paltiel the son of Laish. ¹⁶But her husband went with her, weeping after her all the way to Bahurim. Then Abner said to him, "Go, return"; and he returned.

¹⁷And Abner conferred with the elders of Israel, saying, "For some time past you have been seeking David as king over you. ¹⁸Now then bring it about; for the Lord has promised David, saying, 'By the hand of my servant David I will save my people Israel from the hand of the Philistines, and from the hand of all their enemies.'" ¹⁹Abner also spoke to Benjamin; and then Abner went to tell David at Hebron all that Israel and the whole house of Benjamin thought good to do.

Power is the keynote of this passage—the growing power of David, the power-seeking of Abner, and the weakness of Ish-bosheth.

(i) The paragraph giving details of *David*'s family (verses 2–5), no doubt taken from an ancient archive, has the effect of showing how firmly established David was in Judah. Already he was developing a harem, even if he was king of a very small realm as yet. We know little about most of his wives and their sons. The name of chief interest in the list is Absalom, who would one day turn traitor against his father; what is interesting at this point is to notice that his mother was a princess. *Geshur* was an Aramaean state, lying to the north of Ish-bosheth's kingdom (see Map 1). It is plain that David was making important alliances which would help to weaken his rival's position.

David was also fully determined to retrieve his first wife, Michal (verses 12–16). Nothing is said about David loving her; he was of course entitled to his first wife, but the important issue for him was that she was Saul's daughter. By making her his queen he would divide the loyalties of citizens in the north: did loyalty to Saul's memory mean that they should be the subjects of his son, Ish-bosheth, or of his daughter? By such means David could weaken his opponent without killing a single Israelite soldier and without causing any resentment at all.

(ii) As for *Abner*, naked self-interest motivated him. At first he was content merely to dominate the young king by the force of his own personality, but when he approached one of Saul's concubines he gave every appearance of trying to become king himself. To take over the concubines of a dead king was one way of establishing a claim to the throne (cp. 16:20–23). Either this was Abner's intention, or else he was deliberately picking a quarrel with Ish-bosheth so that he would have an excuse for deserting him. Whichever it was, he did quarrel with Ish-bosheth over the woman, and immediately transferred his allegiance to David. He now admitted to something he had previously ignored, namely the fact that David had been chosen by God to be king. His careful approach to David, making a covenant with him, was designed not only to protect his life but also, we may be sure, to obtain promises about his future position in David's administration. Abner was a very ambitious man, and no doubt he hoped to become David's commander-in-chief as he had been Saul's. He felt no loyalties now to Saul's family; he simply wanted to be on the winning side, come what may.

(iii) By now *Ish-bosheth*'s cause was doomed. Quite apart from the fact that Abner was deserting him, it is clear that many of the most influential citizens in Israel had come to realize that the only hope for the future, the only man who could lead Israel successfully against the Philistines, was David (verse 17).

Ish-bosheth's weakness must have been public knowledge, where his father's concubine and his sister Michal were concerned: he lost one, in a sense, to Abner and the other to David. There is a dramatic contrast with David in all this: while David built up a harem, Ish-bosheth could not control the princesses of his court.

In all this tangle of power politics, it is worth sparing a thought for the concubine and for Michal, whose own wishes nobody consulted. They were mere pawns in the game, and so too was Paltiel, Michal's second husband. Perhaps he had been too ambitious when he had married Michal; be that as it may, his sorrow in losing her now was deep and genuine. The ruthless ambition of a man like Abner leaves many an innocent victim in its train. Ambition is no bad thing in itself, but it can easily become an utterly selfish and cruel motive force in the life of any man or woman. It is probably true that no man achieves a position of leadership without some degree of ambition, but no good and popular leader ever gained his position by trampling on others on the way up.

THE DEATH OF ABNER

2 Samuel 3:20–39

[20]When Abner came with twenty men to David at Hebron, David made a feast for Abner and the men who were with him. [21]And Abner said to David, "I will arise and go, and will gather all Israel to my lord the king, that they may make a covenant with you, and that you may reign over all that your heart desires." So David sent Abner away; and he went in peace.

[22]Just then the servants of David arrived with Joab from a raid, bringing much spoil with them. But Abner was not with David at Hebron, for he had sent him away, and he had gone in peace. [23]When Joab and all the army that was with him came, it was told Joab, "Abner the son of Ner came to the king, and he has let him go, and he has gone in peace." [24]Then Joab went to the king and said, "What have you done? Behold, Abner came to you; why is it that you have sent him away, so that he is gone? [25]You know that Abner the son of Ner came to deceive you, and to know your going out and your coming in, and to know all that you are doing."

[26]When Joab came out from David's presence, he sent messengers after Abner, and they brought him back from the cistern of Sirah; but David did not know about it. [27]And when Abner returned to Hebron, Joab took him aside into the midst of the gate to speak with him privately, and there he smote him in the belly, so that he died, for the blood of Asahel his brother. [28]Afterward, when David heard of it, he said, "I and my kingdom are for ever guiltless before the Lord for the blood of Abner the son of Ner. [29]May it fall upon the

head of Joab, and upon all his father's house; and may the house of Joab never be without one who has a discharge, or who is leprous, or who holds a spindle, or who is slain by the the sword, or who lacks bread!" [30]So Joab and Abishai his brother slew Abner, because he had killed their brother Asahel in the battle at Gibeon.

[31]Then David said to Joab and to all the people who were with him, "Rend your clothes, and gird on sackcloth, and mourn before Abner." And King David followed the bier. [32]They buried Abner at Hebron; and the king lifted up his voice and wept at the grave of Abner; and all the people wept. [33]And the king lamented for Abner, saying,

"Should Abner die as a fool dies?
[34]Your hands were not bound,
  your feet were not fettered;
as one falls before the wicked
  you have fallen."

And all the people wept again over him. [35]Then all the people came to persuade David to eat bread while it was yet day; but David swore, saying, "God do so to me and more also, if I taste bread or anything else till the sun goes down!" [36]And all the people took notice of it, and it pleased them; as everything that the king did pleased all the people. [37]So all the people and all Israel understood that day that it had not been the king's will to slay Abner the son of Ner. [38]And the king said to his servants, "Do you not know that a prince and a great man has fallen this day in Israel? [39]And I am this day weak, though anointed king; these men the sons of Zeruiah are too hard for me. The Lord requite the evildoer according to his wickedness!"

In this narrative once again three men hold the centre of the stage: David and Abner are two of them, and this time the third is Joab, David's nephew and chief soldier. The central event is the murder of Abner by Joab. The space and attention given by the writer to this event shows that it was no minor incident; it was the sort of thing which would nowadays capture the headlines in all the newspapers and invite a great deal of comment. The fact was that Abner was a man of outstanding importance, influence and reputation in Israel. If he had lived, it is certain that he would have been a leading political figure in David's kingdom, though it is impossible to guess whether he would have chosen to put his weight behind the king or, on the other hand, have undermined David's position in order to gain greater power for himself. It seems that David was prepared to trust him, but Joab took a very different view, arguing that Abner was a deceiver and a spy (verse 25). Perhaps Joab would have been proved right in the long term; in the short term the death of Abner was a setback for David which delayed the reunion of Israel and Judah.

(i) *David.* An important aspect of the affair was the question of David's reputation. The murder of Abner was a great embarrassment to him: we could call Abner a foreign dignitary at this stage, and he was killed in Judah, by one of David's closest friends and associates, at a time when he held the promise of David's safe conduct. No wonder tongues wagged and suggested that David was behind the assassination. A number of modern scholars too have questioned David's innocence. Let us suppose that David was indeed anxious about the extent of Abner's power and influence, and saw advantages in planning his murder; he would surely never have carried out any such plan at this critical stage in the negotiations with Israel, when Abner had just promised to persuade all the the northern tribes of Israel to abandon Ish-bosheth and make David their king (verse 21). David was not such a fool as to wreck these negotiations and to risk alienating the northern Israelites permanently. As it was, he had to take public steps to lay the blame where it belonged, and ensure that nobody believed that he was responsible. God's chosen leaders must have not only clear consciences but also good reputations (see 1 Tim. 3:7). The steps David took proved to be sufficient (verses 36f.).

(ii) *Abner.* Abner had a great reputation as a soldier and as a political figure. Probably the lament composed by David had much to say about his abilities and achievements; but the small section of it preserved by the biblical writer in verses 33f. has a single word for him—a *fool.* The man who had survived many battles against the Philistines unscathed was foolish enough to trust Joab, and it was one mistake too many.

David seems to have been surprised by Abner's lack of caution. Indeed, it was a perfect example of pride going before a fall. Abner was too sure of his own importance in David's eyes to suspect that any of David's officers would dare to attack him. And so the man of ruthless ambition in the end achieved nothing but an untimely death; his treachery to Ish-bosheth gained him nothing.

(iii) *Joab*. Joab was already an important figure in David's small kingdom of Judah, and he was soon to become even more important in the reunited kingdom of Israel. Perhaps he was ambitious, and jealous of Abner, who would very likely have been made the commander-in-chief of David's armies, displacing Joab. Perhaps he sincerely believed that Abner was extremely dangerous to David's 'cause, as he claimed, and acted—as he thought—in David's best interests when he assassinated Abner. But probably he was obsessed by one thing and one thing only—personal revenge, because Abner had killed his brother (2:23). Such blood-feuds are utterly destructive to society, as has been proved over and over again in history; it was a wonder that this particular assassination had no repercussions in Israel. Hatred and vengeful feelings are emotions which have no place at all in Christian thinking and behaviour; they are self-centred, warped and destructive emotions, with no positive values at all. Political assassinations are doubly to be deplored: they may cause national turmoil and crisis, and harm many innocent people. In this case only David's good sense and public denunciation of Joab avoided severe political repercussions.

THE DEATH OF ISH-BOSHETH

2 Samuel 4:1-12

[1]When Ish-bosheth, Saul's son, heard that Abner had died at Hebron, his courage failed, and all Israel was dismayed. [2]Now Saul's son had two men who were captains of raiding bands; the name of the one was Baanah, and the name of the other Rechab, sons of

Rimmon a man of Benjamin from Be-eroth (for Be-eroth also is reckoned to Benjamin; 3the Be-erothites fled to Gittaim, and have been sojourners there to this day).

4Jonathan, the son of Saul, had a son who was crippled in his feet. He was five years old when the news about Saul and Jonathan came from Jezreel; and his nurse took him up, and fled; and, as she fled in her haste, he fell, and became lame. And his name was Mephibosheth.

5Now the sons of Rimmon the Be-erothite, Rechab and Baanah, set out, and about the heat of the day they came to the house of Ish-bosheth, as he was taking his noonday rest. 6And behold, the doorkeeper of the house had been cleaning wheat, but she grew drowsy and slept; so Rechab and Baanah his brother slipped in. 7When they came into the house, as he lay on his bed in his bedchamber, they smote him, and slew him, and beheaded him. They took his head, and went by the way of the Arabah all night, 8and brought the head of Ish-bosheth to David at Hebron. And they said to the king, "Here is the head of Ish-bosheth, the son of Saul, your enemy, who sought your life; the Lord has avenged my lord the king this day on Saul and on his offspring." 9But David answered Rechab and Baanah his brother, the sons of Rimmon the Be-erothite, "As the Lord lives, who has redeemed my life out of every adversity, 10when one told me, 'Behold, Saul is dead,' and thought he was bringing good news, I seized him and slew him at Ziklag, which was the reward I gave him for his news. 11How much more, when wicked men have slain a righteous man in his own house upon his bed, shall I not now require his blood at your hand, and destroy you from the earth?" 12And David commanded his young men, and they killed them, and cut off their hands and feet, and hanged them beside the pool at Hebron. But they took the head of Ish-bosheth, and buried it in the tomb of Abner at Hebron.

Abner's importance is demonstrated by the effect which his death had upon Ish-bosheth and his kingdom: both were demoralized, and for a time a political vacuum resulted in Israel. Obviously Ish-bosheth could scarcely be expected to abdicate, and those of his citizens who wanted David to be their king were disheartened by the breakdown of negotiations. So from a human point of view, it is not surprising that somebody should decide to break the deadlock by eliminating Ish-bosheth; by now he was the only real barrier to the reunion of Israel and Judah under David's rule.

Two Israelite army officers, then, took it upon themselves to assassinate the unwanted king. Bringing Ish-bosheth's head by way of proof, they carried the good news, as they supposed it, to David in Hebron. They were sure that they would get a warm welcome, and probably a reward as well: instead they were executed on the spot for murder. Joab, after all, had had some excuse for killing Abner; they had none for killing Ish-bosheth.

Nowadays all sorts of legal problems would be involved: the assassins would need to be extradited, for trial in their own country. Indeed, it is far from clear what actual jurisdiction David had in this matter. Ish-bosheth was not a Judaean, and he had not been killed in Judah. The fact was, in any case, that David made himself their judge; he had the power, and he insisted on his right to act for the welfare of the whole of Israel. His attitude would have been very reassuring to any Israelites who feared that David might show hostility to former associates and supporters of the family of Saul. One man who might well have feared reprisals is mentioned here in passing— Jonathan's son Mephibosheth (verse 4). David's good treatment of him is only hinted at now; the full story is told in chapter 9.

Another reason for David's severity was again the need to demonstrate that he had absolutely no hand in the death of Ish-bosheth. Some cynics might have guessed that David had bribed the assassins, but such suspicions were scotched when David swiftly put them on trial. Evidently they could find nothing to say in their own defence.

A point of special interest is David's description of Ish-bosheth. He did not call him "the Lord's anointed"; he had recognized Saul as such, and refused on that account to lift a finger against him. As he now recalled, too, he had executed the Amalekite who had dared to end the life of the Lord's anointed. Ish-bosheth, in contrast with Saul, ought never to have become king; he had done so without the authority of any prophet, pushed into the position by Abner. By now it was David himself who was the Lord's anointed. However, David could and did acknowledge that Ish-bosheth was *a righteous man* (verse 11). He had promoted the warfare against Judah, it is true, but within his own kingdom he had done nothing to merit treason or assassination. David was simply recognizing facts in so describing his dead rival.

Fairness and justice are essential to all good rule; in the case of Israel and David, it is clear that the proper administration of justice was of great importance to David, especially in the early years of his reign.

We know from many ancient documents that law and justice were matters of very great importance in the whole of the Near East, and that it was viewed as the special duty of the king of each state to maintain the country's laws and to provide justice for all the citizens. Indeed, a sense of fairness and a longing for justice seem to be universal human characteristics; there is scarcely a child who does not now and then voice the protest, "It isn't fair!" This is surely a facet of the nature implanted in us all by the Creator, and it is his concern to promote justice in his world. He is himself "the righteous judge" (cp. Ps. 7:11), and it was the divine intention that his Messiah should bring full justice to the earth (cp. Isa. 11:3ff.). Only the proper punishment of the guilty (though the *means* of their punishment may vary) can bring a sense of security and well-being to ordinary citizens. From the start of his reign over a united Israel David meant to show his passion for justice.

David, then, executed Ish-bosheth's murderers and made it plain to all Israelites that he did not approve of achieving power by such methods. Nevertheless the assassination did his cause no harm, and once again the narrator wishes the reader to see that God stood over the events of history, manipulating them to David's advantage. God can work by means of, as well as in spite of, human misdeeds.

THE CAPTURE OF JERUSALEM

2 Samuel 5:1-16

¹Then all the tribes of Israel came to David at Hebron, and said, "Behold, we are your bone and flesh. ²In times past, when Saul was king over us, it was you that led out and brought in Israel; and the Lord said to you, 'You shall be shepherd of my people Israel, and you shall be prince over Israel.'" ³So all the elders of Israel came to the king at Hebron; and King David made a covenant with them at Hebron before the Lord, and they anointed David king over Israel. ⁴David was thirty years old when he began to reign, and he reigned forty years. ⁵At Hebron he reigned over Judah seven years and six months; and at Jerusalem he reigned over all Israel and Judah thirty-three years.

⁶And the king and his men went to Jerusalem against the Jebusites, the inhabitants of the land, who said to David, "You will not come in here, but the blind and the lame will ward you off"— thinking, "David cannot come in here." ⁷Nevertheless David took the stronghold of Zion, that is, the city of David. ⁸And David said on that day, "Whoever would smite the Jebusites, let him get up the water shaft to attack the lame and the blind, who are hated by David's soul." Therefore it is said, "The blind and the lame shall not come into the house." ⁹And David dwelt in the stronghold, and called it the city of David. And David built the city round about from the Millo inward. ¹⁰And David became greater and greater, for the Lord, the God of hosts, was with him.

¹¹And Hiram king of Tyre sent messengers to David, and cedar trees, also carpenters and masons who built David a house. ¹²And David perceived that the Lord had established him king over Israel, and that he had exalted his kingdom for the sake of his people Israel.

¹³And David took more concubines and wives from Jerusalem, after he came from Hebron; and more sons and daughters were born to David. ¹⁴And these are the names of those who were born to him in Jerusalem: Shammu-a, Shobab, Nathan, Solomon, ¹⁵Ibhar, Elishu-a, Nepheg, Japhia, ¹⁶Elishama, Eliada, and Eliphelet.

Two of the most significant events in world history now took place. The first was when David became king of a united Israel. The second was when he made Jerusalem the capital of his united realm. We must not exaggerate the *political* importance of either event; Israel was never a major world power, not even under David himself, and Jerusalem has never been a city to rival Babylon or Rome, London or New York, in terms of political power and influence. At the time when David became king and captured Jerusalem, none of the major kingdoms around (such as Egypt) would have been very interested or impressed. But the two events were of great and lasting *religious* significance.

(i) *David* began a line of kings which lasted for over four hundred years, and left behind the hope of a second and greater David, who would claim the historical David as his ancestor. This hope was fulfilled in the birth of Jesus Christ, as every Christmas reminds us. So the figure of David lies behind the whole of Christianity, with all its vast effects upon the world. (In that sense, David has after all helped to shape the world political scene.) Christians as well as Jews have grounds for being grateful to David's memory.

(ii) *Jerusalem* was till now a foreign city inside Israel; its occupants were a Canaanite group called Jebusites. David determined to conquer it, and managed to do so easily enough, even though it was well defended—its walls and steep slopes were such a natural defence that a garrison of cripples could have kept David out, the Jebusites wrongly supposed! David went on to make it a *military headquarters*, for which it was well suited, and the *national capital* too. This was a shrewd move, because Jerusalem lay on the frontier between the tribes of Judah and Benjamin, so by making it his capital David avoided favouring any tribe, north or south.

Most important of all, he made it the *religious capital*. It gradually came to displace all other sanctuaries and shrines in Israel, and eventually provided the only accepted religious centre for the Jews. It stands without a rival in Christian affection too, as the city not only of David's triumphs but also of Jesus' crucifixion and resurrection. Muslims too view it as a holy city, along with Mecca and Medina. For David's capture and transformation of Jerusalem, then, the world owes him an enormous debt.

The chief emphasis in this passage is on the security and stability of David and his kingdom; the second half of the chapter indicates that this security did not come easily or automatically, but that is another matter. From the standpoint of history, it was God's firm intention to provide Israel with a period of success, power and prosperity, under David's leadership—a golden age which would never be forgotten and which would set standards for the future. Golden ages may be few in human history, but they have provided not merely nostalgia but positive values, targets to aim at, ideals to be pursued. That they are possible at all renews hope in times of widespread despair and intractable problems. The expectation of a Messianic king who would one day usher in a kingdom of power, peace and every prosperity buoyed up Jewish hopes over many centuries, and the New Testament is full of promises to Christians about our returning King. In our present age of gloom and pessimism we do well to remember that the Scriptures and the Church have always taught that ultimately God will reign supreme, and all will be prosperity and peace. Till then our sincere prayer should be, "Thy kingdom come, thy will be done . . . ".

VICTORY OVER THE PHILISTINES

2 Samuel 5:17–25

[17]When the Philistines heard that David had been anointed king over Israel, all the Philistines went up in search of David; but David heard of it and went down to the stronghold. [18]Now the Philistines had come and spread out in the valley of Rephaim. [19]And David inquired of the Lord, "Shall I go up against the Philistines? Wilt thou give them into my hand?" And the Lord said to David, "Go up; for I will certainly give the Philistines into your hand." [20]And David came to Baal-perazim, and David defeated them there; and he said, "The Lord has broken through my enemies before me, like a bursting flood." Therefore the name of that place is called Baal-perazim. [21]And the Philistines left their idols there, and David and his men carried them away.

22And the Philistines came up yet again, and spread out in the valley of Rephaim. 23And when David inquired of the Lord, he said, "You shall not go up; go around to their rear, and come upon them opposite the balsam trees. 24And when you hear the sound of marching in the tops of the balsam trees, then bestir yourself; for then the Lord has gone out before you to smite the army of the Philistines." 25And David did as the Lord commanded him, and smote the Philistines from Geba to Gezer.

All the while Israel was split into two small kingdoms at war with each other, the Philistines seem to have taken little action, but as soon as David became king of a united Israel they attacked. Probably their first invasion took place even before David captured Jerusalem; the *stronghold* mentioned in verse 17 is probably Adullam, which had been David's headquarters for a time when Saul was pursuing him (see Map 2). The valley of Rephaim lay to the south of Jerusalem, and here the Philistines stationed an army on two separate occasions, forcing David to attack them on ground of their own choosing. This was a tactic which had proved very successful against Saul at Gilboa (cp. 1 Sam. 31), but they now suffered two defeats at the hands of David. It looks as if the first victory for Israel was gained by a frontal assault; in the second David changed his tactics and surprised them from the cover of balsam trees in their rear. Such victories, no doubt including others which the Bible does not recount, resulted in the Philistines being driven back finally into their own territory on the Mediterranean coastal plain. That is the point of the mention of *Gezer* in verse 25; see the map.

It goes without saying that David must have been a brilliant soldier. He had proved that fact when in Saul's employ, and these great victories now against the Philistines proved it once again. However, the narrative makes it clear that he did not take a single step without seeking God's approval. He must have used the ephod, still in Abiathar's custody, as the method of finding out God's will. As can be seen from a study of 1 Sam. 23:9–12, one could ask direct questions of the ephod and receive simple answers (basically a simple "yes" or "no"). In other words, the initiative and tactical ideas were David's but he asked God, through the ephod, to say yes or no to them. This is a model for Christian activity and Christian leadership. We should use the brains and talents which God has given us in order to cope with the problems and needs of the time, not sit back and pray for God to do our thinking for us. But each scheme and project should be submitted to God in prayer; without him it cannot succeed.

David's victories, then, were rightly credited to God. It should be remembered that the two occasions when Saul had disobeyed God were precisely battle situations (cp. 1 Sam. 13 and 15). The true leader, however, not only used his native talents and abilities but also dedicated them to God; and Israel prospered as a result.

The scenes of great battles are often remembered for long years, even for centuries. The Battle of Hastings (1066), for instance, has given its name to the site—"Battle". In ancient Israel, too, place-names were often associated with events that happened there. It was long remembered that David's first victory occurred at Baal-perazim, literally "the Lord of breaking-through" (verse 20). This very name recalled that the victory was achieved not by David but by God. This was as it should be, because David eventually died and could fight Israel's battles no longer; but the God of Israel did not die, and he was the source of hope and courage for later generations of Israelites, especially in days when other enemies (such as Assyrians and Babylonians) had the upper hand.

The Philistines were so thoroughly beaten that they abandoned their idols (verse 21); a generation or so earlier they had captured the ark of the covenant (1 Sam. 4), but they had never defeated Israel's God. Now the tables were turned, but the Philistine gods were only man-made images and their capture was the end of the story. The Philistines were never again strong enough to threaten Israel; their power was permanently broken. This was David's most notable achievement, and the proof that he was God's chosen king.

THE ARK COMES TO JERUSALEM

2 Samuel 6:1–23

¹David again gathered all the chosen men of Israel, thirty thousand. ²And David arose and went with all the people who were with him from Baale-judah, to bring up from there the ark of God, which is called by the name of the Lord of hosts who sits enthroned on the cherubim. ³And they carried the ark of God upon a new cart, and brought it out of the house of Abinadab which was on the hill; and Uzzah and Ahio, the sons of Abinadab, were driving the new cart ⁴with the ark of God; and Ahio went before the ark. ⁵And David and all the house of Israel were making merry before the Lord with all their might, with songs and lyres and harps and tambourines and castanets and cymbals.

⁶And when they came to the threshing floor of Nacon, Uzzah put out his hand to the ark of God and took hold of it, for the oxen stumbled. ⁷And the anger of the Lord was kindled against Uzzah; and God smote him there because he put forth his hand to the ark; and he died there beside the ark of God. ⁸And David was angry because the Lord had broken forth upon Uzzah; and that place is called Perez-uzzah, to this day. ⁹And David was afraid of the Lord that day; and he said, "How can the ark of the Lord come to me?" ¹⁰So David was not willing to take the ark of the Lord into the city of David; but David took it aside to the house of Obed-edom the Gittite. ¹¹And the ark of the Lord remained in the house of Obed-edom the Gittite three months; and the Lord blessed Obed-edom and all his household.

¹²And it was told King David, "The Lord has blessed the household of Obed-edom and all that belongs to him, because of the ark of God." So David went and brought up the ark of God from the house of Obed-edom to the city of David with rejoicing; ¹³and when those who bore the ark of the Lord had gone six paces, he sacrificed an ox and a fatling. ¹⁴And David danced before the Lord with all his might; and David was girded with a linen ephod. ¹⁵So David and all the house of Israel brought up the ark of the Lord with shouting, and with the sound of the horn.

¹⁶As the ark of the Lord came into the city of David, Michal the

daughter of Saul looked out of the window, and saw King David
leaping and dancing before the Lord; and she despised him in her
heart. ¹⁷And they brought in the ark of the Lord, and set it in its
place, inside the tent which David had pitched for it; and David
offered burnt offerings and peace offerings before the Lord. ¹⁸And
when David had finished offering the burnt offerings and the peace
offerings, he blessed the people in the name of the Lord of hosts,
¹⁹and distributed among all the people, the whole multitude of
Israel, both men and women, to each a cake of bread, a portion of
meat, and a cake of raisins. Then all the people departed, each to his
house.

²⁰And David returned to bless his household. But Michal the
daughter of Saul came out to meet David, and said, "How the king
of Israel honoured himself today, uncovering himself today before
the eyes of his servants' maids, as one of the vulgar fellows
shamelessly uncovers himself!" ²¹And David said to Michal, "It was
before the Lord, who chose me above your father, and above all his
house, to appoint me as prince over Israel, the people of the Lord—
and I will make merry before the Lord. ²²I will make myself yet more
contemptible than this, and I will be abased in your eyes; but by the
maids of whom you have spoken, by them I shall be held in honour."
²³And Michal the daughter of Saul had no child to the day of her
death.

This chapter describes David's first steps in making Jerusalem
his religious capital. Much remained to be done afterwards;
even the permanent site for a sanctuary had yet to be found (see
chapter 24), and not till after David's death would a proper
temple be erected. Even so, the act of bringing the ark of the
covenant to Jerusalem, where it was to remain, was a very
significant one. The capture of Jerusalem had of course been
necessary first, and it is quite likely that the defeat of the
Philistines was equally essential, because Baale-judah (verse 2),
called Kiriath-jearim in 1 Sam. 7:2, was very close to Philistine
territory and may well have been under their control. At any
rate, the way was now open for the recovery of the ark, which
had been neglected for many years. David made its journey to
Jerusalem a national affair, as the huge numbers of people
present reveals (verse 1). The details given indicate something

of the joy and festivity that surrounded the two stages of the ark's journey from Baale-judah to the capital.

The ark of the covenant was something of a national symbol, as well as the visible sign of God's presence. Patriotic fervour as well as religious devotion marked the occasion; God's presence was now known to be located in the centre of the nation, in its new capital city. It was a sign of God's favour to Israel and to David. In the pilgrimages to Jerusalem that would follow year after year, down to New Testament times and beyond, the Jews' love for their country and people would grow only more strong and deeply rooted. Creatures of time and space as we are, we all need some sort of centre for our faith. The local church may suffice for many of us, but there is undoubtedly a place for great cathedrals and all that they signify to many Christians. So long as they strengthen and enrich faith, they are assets indeed. It is sometimes claimed that in Islam, the rites of the pilgrimage to Mecca provide one of the strongest sources of unity, faith and sense of brotherhood which that religion possesses. It may be that in Protestantism (as opposed to Roman Catholicism with its visible centre at Rome) we have lost our sense of unity together with the loss of any particular geographical centre. Perhaps we need some substitute for our lost "Jerusalem"; on the other hand, Heb. 13:14 serves to remind all Christians that "here we have no continuing city".

For David, the joy of the occasion was marred by two incidents, one public and one private; the death of Uzzah and the estrangement between himself and his wife Michal. Both caused him some concern, since they seemed to suggest that God himself had frowned on the removal of the ark from its previous resting-place. The setback was in fact only temporary (see chapter 7) but still serious enough for hesitation at the time.

(i) *Uzzah.* It is easy enough to explain the death of Uzzah in modern-day terms. To lay a casual hand on the sacred ark was considered to be a sacrilege; holy things must not be handled, or mishandled, by anybody except those specially appointed and dedicated as "holy" men. Uzzah, with the best intentions in the world, instinctively put out a hand to steady the ark, and having done so was horrifed at his own action, and overcome by fear suffered a heart attack or something of the sort. The Old Testament writers invariably saw God's hand in things which we would attribute to natural causes.

The lesson taken from this unexpected and unwelcome event was a fresh recognition of God's awesome power, shown in and through the ark. The ark was just a box, physically speaking, and could be moved as and where men pleased; the God whom it symbolized could not be manipulated nor pushed around. Israel must beware of God's anger just as much as the Philistines. It is still a temptation for God's people to suppose that he is at their beck and call, and that his thinking is sure to correspond with their thinking. Such an attitude is not far removed from blasphemy. Nevertheless, as the three months' delay proved to David, God's presence primarily means blessing and well-being (verse 11).

(ii) *Michal.* It is not wholly clear why Michal disapproved of what was going on. Obviously her outburst to David was the tip of an iceberg. Perhaps she already felt at odds with her husband, or—more probably—she had some kind of religious objection to the ark's move to Jerusalem, with the "new-fangled" ceremonies which accompanied it. The estrangement that followed resulted in her barrenness (verse 23). This was a punishment to her, but a cause of some concern to David too, who must have hoped to heal the relationship between Saul's family and himself by this marriage and its offspring. A son of the marriage would have been an excellent crown prince, the obvious successor to David in due course; but it was not to be.

Verse 23 stresses that Michal was *the daughter of Saul*; it was not God's will that *any* son of Saul should hold the throne of Israel, not even if he was also David's son. Even so, Michal's loss was equally due to her own unwillingness to co-operate in the new religious structure of the kingdom. We must remember that Jerusalem then had no tradition behind it for the Israelites, and must have been viewed as still half a pagan and foreign city. David himself was only cautiously feeling his way towards making it his religious centre, so it is not surprising that some people had objections. There is a tendency in all of us to be very conservative, even reactionary, where religion is concerned. But new situations demand fresh thinking and sometimes demand radical departures from long-accepted ways. If so, our traditionalist objections will not only fail to thwart God's purposes but also bring distress and frustration to ourselves. We must be as sensitive to God's will as David was.

NATHAN'S PROPHECY

2 Samuel 7:1–17

¹Now when the king dwelt in his house, and the Lord had given him rest from all his enemies round about, ²the king said to Nathan the prophet, "See now, I dwell in a house of cedar, but the ark of God dwells in a tent." ³And Nathan said to the king, "Go, do all that is in your heart; for the Lord is with you."

⁴But that same night the word of the Lord came to Nathan, ⁵"Go and tell my servant David, 'Thus says the Lord: Would you build me a house to dwell in? ⁶I have not dwelt in a house since the day I brought up the people of Israel from Egypt to this day, but I have been moving about in a tent for my dwelling. ⁷In all places where I have moved with all the people of Israel, did I speak a word with any of the judges of Israel, whom I commanded to shepherd my people Israel, saying, "Why have you not built me a house of cedar?"' ⁸Now therefore thus you shall say to my servant David, 'Thus says the Lord of hosts, I took you from the pasture, from following the sheep, that you should be prince over my people Israel; ⁹and I have been with you wherever you went, and have cut off all your enemies from before you; and I will make for you a great name, like the name of the great ones of the earth. ¹⁰And I will appoint a place for my people Israel, and will plant them, that they may dwell in their own place, and be disturbed no more; and violent men shall afflict them no more, as formerly, ¹¹from the time that I appointed judges over my people Israel; and I will give you rest from all your enemies. Moreover the Lord declares to you that the Lord will make you a house. ¹²When your days are fulfilled and you lie down with your fathers, I will raise up your offspring after you, who shall come forth from your body, and I will establish his kingdom. ¹³He shall build a

house for my name, and I will establish the throne of his kingdom for ever. [14]I will be his father, and he shall be my son. When he commits iniquity, I will chasten him with the rod of men, with the stripes of the sons of men; [15]but I will not take my steadfast love from him, as I took it from Saul, whom I put away from before you. [16]And your house and your kingdom shall be made sure for ever before me; your throne shall be established for ever.'" [17]In accordance with all these words, and in accordance with all this vision, Nathan spoke to David.

Two questions were raised by the events recorded in chapter 6: (a) what was the future of the Jerusalem shrine to be? and (b) who was to be David's successor, seeing that Michal had no children? Both were extremely important issues. In the short term, both were important for the stability of the kingdom of Israel. In the longer term, the answers to both questions would have a permanent effect on Jewish thought and practice, and indeed on Christian ideas as well.

The questions were vital enough to demand an answer from God himself, and this was provided by a prophet, Nathan by name. Though the two questions are separate, they were linked together by the use of a single Hebrew word, *bayith* or *house*. As in English, the word can mean a dynasty (e.g. the House of Windsor, the present British royal family); but unlike normal English, the Hebrew noun can also mean a temple. So the theme of Nathan's prophecy to David can be expressed in one sentence: "You are not to build a *house* for God, but he will raise a *house* for you." In terms of relative importance, then, the dynasty is more important than the temple.

(i) *The Temple.* The instructions to David about his proposed temple are clear enough: he was not given permission to build it, although this is implied rather than stated in so many words, but his son would do so (verse 13). The reason for such a decision is not so clear, however. The only reason given here is that till now Israelite sanctuaries dedicated to Yahweh had always been tents, not permanent buildings; this meant that a temple was unnecessary, but not wrong in itself, otherwise David's son (Solomon, cp. 1 Kings 6) would not have been allowed to build one. (Elsewhere we are told that David was prohibited from building a temple because he was a man of warfare and bloodshed (cp. 1 Chr. 22:8), but that point is not made here.) The virtue of a tent-shrine is that it can move when its worshippers have to move; but Israel was now a fully settled people, given new political stability under David. The chief thrust of Nathan's words was as a lesson for later generations. The time came when the people of Judah became arrogantly confident that the presence of a permanent temple in their city guaranteed them God's permanent protection (see Jer. 7:4), and they were to learn how wrong they were, when—as Jeremiah predicted—the Babylonians destroyed the temple and the city too. God dwells with his people, wherever they may be; elaborate buildings do not contain him, though he may be pleased to reveal his presence in them, and they certainly never restrict him. Fine temples both hinder and help the worship of God; it all depends on the worshipper.

(ii) *The Dynasty.* The first king of Israel, Saul, had not founded a dynasty: the crown had gone to a man from another family and a different tribe. Would David in turn lose the crown to some other family? The answer was direct and clear: God had determined that David's family should retain the throne—*for ever* (verse 13). This is not so final as the English translation suggests; the Hebrew can mean "for ever" but equally "for a long time". The four hundred years of David's dynasty amply fulfilled the prophecy; but in fact the *for ever* proved to be true as well, since David's descendant long after the fall of his dynasty was Jesus Christ, the Messiah and anointed King, whose reign knows no end. James Montgomery's well-known hymn, which begins by hailing "Great David's greater Son", reminds us that his is "a Kingdom without end" and that:

> The tide of time shall never
> His covenant remove;
> His Name shall stand for ever;
> That Name to us is Love.

But might not some son of David prove as disobedient to

God as Saul had been? True enough—many in fact did, as the
books of Kings show. But the stability of the nation was God's
chief concern, so the individual king would merit God's
condemnation and punishment, but the dynasty would not be
broken (verses 14f.). As long as Davidic kings reigned in
Jerusalem, then, however gloomy the political situation might
be, there was this reminder to Israel of the faithfulness of God's
promise.

Once the dynasty had fallen (in 587 B.C.), devout Jews
continued to treasure the divine promises made to David,
confident that eventually God would again fulfil them in a very
special son of David whom they called the Messiah. This
continuing hope was based on later prophecies too, such as Isa.
11, but 2 Sam. 7 has never lost its value for those Jews and
Christians who have continued to believe that God works
actively in history.

This chapter marks a most important stage in the
development of the faith of ancient Israel. Israel came to
treasure and commemorate two divine promises, both of them
embodied in covenants. The first was the covenant at Sinai
(Exod. 19:3-6), when God made Israel his people and promised
to be their God and to look after their welfare. This covenant
and promise, of course, were in existence long before David's
time. 2 Sam. 7 tells of a new divine promise, which would
further the welfare of Israel; this Davidic covenant was God's
solemn promise to provide his people with the leadership they
needed, in the person of David and his family after him. God
had chosen the man and the dynasty and would equip them for
leadership. This promise was not only gladly received by Israel
but it also became embodied in their worship (as Ps. 2
demonstrates); it was recalled and reinforced by several
prophets (see Isa. 11:1-5; Mic. 5:2-5; Jer. 23:5f; Ezek. 34:23),
and after the fall of the dynasty in 587 B.C., it served as the basis
for fresh promises which looked into the future (see Amos
9:11). Once given, the promise that a king of David's line would
fulfil God's purposes for his people was never abrogated, and so
held out hope in hard times. It is no coincidence that the New

Testament from the start (Matt. 1) emphasizes that Jesus was "the son of David".

DAVID'S PRAYER

2 Samuel 7:18–29

[18]Then King David went in and sat before the Lord, and said, "Who am I, O Lord God, and what is my house, that thou has brought me thus far? [19]And yet this was a small thing in thy eyes, O Lord God; thou hast spoken also of thy servant's house for a great while to come, and hast shown me future generations, O Lord God! [20]And what more can David say to thee? For thou knowest thy servant, O Lord God! [21]Because of thy promise, and according to thy own heart, thou hast wrought all this greatness, to make thy servant know it. [22]Therefore thou art great, O Lord God; for there is none like thee, and there is no God besides thee, according to all that we have heard with our ears. [23]What other nation on earth is like thy people Israel, whom God went to redeem to be his people, making himself a name, and doing for them great and terrible things, by driving out before his people a nation and its gods? [24]And thou didst establish for thyself thy people Israel to be thy people for ever; and thou, O Lord, didst become their God. [25]And now, O Lord God, confirm for ever the word which thou hast spoken concerning thy servant and concerning his house, and do as thou hast spoken; [26]and thy name will be magnified for ever, saying, 'The Lord of hosts is God over Israel,' and the house of thy servant David will be established before thee. [27]For thou, O Lord of hosts, the God of Israel, hast made this revelation to thy servant, saying, 'I will build you a house'; therefore thy servant has found courage to pray this prayer to thee. [28]And now, O Lord God, thou art God, and thy words are true, and thou hast promised this good thing to thy servant; [29]now therefore may it please thee to bless the house of thy servant, that it may continue for ever before thee; for thou, O Lord God, hast spoken, and with thy blessing shall the house of thy servant be blessed for ever."

From one point of view David's prayer is a natural and proper response to the promises made to him; from the reader's point of view, the prayer provides a pause for thought, a chance to reflect on the situation in Israel following the many events and changes of recent years. The prayer is therefore both a thanksgiving and a meditation; the two are interwoven. Both David and his nation were on the crest of the wave. The enemies of the past, especially the Philistines, were crushed (see verse 1); the Israelite tribes were united and beginning to be economically prosperous; the new constitution, that is to say the monarchy, was now stable and accepted by all; and now God had given his sign of approval to the new shrine in Jerusalem and to the rule of David and his family after him.

(i) The first response was *humility* (verse 18). It was a proud moment for David and for Israel alike, but grateful humility, not boastful arrogance, was the proper response. David's rise was not due to his talents but to God's goodness.

(ii) *Gratitude* for the extent of God's favours came next (verse 19). God had not only brought David to the pinnacle of success, but had made him firm promises for the future. There was no fear that tomorrow would bring unexpected disaster when God had declared his future purposes. For a contrast, we might consider the concept of nemesis in ancient Greek thought and mythology. It seems that to the Greeks all too often prosperity today heralded and indeed invited disaster tomorrow—success breeds arrogance, and arrogance brings nemesis. But David was assured that God's plans held no threat for him.

(iii) *Praise* (verse 22): David's gratitude expressed itself in a recognition of God's goodness and greatness. In a world where many gods were worshipped, it was appropriate to contrast the God of Israel and all his very real and tangible achievements for his people with other deities; but in the last resort he is beyond comparison.

(iv) *Remembrance*: verses 23f. place the new gifts of God to David in an historical setting and sequence. The exodus from Egypt, the covenant at Sinai, and the conquest of Canaan are all summed up in a couple of verses. In these three basic events in Israel's earlier history God had demonstrated his special choice of Israel, his loving relationship with them, and his protective care towards them. Israel always recalled these events with gratitude and praise, but it was equally important to seek to apply the lessons of them to the contemporary situation. David's victories had been but a continuation of God's purposes to establish the nation firmly and securely in their own land; the new shrine in Jerusalem was the place where Israel could renew her covenant with God, giving him his rightful place in the very heart of the nation.

(v) *Acknowledgment*: the rest of the prayer (verses 25-29) is an acknowledgment of what God had now promised, together with a prayer that he would indeed bring the promises to fruition. The chief purpose of these verses may well have been for later generations, in times when the *blessing* mentioned in verse 29 seemed rather doubtful. David's dynasty lasted for four centuries, but the glories of his reign did not last, and eventually his descendants reigned in the dark shadow of military threats from the East. It must have been easy then to forget the promises of God—and even to look to other gods for *their* "blessing". Faith in God is sustained by recalling his past gifts, his former promises, and his future intentions.

POWER AND SUCCESS

2 Samuel 8:1-18

¹After this David defeated the Philistines and subdued them, and David took Metheg-ammah out of the hand of the Philistines.

²And he defeated Moab, and measured them with a line, making them lie down on the ground; two lines he measured to be put to death, and one full line to be spared. And the Moabites became servants to David and brought tribute.

³David also defeated Hadadezer the son of Rehob, king of Zobah, as he went to restore his power at the river Euphrates. ⁴And David took from him a thousand and seven hundred horsemen, and twenty thousand foot soldiers; and David hamstrung all the chariot horses,

but left enough for a hundred chariots. 5And when the Syrians of Damascus came to help Hadadezer king of Zobah, David slew twenty-two thousand men of the Syrians. 6Then David put garrisons in Aram of Damascus; and the Syrians became servants to David and brought tribute. And the Lord gave victory to David wherever he went. 7And David took the shields of gold which were carried by the servants of Hadadezer, and brought them to Jerusalem. 8And from Betah and from Berothai, cities of Hadadezer, King David took very much bronze.

9When Toi king of Hamath heard that David had defeated the whole army of Hadadezer, 10Toi sent his son Joram to King David, to greet him, and to congratulate him because he had fought against Hadadezer and defeated him; for Hadadezer had often been at war with Toi. And Joram brought with him articles of silver, of gold, and of bronze; 11these also King David dedicated to the Lord, together with the silver and gold which he dedicated from all the nations he subdued, 12from Edom, Moab, the Ammonites, the Philistines, Amalek, and from the spoil of Hadadezer the son of Rehob, king of Zobah.

13And David won a name for himself. When he returned, he slew eighteen thousand Edomites in the Valley of Salt. 14And he put garrisons in Edom; throughout all Edom he put garrisons, and all the Edomites became David's servants. And the Lord gave victory to David wherever he went.

15So David reigned over all Israel; and David administered justice and equity to all his people. 16And Joab the son of Zeruiah was over the army; and Jehoshaphat the son of Ahilud was recorder; 17and Zadok the son of Ahitub and Ahimelech the son of Abiathar were priests; and Seraiah was secretary; 18and Benaiah the son of Jehoiada was over the Cherethites and the Pelethites; and David's sons were priests.

From the religious heights of chapter 7 we descend again to the everyday world of battles and bloodshed in chapter 8. The military action picks up where the story left off at the end of chapter 5. The Philistines, driven back to Gezer (5:25), now had the war brought into their homeland, although David was not concerned to conquer it and become their king. It was enough that they should be *subdued*. It is not at all certain what is meant by *Metheg-ammah* (verse 1). It is unknown as a place-name, and perhaps means rather "the control exercised by the metropolis". It is at any rate a fact that the role of empire-builders now passed from the Philistines to the Israelites, as the rest of the chapter demonstrates.

Verse 11 gives us some idea of the wide range of wars which David fought. We have no information as to how most of these wars began. David was certainly not the aggressor where the Philistines were concerned, and in the war with Ammon he was provoked into action (cp. 10:1–7); so it is quite possible that he never set out on conquest with the fixed intention of building an empire. To the north of Israel lay several Aramaean states, and one or more of them very probably endeavoured to assert a commercial supremacy over their neighbours. Some very important trade routes passed through Palestine, and the Aramaeans were great traders. We may guess, then, that the wars between Aram and David were for the mastery of the trade routes vital to Israel's prosperity.

Moab and Edom were quite different; they were only small kingdoms, distantly related to Israel, and they posed no threat to David at all. However, they too held territory through which a vital trade link ran, and there is good reason to suppose that they sided with David's enemies in a trade war. That would explain the fierce reprisals which David took against the Moabites (verse 2) and perhaps against the Edomites too (verse 13). At any rate, the Moabites must have taken some very hostile action to provoke such reprisals, especially when we consider the earlier good relations between them and David, cp. 1 Sam. 22:3f.

The biblical writer is not concerned to explain these wars; he certainly did not feel on the defensive about colonialism, as a modern writer might do. So far as he was concerned, the simple truth was that God gave David victory *wherever he went* (verse 14). For our part, we must not use such Old Testament stories as a warrant for aggression or colonialism; basically David's intentions were the defence and consolidation of his own realm, after throwing off the yoke of an oppressor—the Philistines. The biblical writers did however see another dimension to

David's successes. Believing in one God and one God only, who had chosen Israel as his special nation, they came to realize that God must have purposes for the world and not just for Israel. While in our era we emphasize the rights of self-determination and nationalism, the Old Testament writers believed that God's ultimate purpose was a unified world: and who better to rule over it than God's anointed leader? This is in a sense still the Christian aspiration for the world—that all lands and peoples should become subject to God's Messiah, the Christ. David's victories over neighbouring countries, then, could be seen not as an exercise in power politics but as a symbol of the future triumph of good over evil. Besides, some great empires have for all their faults left noble and useful legacies behind them: one thinks immediately of Roman law and Roman roads, for instance. David's small and short-lived empire left behind it the promise that eventually the knowledge of the one true God would be available to all mankind.

The list of David's officers and officials in verses 15–18 gives some idea of the development of administration in Israel, as the monarchy took full control of the nation's affairs. There are two important aspects to the list. (a) The first is the fact that David kept the administration of law to himself. Justice was a vital consideration, and he was determined to ensure that it should be thorough and impartial. (b) The second is the name of *Zadok*, as chief priest alongside Abiathar, who had long been a friend and companion to David. Nothing is known about Zadok's life till now, but he was the man whose family would provide Jerusalem's high priests for many generations, almost into New Testament times. Just as God·had now designated David's family as kings, so too he overruled in the provision of the high priestly family which would give Israel stability in the sphere of their worship and religious practice.

What priestly duties were carried out by David's *sons* (verse 18) is a puzzle; it seems to have been just a temporary arrangement, in any case (see 20:26). Generally speaking the principle of the division of power in Israel under the monarchy was that the offices of king, priest and prophet should be quite distinct; the ideal was that the three should act in full harmony and co-operation.

DAVID AND MEPHIBOSHETH

2 Samuel 9:1–13

[1]And David said, "Is there still any one left of the house of Saul, that I may show him kindness for Jonathan's sake?" [2]Now there was a servant of the house of Saul whose name was Ziba, and they called him to David; and the king said to him, "Are you Ziba?" And he said, "Your servant is he." [3]And the king said, "Is there not still some one of the house of Saul, that I may show the kindness of God to him?" Ziba said to the king, "There is still a son of Jonathan; he is crippled in his feet." [4]The king said to him, "Where is he?" And Ziba said to the king, "He is in the house of Machir the son of Ammiel, at Lo-debar." [5]Then King David sent and brought him from the house of Machir the son of Ammiel, at Lo-debar. [6]And Mephibosheth the son of Jonathan, son of Saul, came to David, and fell on his face and did obeisance. And David said, "Mephibosheth!" And he answered, "Behold, your servant." [7]And David said to him, "Do not fear; for I will show you kindness for the sake of your father Jonathan, and I will restore to you all the land of Saul your father; and you shall eat at my table always." [8]And he did obeisance, and said, "What is your servant, that you should look upon a dead dog such as I?"

[9]Then the king called Ziba, Saul's servant, and said to him, "All that belonged to Saul and to all his house I have given to your master's son. [10]And you and your sons and your servants shall till the land for him, and shall bring in the produce, that your master's son may have bread to eat; but Mephibosheth your master's son shall always eat at my table." Now Ziba had fifteen sons and twenty servants. [11]Then Ziba said to the king, "According to all that my lord the king commands his servant, so will your servant do." So Mephibosheth ate at David's table, like one of the king's sons. [12]And Mephibosheth had a young son, whose name was Mica. And all who dwelt in Ziba's house became Mephibosheth's servants. [13]So Mephibosheth dwelt in Jerusalem; for he ate always at the king's table. Now he was lame in both his feet.

In Christian preaching, this story of David and Mephibosheth has often been used as an illustration of "unmerited grace": the great king (Christ) goes out of his way to bring even a moral cripple to eat at his table. Clearly that is one possible way of looking at the story told in this chapter, but such an interpretation hardly explains why it was told in the first place. Besides, an application like this ignores two important aspects of the matter:

(a) Mephibosheth was not just anybody, but a member of a very important family, that of Saul. He was in fact the son of David's best friend and the grandson of David's fiercest enemy: the very intriguing question which arises from this fact is whether he would prove to be another Saul or another Jonathan so far as David was concerned.

(b) The story neither begins nor ends with this chapter. David's act of charity arose from his friendship with Jonathan; more than that, he was fulfilling the spirit of a promise made long before to Jonathan (cp. 1 Sam. 20:15). To *show kindness* (verse 1) is not precisely what the Hebrew phrase means; the noun includes the idea of loyalty, and so picks up the theme of the covenant between David and Jonathan. So the chapter begins by recalling David's duty to his dead friend; and it ends with Mephibosheth in an honoured position at court, but it remains to be seen how he will use that position—the sequel is to be found in chapters 16 and 19.

The story, then, is not so much about undeserved charity as about loyalty. It is not easy to read the mind of either man. Should we take their words at face value or not?

(i) *David's* words (verses 1, 7) seem admirable, on the face of it. Nobody, then or now, could fault a sincere desire on David's part to honour Jonathan's memory in such a practical fashion. But how sincere was it? It has often been observed that other members of Saul's family suffered terribly, due at least in part to David: cp. chapter 21. It is also often suggested that in bringing Mephibosheth to the royal court David was outwardly honouring him but in reality placing him where he could keep an eye on him and make sure that he was taking no action against David's interests. Perhaps, then, David had ulterior motives, or at any rate mixed motives.

(ii) As for *Mephibosheth*, his reply to David (verse 8) really tells us nothing. What else could he say to the king, especially in the circumstances of an oriental court where it was only customary to speak in terms of deep humility?

When a passage sets us problems like these, we should always ask ourselves not only about historical probabilities but also about the narrator's intentions. In this case, it seems clear enough that the writer did not mean the reader to be cynical about David's motives. In any case, we may reasonably doubt whether Mephibosheth was less of a potential danger to David at the royal court than he was at Lo-debar, a remote farming community on the north-east frontiers of Israel. Besides, it is doubtful if Mephibosheth, crippled as he was, was likely to pose much of a threat to David in either Lo-debar or Jerusalem. It is clear from other passages that ordinary Israelites liked their kings to be handsome, strong men (cp. 1 Sam. 9:2; 16:6f., 12). But the narrative gives us no clue as to Mephibosheth's real sentiments, and that is probably intentional.

Here, then, we can see David taking a risk with one of Saul's family, giving him a place of privilege and opportunity, and we do not yet know how he will use it. The story is part of the larger narrative of the complex relationships between Saul and his family, on the one side, and David on the other. The biblical writer once again stresses that David showed unfailing kindness to Saul and to his family. Michal (though still alive, presumably) has dropped out of the story, estranged from David; in a sense Mephibosheth takes her place now, as the member of Saul's family with most potential for action, good or bad.

David, as we have said, was above all showing loyalty to Jonathan and fulfilling his promise to him. The promise had been made many years earlier, and Jonathan had been dead many years; in the interval Mephibosheth had grown from boyhood to manhood. There was nobody to press David even to remember, still less to honour, this old vow; but he did it nevertheless. It was not unusual in the ancient world for a new king to massacre all the members of his predecessor's family, in order to make absolutely sure that they could be no danger to him. David's action towards Mephibosheth was the very opposite of this, and underlines the degree to which David was a man of his word. The favour was not exactly "unmerited", then; but it was both real and rare if not astonishing. But how would it be repaid? That remained to be seen.

If we wish to treat the story as a parable, we may indeed see ourselves in Mephibosheth; as Christians we have been brought from darkness into light, and given what Paul calls "the immeasurable riches of his grace in kindness toward us in Christ Jesus" (Eph. 2:7). In our individual cases too an unanswered question remains: how will God's goodness be repaid?

THE DEFEAT OF AMMON

2 Samuel 10:1-19

¹After this the king of the Ammonites died, and Hanun his son reigned in his stead. ²And David said, "I will deal loyally with Hanun the son of Nahash, as his father dealt loyally with me." So David sent by his servants to console him concerning his father. And David's servants came into the land of the Ammonites. ³But the princes of the Ammonites said to Hanun their lord, "Do you think because David has sent comforters to you, that he is honouring your father? Has not David sent his servants to you to search the city, and to spy it out, and to overthrow it?" ⁴So Hanun took David's servants, and shaved off half the beard of each, and cut off their garments in the middle, at their hips, and sent them away. ⁵When it was told David, he sent to meet them, for the men were greatly ashamed. And the king said, "Remain at Jericho until your beards have grown, and then return."

⁶When the Ammonites saw that they had become odious to David, the Ammonites sent and hired the Syrians of Beth-rehob, and the Syrians of Zobah, twenty thousand foot soldiers, and the king of Maacah with a thousand men, and the men of Tob, twelve thousand men. ⁷And when David heard of it, he sent Joab and all the host of the mighty men. ⁸And the Ammonites came out and drew up

in battle array at the entrance of the gate; and the Syrians of Zobah and of Rehob, and the men of Tob and Maacah, were by themselves in the open country.

⁹When Joab saw that the battle was set against him both in front and in the rear, he chose some of the picked men of Israel, and arrayed them against the Syrians; ¹⁰the rest of his men he put in the charge of Abishai his brother, and he arrayed them against the Ammonites. ¹¹And he said, "If the Syrians are too strong for me, then you shall help me; but if the Ammonites are too strong for you, then I will come and help you. ¹²Be of good courage, and let us play the man for our people, and for the cities of our God; and may the Lord do what seems good to him." ¹³So Joab and the people who were with him drew near to battle against the Syrians; and they fled before him. ¹⁴And when the Ammonites saw that the Syrians fled, they likewise fled before Abishai, and entered the city. Then Joab returned from fighting against the Ammonites, and came to Jerusalem.

¹⁵But when the Syrians saw that they had been defeated by Israel, they gathered themselves together. ¹⁶And Hadadezer sent, and brought out the Syrians who were beyond the Euphrates; and they came to Helam, with Shobach the commander of the army of Hadadezer at their head. ¹⁷And when it was told David, he gathered all Israel together, and crossed the Jordan, and came to Helam. And the Syrians arrayed themselves against David, and fought with him. ¹⁸And the Syrians fled before Israel; and David slew of the Syrians the men of seven hundred chariots, and forty thousand horsemen, ahd wounded Shobach the commander of their army, so that he died there. ¹⁹And when all the kings who were servants of Hadadezer saw that they had been defeated by Israel, they made peace with Israel, and became subject to them. So the Syrians feared to help the Ammonites any more.

The story-teller is content to leave Mephibosheth as an enigma for the time being, and reverts to giving us information about David's wars. Once again (as in chapter 8) the Aramaeans (or Syrians) were involved and were defeated; but this time the story is chiefly to do with the Ammonites, a small kingdom in Transjordan, just north of Moab and Edom (see Map 1), formerly defeated by Saul, cp. 1 Sam. 11. It was much to Israel's commercial advantage to dominate these three small kingdoms, but as the story shows, David did not have any hostile intentions towards Ammon in the first place.

In fact, this chapter provides an object lesson—if one were needed—as to how wars can develop out of nothing. A friendly act (by David) was misinterpreted (by the Ammonite king) and was repaid by a gross insult; the next step was to look round for allies, and before long three nations were at war. What really caused the war, then? Undoubtedly it was suspicion and mistrust, otherwise David's friendly gesture would have been accepted as such. Where suspicion and mistrust exist, it is possible for any and every action to be misjudged.

Previously, verse 2 reveals, there had been a treaty relationship between David and the Ammonites. No doubt the treaty dated either from Saul's lifetime or else from the years when David had ruled in Judah and Ish-bosheth in Israel. Just as the Philistines had changed their attitude towards David abruptly when they discovered that he was king of a united and potentially strong Israel, so too the Ammonites suddenly became aware that this ally against Saul and Ish-bosheth was now strong enough to attack them if he wished. Thus fear lay behind their mistrust.

Even if the Ammonites had good reason for suspicion, the action they took was the height of folly, amounting to a declaration of war. Even today if ambassadors were subjected to such indignities a major "incident" would be inevitable; and in ancient Israel and its world to touch a man's beard was in itself a most hostile act, while the exposure of the buttocks was particularly horrifying in a society somewhat prudish by modern Western standards. It was impossible for David to ignore such an incident, and the Ammonites knew it. They could not hope to defeat Israel without outside help, so their action immediately jeopardized their land and people. It is surprising how often in history national pride has led to foolish actions which have ended in disaster for the nation concerned.

As for David, his motivation at the beginning of the story was again *loyalty*, just as in chapter 9. His intention to honour a promise made to a man now dead provides an interesting link between the two chapters. This is clearer in Hebrew than in English; the phrase to *deal loyally* in 10:2 is exactly the same as to *show kindness* in 9:1. Mephibosheth and Hanun were very different men in very different positions, but to both of them it was David's purpose to fulfil promises made to their fathers. The ideal leader of God's people is one who shows complete loyalty and trustworthiness in all his dealings, at a personal level and at a national and international level equally. Honour and trustworthiness are the only hope of allaying natural human suspicions, at all levels of society. Peace between individuals and between nations is promoted by men of honour, and destroyed by men whose word can never be trusted.

In this case, however, loyalty was defeated by folly, in the sense that the treaty David wished to honour was torn up by the Ammonite king; David of course won the war—the chapter ends with the Aramaean allies paying tribute to David and the Ammonites' capital about to be besieged (see 11:1). In our continuing study of leadership we see the importance of good counsel. Every king needs competent, reliable advisers; and secondly, he needs the judgement and discernment to distinguish good counsel from bad. Hanun—just like David's own grandson Rehoboam some fifty or sixty years later (see 1 Kings 12)—made the fatal mistake of acting on the worst possible advice. Here, then, we have two contrasting pictures of leadership: David is the honourable king, following the dictates of conscience and the stipulations of a treaty; Hanun is the foolish leader who follows ill-natured and ill-conceived advice—and leads his nation into warfare and humiliation. It is always foolish to refuse even to seek advice, but it may be foolish sometimes to follow the advice we get. Whether or not we are blessed with the gift of discernment, it is often easy enough to guess the likely outcome of our actions. Hanun failed totally to count the cost beforehand; cp. Luke 14:31f.

ADULTERY AND MURDER

2 Samuel 11:1–27

[1]In the spring of the year, the time when kings go forth to battle, David sent Joab, and his servants with him, and all Israel; and they ravaged the Ammonites, and besieged Rabbah. But David remained at Jerusalem.

[2]It happened, late one afternoon, when David arose from his couch and was walking upon the roof of the king's house, that he saw from the roof a woman bathing; and the woman was very beautiful. [3]And David sent and inquired about the woman. And one said, "Is not this Bathsheba, the daughter of Eliam, the wife of Uriah the Hittite?" [4]So David sent messengers, and took her; and she came to him, and he lay with her. (Now she was purifying herself from her uncleanness.) Then she returned to her house. [5]And the woman conceived; and she sent and told David, "I am with child."

[6]So David sent word to Joab, "Send me Uriah the Hittite." And Joab sent Uriah to David. [7]When Uriah came to him, David asked how Joab was doing, and how the people fared, and how the war prospered. [8]Then David said to Uriah, "Go down to your house, and wash your feet." And Uriah went out of the king's house, and there followed him a present from the king. [9]But Uriah slept at the door of the king's house with all the servants of his lord, and did not go down to his house. [10]When they told David, "Uriah did not go down to his house," David said to Uriah, "Have you not come from a journey? Why did you not go down to your house?" [11]Uriah said to David, "The ark and Israel and Judah dwell in booths; and my lord Joab and the servants of my lord are camping in the open field; shall I then go to my house, to eat and to drink, and to lie with my wife? As you live, and as your soul lives, I will not do this thing." [12]Then David said to Uriah, "Remain here today also, and tomorrow I will let you depart." So Uriah remained in Jerusalem that day, and the next. [13]And David invited him, and he ate in his presence and drank, so that he made him drunk; and in the evening he went out to lie on his couch with the servants of his lord, but he did not go down to his house.

[14]In the morning David wrote a letter to Joab, and sent it by the hand of Uriah. [15]In the letter he wrote, "Set Uriah in the forefront of

the hardest fighting, and then draw back from him, that he may be struck down, and die." 16And as Joab was besieging the city, he assigned Uriah to the place where he knew there were valiant men. 17And the men of the city came out and fought with Joab; and some of the servants of David among the people fell. Uriah the Hittite was slain also. 18Then Joab sent and told David all the news about the fighting; 19and he instructed the messenger, "When you have finished telling all the news about the fighting to the king, 20then, if the king's anger rises, and if he says to you, 'Why did you go so near the city to fight? Did you not know that they would shoot from the wall? 21Who killed Abimelech the son of Jerubbesheth? Did not a woman cast an upper millstone upon him from the wall, so that he died at Thebez? Why did you go so near the wall?' then you shall say, 'Your servant Uriah the Hittite is dead also.'"

22So the messenger went, and came and told David all that Joab had sent him to tell. 23The messenger said to David, "The men gained an advantage over us, and came out against us in the field; but we drove them back to the entrance of the gate. 24Then the archers shot at your servants from the wall; some of the king's servants are dead; and your servant Uriah the Hittite is dead also." 25David said to the messenger, "Thus shall you say to Joab, 'Do not let this matter trouble you, for the sword devours now one and now another; strengthen your attack upon the city, and overthrow it.' And encourage him."

26When the wife of Uriah heard that Uriah her husband was dead, she made lamentation for her husband. 27And when the mourning was over, David sent and brought her to his house, and she became his wife, and bore him a son. But the thing that David had done displeased the Lord.

The continuing warfare with Ammon and the siege of its capital city Rabbah form the background to the well-known story of David and Bathsheba. David made use of the perfectly legitimate war against Ammon to cover up his murderous intentions towards an innocent man, who happened to be one of his own most loyal and able officers: David's leading soldiers are listed in 23:8-39, and Uriah's name is among them (verse 39).

Nobody would defend David's actions towards Uriah, though in the modern world his adultery with Bathsheba would be condoned by many people. In the ancient world, too, double standards prevailed. On the one hand, the marriage bond was sacred and penalties against breaking it were severe, cp. Lev. 20:10. (In fact David broke no fewer than three of Israel's basic laws, the Ten Commandments: he coveted another man's wife, he committed adultery with her, and then he killed.) On the other hand, whatever the laws of Israel and neighbouring countries might say, it was by no means unusual for kings to ride roughshod over the laws when it pleased them. One does not have to delve very deep into one's own nation's history, for that matter, to learn of adulteries and immoralities by former monarchs, rulers and statesmen. Kings *made* laws; they did not always feel bound to *keep* them, and their courtiers were only too willing to turn a blind eye. There was undoubtedly one law for the rich and another for the poor—or rather, one standard for the king and another for the common man. Indeed, it says something for Israel's laws and standards that David felt obliged to cover up his relationship with Bathsheba. In another country he would either have abandoned her or else taken her from her previous husband, to suit his own pleasure. Presumably David's intentions changed as time passed. At first he had no plan to marry Bathsheba; he simply wanted to bring Uriah together with her, so that the child, when it was born, should seem to be Uriah's. But since Uriah proved so obstinate, from David's point of view, he realized that murder would not only solve the problem of Bathsheba's pregnancy but also permit him to marry the widow.

Bathsheba is a completely passive character in the story; we do not know her feelings about either David or Uriah, nor what her wishes were. *Joab* too, though usually a forceful character, is here presented in neutral terms. He did venture to modify David's orders, probably because he felt that David's plan was too obvious and would be certain to arouse comment and criticism, but he never questioned the instructions he received. So in a sense there are only two real actors in the drama, David and Uriah. *David* is the man with all the power; he can command Bathsheba and he can command Joab, and for that matter he can manoeuvre Uriah more or less as he pleases. *Uriah*, on the other hand, is the man with the single-minded dedication to the nation's cause. He was not obstinate, except in David's estimation, and there is no good reason to suppose that he had heard rumours of his wife's adultery and therefore refused to visit her. He can scarcely have been particularly suspicious of David if he soon after carried his own death warrant to Joab. Rather, he is portrayed as a fully dedicated soldier in a war being carried out on God's behalf: it was simply against the rules for him to have sexual intercourse with his wife until the campaign was over. His words in verse 11 show the extent of his piety.

When piety clashes with power, piety comes off worse. Here, for the first time in the career of David, we see the moral dangers inherent in the possession of power. The parallel in Saul's case was his treatment of the priesthood and citizens of Nob, cp. 1 Sam. 22. David, to do him what little justice we can, wanted to harm nobody except Uriah, but in fact several other good soldiers met their deaths alongside Uriah (verses 16f.), and when he heard about it the king's attitude was completely callous (verse 25).

The chapter ends with an unrepentant David enjoying the results of his abuse of royal power. All too often kings and national leaders are able to get away with their misdeeds. Even when rumour is rife, there may be no machinery for bringing a king to trial. This was certainly the case in Israel, where David himself was the chief judge, and perhaps the only judge. Was David then above the law? The last sentence of the chapter reminds us that no man is above God's law, even when human courts are powerless, or for that matter, when one's sins never see the light of day. Adultery may often be very difficult to prove; such sins as envy, pride and covetousness are all in the mind and so are quite beyond the range of human laws, for all their grim effects on human conduct. But no such misdeed is hidden from God's eye; cp. Matt. 5:21-30.

NATHAN'S PARABLE

2 Samuel 12:1–15(a)

[1]And the Lord sent Nathan to David. He came to him, and said to him, "There were two men in a certain city, the one rich and the other poor. [2]The rich man had very many flocks and herds; [3]but the poor man had nothing but one little ewe lamb, which he had bought. And he brought it up, and it grew up with him and with his children; it used to eat of his morsel, and drink from his cup, and lie in his bosom, and it was like a daughter to him. [4]Now there came a traveller to the rich man, and he was unwilling to take one of his own flock or herd to prepare for the wayfarer who had come to him, but he took the poor man's lamb, and prepared it for the man who had come to him." [5]Then David's anger was greatly kindled against the man; and he said to Nathan, "As the Lord lives, the man who has done this deserves to die; [6]and he shall restore the lamb fourfold, because he did this thing, and because he had no pity."

[7]Nathan said to David, "You are the man. Thus says the Lord, the God of Israel, 'I anointed you king over Israel, and I delivered you out of the hand of Saul; [8]and I gave you your master's house, and your master's wives into your bosom, and gave you the house of Israel and of Judah; and if this were too little, I would add to you as much more. [9]Why have you despised the word of the Lord, to do what is evil in his sight? You have smitten Uriah the Hittite with the sword, and have taken his wife to be your wife, and have slain him with the sword of the Ammonites. [10]Now therefore the sword shall never depart from your house, because you have despised me and have taken the wife of Uriah the Hittite to be your wife.' [11]Thus says the Lord, 'Behold, I will raise up evil against you out of your own house; and I will take your wives before your eyes, and give them to your neighbour, and he shall lie with your wives in the sight of this sun. [12]For you did it secretly; but I will do this thing before all Israel, and before the sun.'" [13]David said to Nathan, "I have sinned against the Lord." And Nathan said to David, "The Lord also has put away your sin; you shall not die. [14]Nevertheless, because by this deed you have utterly scorned the Lord, the child that is born to you shall die." [15]Then Nathan went to his house.

Nathan's is the most famous parable in the Old Testament. Like many of the parables of Jesus, it was told in order to get the listener to judge himself. Jesus told so many parables that his listeners came to expect them, and knew that he did not mean them literally; but the effectiveness of Nathan's parable lay precisely in this, that David was fooled into thinking that the prophet was telling him about a real-life incident. David was the chief judge in Israel, and we could well imagine that Nathan regularly discussed current affairs of various kinds with the king. We are not meant to suppose that David was pronouncing an official verdict on the wrongdoer; proper court procedure must have allowed an accused man to speak in his own defence before sentence was pronounced (see 1 Sam. 22:11–16). Rather, David's response was a spontaneous reaction to the story he had just heard. Besides, it is not even clear what the rich man was guilty of: did he steal the other man's lamb, or had he some right in law to it? The application of the parable lay not so much in its exact details as in the impression of greed and injustice which the story created. That is what David reacted to, and we can reasonably imagine that Nathan was voicing public opinion. It is unlikely that the story in chapter 11 would ever have been written if David had been able to hush the matter up; it is not easy for people in the public eye to keep secrets.

Nathan was not really the voice of the people nor yet of David's conscience: he was convinced that he went to confront the king as God's spokesman. He exhibited several signs of the true prophet:

(i) He believed implicitly that he had a commission from God.

(ii) He had the courage to challenge the king to his face—a serious risk to take, for which some later prophets paid with their lives.

(iii) He pronounced judgement on specific wrongs.

(iv) He predicted the future in a certain amount of detail.

The last of these is the most mysterious and unfamiliar to us nowadays. It is idle to deny that some men and women, not just Old Testament prophets, have been gifted with occasional glimpses of the future and have made some remarkable predictions, however they are to be explained. However, it is wrong to think that every prediction made by the biblical prophets was literally and exactly fulfilled. Often there was a conditional element in what they said: "If you continue to do such-and-such, then God will punish you by doing such-and-such." Just as judges today sometimes commute a sentence, so too God has the right and the power to modify or even cancel his own decisions in the light of the human response. In this case David's immediate signs of remorse allowed immediate forgiveness; but the deed itself could not be undone, and some consequences were inevitable.

There are two principles involved in the punishment prescribed by Nathan. (a) *The punishment must fit the crime.* David had been guilty of adultery and murder; very well, then lust and violence would in turn afflict his own family. We should see this not so much as a punishment inflicted from above as a logical consequence—if the father acts so irresponsibly, it is only natural for the sons to follow the example he has set. (b) *Justice must be seen to be done.* David had, it is true, acted secretly (verse 12), but in fact a public scandal had resulted. Very well, God's punishment would be no less public.

What a sorry train of events David's first lapse had caused! One lustful look had started it all: one can appreciate the force of Jesus' words in the Sermon on the Mount: "If your right eye causes you to sin, pluck it out and throw it away" (Matt. 5:29). The real fault was deeper than this, though, for it lay in David's attitude to God. At this stage in his career, said Nathan, David *despised* God, indeed *utterly scorned the Lord.* Such an attitude was no doubt completely subconscious, but it revealed itself in David's willingness to break God's commandments. Just as we can grow away from people we once loved and respected, so too we are all prone, like the church at Ephesus in Rev. 2:4, to abandon our first love towards God.

THE BIRTH OF SOLOMON

2 Samuel 12:15(b)–31

And the Lord struck the child that Uriah's wife bore to David, and it became sick. 16David therefore besought God for the child; and David fasted, and went in and lay all night upon the ground. 17And the elders of his house stood beside him, to raise him from the ground; but he would not, nor did he eat food with them. 18On the seventh day the child died. And the servants of David feared to tell him that the child was dead; for they said, "Behold, while the child was yet alive, we spoke to him, and he did not listen to us; how then can we say to him the child is dead? He may do himself some harm." 19But when David saw that his servants were whispering together, David perceived that the child was dead; and David said to his servants, "Is the child dead?" They said, "He is dead." 20Then David arose from the earth, and washed, and anointed himself, and changed his clothes; and he went into the house of the Lord, and worshipped; he then went to his own house; and when he asked, they set food before him, and he ate. 21Then his servants said to him, "What is this thing that you have done? You fasted and wept for the child while it was alive; but when the child died, you arose and ate food." 22He said, "While the child was still alive, I fasted and wept; for I said, 'Who knows whether the Lord will be gracious to me, that the child may live?' 23But now he is dead; why should I fast? Can I bring him back again? I shall go to him, but he will not return to me."

24Then David comforted his wife, Bathsheba, and went in to her, and lay with her; and she bore a son, and he called his name Solomon. And the Lord loved him, 25and sent a message by Nathan the prophet; so he called his name Jedidiah, because of the Lord.

26Now Joab fought against Rabbah of the Ammonites, and took the royal city. 27And Joab sent messengers to David, and said, "I have fought against Rabbah; moreover, I have taken the city of waters. 28Now, then, gather the rest of the people together, and encamp against the city, and take it; lest I take the city, and it be called by my name." 29So David gathered all the people together and went to Rabbah, and fought against it and took it. 30And he took the crown of their king from his head; the weight of it was a talent of gold, and in it was a precious stone; and it was placed on David's head. And he brought forth the spoil of the city, a very great amount. [31] And he brought forth the people who were in it, and set them to labour with saws and iron picks and iron axes, and made them toil at the brick-kilns; and thus he did to all the cities of the Ammonites. Then David and all the people returned to Jersualem.

Nathan's final prediction (verse 14) was the first to come true: Bathsheba's son, conceived out of wedlock, died in infancy. The story of his death is told vividly and with pathos; it is obvious that the child was very precious to David, and that the boy's death was truly a punishment to him. In passing, it is worth remembering that this death was a punishment for David, not for the child himself; death is not invariably seen as a punishment in the Old Testament, though at times it could be.

The surprise of David's courtiers arose from the fact that he reversed the normal mourning conventions, fasting and weeping for a week before the boy died but not at all afterwards. His unusual actions needed explanation. It was a situation where a prophet's judgement might perhaps be averted, or so David hoped and prayed; but once death had intervened, the matter was finished. By declining to mourn publicly after the child's death, David demonstrated his acceptance of God's will; there is no suggestion that he did not suffer inwardly.

The most important section in this part of the chapter is in verses 24f., which introduce the reader to the next king of Israel—Solomon. Saul and David had both been anointed for kingship when in young manhood, but Solomon was in a way marked out from birth. David already had several sons, but this one was singled out by a prophet, just as Saul and David had been, though with less clarity. In this context *the Lord loved him* has much the same meaning as "the Lord chose him". Here as often in the Bible we find the theme of the mystery of God's choosing. No reason is ever given why Solomon rather than one of his brothers should have been marked out to succeed David. On the contrary, we might have expected that the union between David and Bathsheba, based as it was on the murder of her first husband, would never be blessed; but to our surprise, the same prophet who had denounced the murder now prompted a name for this child, Jedidiah, which would always be a reminder of God's favourable attitude to this boy. *Jedidiah* means "beloved by the Lord"; oddly enough the name is nowhere else mentioned in the Bible, but almost certainly it must have been his everyday name. Very probably Solomon was the name he took when he became king, just as in Great Britain Prince Albert took the title "King George VI" when he succeeded to the throne.

In this way David's punishment in the death of Bathsheba's first son was soon followed by an unexpected sign of God's favour. It was a sign not only to David but also to the nation, because—as the next few chapters will tell—dark days lay ahead, when David's throne seemed shaky indeed. It must have been reassuring to see that this boy, unlike his older brothers, lived and prospered, his very name a promise for the future.

Verses 24f. also held a message for later Israelites. As told in 1 Kings 1f., the story of Solomon's accession to the throne looks very much like a matter of brute force and power politics; here is reassurance that whatever the actions of men, God himself stood behind Solomon's rule. God had designed and planned it many years before David's death. All of us at times feel helpless when we consider the power politics of our own country or our world; it is comforting to know that the same God continues to act, usually in a quiet, unseen, and indeed mysterious way, in the affairs of human history.

The final paragraph of the chapter rounds off the account of the war against Ammon. Once Joab captured the water supplies of the Ammonite capital, Rabbah, its fall was sure to follow swiftly, and so David was now invited by his commander-in-chief to assume direct command of the Israelite troops for the final assault. Ammon was possibly the first territory outside Israel to be annexed to the Israelite throne. The insult paid to David's envoys (cp. 10:4) was now amply avenged, as the citizens of the Ammonite capital were put to hard labour (verse 31). This was not deliberate cruelty but a normal use, at the time, of prisoners of war. The growth of the

Israelite state, especially its building programme, needed more labourers than Israel itself could readily find. Even so, the Ammonite prisoners undoubtedly suffered hardship—and all because of the folly of their king. Once again we note how true it is that the actions, wise or foolish, of political leaders inevitably affect the fortunes of their citizens. But as the Ammonites paid dearly for the past folly of their king, the Israelites enjoyed both the present success of their king and the future promise that the birth of Solomon symbolized.

THE RAPE OF TAMAR

2 Samuel 13:1–19

[1]Now Absalom, David's son, had a beautiful sister, whose name was Tamar; and after a time Amnon, David's son, loved her. [2]And Amnon was so tormented that he made himself ill because of his sister Tamar; for she was a virgin, and it seemed impossible to Amnon to do anything to her. [3]But Amnon had a friend, whose name was Jonadab, the son of Shimeah, David's brother; and Jonadab was a very crafty man. [4]And he said to him, "O son of the king, why are you so haggard morning after morning? Will you not tell me?" Amnon said to him, "I love Tamar, my brother Absalom's sister." [5]Jonadab said to him, "Lie down on your bed, and pretend to be ill; and when your father comes to see you, say to him, 'Let my sister Tamar come and give me bread to eat, and prepare the food in my sight, that I may see it, and eat it from her hand.'" [6]So Amnon lay down, and pretended to be ill; and when the king came to see him, Amnon said to the king, "Pray let my sister Tamar come and make a couple of cakes in my sight, that I may eat from her hand."

[7]Then David sent home to Tamar, saying, "Go to your brother Amnon's house, and prepare food for him." [8]So Tamar went to her brother Amnon's house, where he was lying down. And she took dough, and kneaded it, and made cakes in his sight, and baked the cakes. [9]And she took the pan and emptied it out before him, but he refused to eat. And Amnon said, "Send out every one from me." So every one went out from him. [10]Then Amnon said to Tamar, "Bring the food into the chamber, that I may eat from your hand." And

Tamar took the cakes she had made, and brought them into the chamber to Amnon her brother. [11]But when she brought them near him to eat, he took hold of her, and said to her, "Come, lie with me, my sister." [12]She answered him, "No, my brother, do not force me; for such a thing is not done in Israel; do not do this wanton folly. [13]As for me, where could I carry my shame? And as for you, you would be as one of the wanton fools in Israel. Now therefore, I pray you, speak to the king; for he will not withhold me from you." [14]But he would not listen to her; and being stronger than she, he forced her, and lay with her.

[15]Then Amnon hated her with very great hatred; so that the hatred with which he hated her was greater than the love with which he had loved her. And Amnon said to her, "Arise, be gone." [16]But she said to him, "No, my brother; for this wrong in sending me away is greater than the other which you did to me." But he would not listen to her. [17]He called the young man who served him and said, "Put this woman out of my presence, and bolt the door after her." [18]Now she was wearing a long robe with sleeves; for thus were the virgin daughters of the king clad of old. So his servant put her out, and bolted the door after her. [19]And Tamar put ashes on her head, and rent the long robe which she wore; and she laid her hand on her head, and went away, crying aloud as she went.

Solomon will not appear in the narratives of 2 Samuel again; his story is resumed in 1 Kings. Our attention is switched to two older sons of David, Amnon and Absalom. If the ordinary rules of inheritance had operated, then Amnon as the eldest son would have expected to succeed David as king in due course. Absalom was the third son, and it is quite likely that the second son had died before now—at least, we never hear anything of him (see 3:2f.). If so, Absalom was second in line to the throne, at least in his own estimation. So a great deal of human interest naturally surrounds the careers of these two young men. It soon turns out that Amnon was a most unpleasant character, and one can only suppose that any Israelite reader will have felt a great sense of relief that such a man never became king.

In fact, we have in this section one of the most sordid stories in the whole of the Bible, and one told in considerable detail. Why, one is tempted to ask, does the Bible devote so much space to incidents like this? What spiritual profit is there in considering such an episode? To answer this latter question we have to ask another: what is the narrator's purpose in including this story at all? We can give four separate answers to this question:

(i) *The story describes part of David's punishment.* As Nathan foretold, God's punishment of David would be public, and the detailed narrative makes it public even to us many centuries later. We are left to imagine the distress and unhappiness Amnon's conduct brought to his father; but David had brought it on himself, having taught his son to yield to lust and to use violence if need be.

(ii) *It explains subsequent events.* This sordid episode did not take place in a vacuum: it not only had a cause (in David's previous actions) but also an effect, upon Absalom. If David had not set a bad example, Amnon might not have raped Tamar; then Absalom would not have hated his eldest brother and he would not have turned against first Amnon and later his own father. David's violation of Bathsheba and Amnon's violation of Tamar both point the same moral, that illicit sexual indulgence is no private sin without any serious consequences for anyone, as so many of our contemporaries fondly imagine. Such acts raise the most basic and ungovernable of all human passions, and nobody can foresee their full consequences.

(iii) *It offers a cautionary tale.* This fine character study offers any reader an example to avoid at all costs. In particular, it gives us another portrait of kingship, in the sense that Amnon was brought up as a prince and probably saw himself as the next king of Israel. Seen in this light, the story warns against the moral dangers of a high position in society. It is all too easy for such a man, since he is denied practically nothing, to believe that he has the right to anything he fancies, even in the whim of the moment. Amnon's cold-blooded scheming, his callous disregard of his sister's feelings (to say nothing of her future disgrace), his brutality both in the deed and after it, all show his arrogant self-centredness and lack of restraint. Few leaders, fortunately, go to such extremes as Amnon; but wherever there is power, however little, there is a degree of freedom—freedom to make use of the power and to abuse it.

(iv) *It shows God's goodness to his people.* Here is a good example of how the very complexity of personalities and events can bring about God's purposes. Amnon's vicious act was part of David's punishment, but it was also part of the chain of events which rid Israel of such an unsuitable leader. It was Solomon whom God had determined should succeed David as king; this potentially dangerous rival, Amnon, in fact eliminated himself, as the sequel will soon reveal. Later Israelites reading this story could well thank their God that a man like Amnon was never their king. He showed himself to be a *wanton fool*, to use Tamar's own words (verse 13). The Old Testament recognizes that folly consists in deliberate wrongdoing just as much as in dim-witted stupidity.

One uncertainty in the story is whether marriage was a possibility between Amnon and Tamar or not. Tamar hinted that it was (verse 13), but perhaps in her desperation she was voicing a very remote possibility. Marriage between half-brother and half-sister was normally prohibited by Israelite law (Lev. 18:11). At any rate, it looks very much as if Amnon was not planning for a marriage but simply gratifying his lust. Genuine love shows itself in gentleness and consideration, however strong the sexual desire may be.

ABSALOM'S REVENGE

2 Samuel 13:20–39

20And her brother Absalom said to her, "Has Amnon your brother been with you? Now hold your peace, my sister; he is your brother; do not take this to heart." So Tamar dwelt, a desolate woman, in her brother Absalom's house. 21When King David heard of all these things, he was very angry. 22But Absalom spoke to Amnon neither good nor bad; for Absalom hated Amnon, because he had forced his sister Tamar.

23After two full years Absalom had sheepshearers at Baal-hazor, which is near Ephraim, and Absalom invited all the king's sons.

²⁴And Absalom came to the king, and said, "Behold, your servant has sheepshearers; pray let the king and his servants go with your servant." ²⁵But the king said to Absalom, "No, my son, let us not all go, lest we be burdensome to you." He pressed him, but he would not go but gave him his blessing. ²⁶Then Absalom said, "If not, pray let my brother Amnon go with us." And the king said to him, "Why should he go with you?" ²⁷But Absalom pressed him until he let Amnon and all the king's sons go with him. ²⁸Then Absalom commanded his servants, "Mark when Amnon's heart is merry with wine, and when I say to you, 'Strike Amnon,' then kill him. Fear not; have I not commanded you? Be courageous and be valiant." ²⁹So the servants of Absalom did to Amnon as Absalom had commanded. Then all the king's sons arose, and each mounted his mule and fled.

³⁰While they were on the way, tidings came to David, "Absalom has slain all the king's sons, and not one of them is left." ³¹Then the king arose, and rent his garments, and lay on the earth; and all his servants who were standing by rent their garments. ³²But Jonadab the son of Shime-ah, David's brother, said, "Let not my lord suppose that they have killed all the young men the king's sons, for Amnon alone is dead, for by the command of Absalom this has been determined from the day he forced his sister Tamar. ³³Now therefore let not my lord the king so take it to heart as to suppose that all the king's sons are dead; for Amnon alone is dead."

³⁴But Absalom fled. And the young man who kept the watch lifted up his eyes, and looked, and behold, many people were coming from the Horonaim road by the side of the mountain. ³⁵And Jonadab said to the king, "Behold, the king's sons have come; as your servant said, so it has come about." ³⁶And as soon as he had finished speaking, behold, the king's sons came, and lifted up their voice and wept; and the king also and all his servants wept very bitterly.

³⁷But Absalom fled, and went to Talmai the son of Ammihud, king of Geshur. And David mourned for his son day after day. ³⁸So Absalom fled, and went to Geshur, and was there three years. ³⁹And the spirit of the king longed to go forth to Absalom; for he was comforted about Amnon, seeing he was dead.

The narrative tells us the consequences of Amnon's rape of his half-sister, and in doing so switches the reader's attention from Amnon to Absalom, who as Tamar's full brother was naturally enraged by what Amnon had done. So now the writer gives us not only a record of events but at the same time a character study of this son of David. He was a more complex and more interesting man than Amnon, and at first we are bound to feel considerable sympathy for him, in his kindliness and concern for his sister, his hostility towards Amnon, and his impatience when his father took no action. However, two aspects of his attitude towards Amnon are less commendable. He hated him; but said not a word to him. There are two ways of understanding verse 22. The Hebrew idiom "to speak *neither good nor bad*" could mean that he sent Amnon to "Coventry", and refused to have any dealings with him at all; or (more probably) it means that he never discussed the rape with Amnon. It would have been far better if he had given vent to his natural anger straight away; the New Testament does not condemn justifiable anger, but its plea that we should not "let the sun go down" on our anger (cp. Eph. 4:26) is wise indeed. The result was not only fatal for Amnon but very harmful to Absalom's character and wrecked his whole career.

So Absalom nursed his hatred and his desire for revenge, waiting patiently for his opportunity. Both he and Amnon showed that they could be patient, cold-blooded and deceitful men in obtaining their objectives; they were brothers, and evidently shared the same temperament. David was the man whom both of them deceived, Amnon when he pretended to be ill and Absalom when he asked that his brother should attend a feast as David's representative.

Vengeance is a powerful human motive, and nowhere more so than in the East. That is the reason why "an eye for an eye" (cp. Exod. 21:24) was such an important principle. This principle did not, as is widely but quite wrongly supposed, insist that the loss of an eye demanded that an eye should be forfeited in compensation. Rather, it laid down that in no circumstances should *more* than an eye be forfeited. Rape is a serious crime, but murder is very much more serious. Absalom's deed was by any standards inexcusable, then. The story also illustrates why punishment should always be left to a third party to impose, someone with no personal involvement in the case. Where human law courts cannot or do not deal with the case, then "leave it to the wrath of God", as St. Paul advised, cp. Rom. 12:19.

Absalom thus proved that he was as unfit as Amnon to rule Israel. He was a man with none of the magnanimity of his father; he could nurse a hatred against an opponent for a very long time. A national leader, by contrast, must be cool and objective in his judgements, willing to forgive or at least to ignore wrongs done to him. He must uphold and maintain justice, not flout it as Absalom did.

Absalom, then, was not the right man to rule Israel; yet by killing Amnon he seems to have made himself next in line to the throne, certainly in his own mind and quite possibly in the minds of many Israelites at the time. It is not at all improbable that his own status was in his mind when he decided to kill his elder brother rather than hurt him in some other fashion. However, he dared not stay in Israel immediately after committing a murder, so as a temporary measure he fled to his grandfather's court (3:3) in the neighbouring Aramaean kingdom of Geshur.

David's role in this chapter is rather a passive one, but what little is said about his reactions to first Amnon and then Absalom is of interest and offers a sidelight on his character. The writer tells us of his natural and very proper anger at the rape of Tamar but leaves the reader to guess for himself that David did nothing; if he had punished Amnon in some way, Absalom might have been satisfied. The ancient Greek translation of verse 21 adds the information "but he [David] would not hurt Amnon because he was his eldest son and he loved him" (see the NEB), which may well be true. Love, just as much as hatred, can result in unwise or wrongful conduct. David's failure to punish Amnon may have been due to over-indulgence of his sons; or perhaps he was now beginning to age and was less decisive then he had been; or his own recent misconduct may have weakened his moral position in his own family. Whichever might be the cause, we can see a certain weakness developing in this strong king. For all his achievements, he was no ideal ruler and the Bible does not idealize him.

At the end of the chapter we find him beginning to feel indulgent towards Absalom, and the reader starts to wonder if Absalom like Amnon will go unpunished. Again the hint of weakness is plain to see; and in this situation weakness meant injustice.

JOAB'S INTERVENTION

2 Samuel 14:1–20

[1]Now Joab the son of Zeruiah perceived that the king's heart went out to Absalom. [2]And Joab sent to Tekoa, and fetched from there a wise woman, and said to her, "Pretend to be a mourner, and put on mourning garments; do not anoint yourself with oil, but behave like a woman who has been mourning many days for the dead; [3]and go to the king, and speak thus to him." So Joab put the words in her mouth.

[4]When the woman of Tekoa came to the king, she fell on her face to the ground, and did obeisance, and said, "Help, O king." [5]And the king said to her, "What is your trouble?" She answered, "Alas, I am a widow; my husband is dead. [6]And your handmaid had two sons, and they quarrelled with one another in the field; there was no one to part them, and one struck the other and killed him. [7]And now the whole family has risen against your handmaid, and they say, 'Give up the man who struck his brother, that we may kill him for the life of his brother whom he slew'; and so they would destroy the heir also. Thus they would quench my coal which is left, and leave to my husband neither name nor remnant upon the face of the earth."

[8]Then the king said to the woman, "Go to your house, and I will give orders concerning you." [9]And the woman of Tekoa said to the king, "On me be the guilt, my lord the king, and on my father's house; let the king and his throne be guiltless." [10]The king said, "If any one says anything to you, bring him to me, and he shall never touch you again." [11]Then she said, "Pray let the king invoke the Lord your God, that the avenger of blood slay no more, and my son be not destroyed." He said, "As the Lord lives, not one hair of your son shall fall to the ground."

¹²Then the woman said, "Pray let your handmaid speak a word to my lord the king." He said, "Speak." ¹³And the woman said, "Why then have you planned such a thing against the people of God? For in giving this decision the king convicts himself, inasmuch as the king does not bring his banished one home again. ¹⁴We must all die, we are like water spilt on the ground, which cannot be gathered up again; but God will not take away the life of him who devises means not to keep his banished one an outcast. ¹⁵Now I have come to say this to my lord the king because the people have made me afraid; and your handmaid thought, 'I will speak to the king; it may be that the king will perform the request of his servant. ¹⁶For the king will hear, and deliver his servant from the hand of the man who would destroy me and my son together from the heritage of God.' ¹⁷And your handmaid thought, 'The word of my lord the king will set me at rest'; for my lord the king is like the angel of God to discern good and evil. The Lord your God be with you!"

¹⁸Then the king answered the woman, "Do not hide from me anything I ask you." And the woman said, "Let my lord the king speak." ¹⁹The king said, "Is the hand of Joab with you in all this?" The woman answered and said, "As surely as you live, my lord the king, one cannot turn to the right hand or to the left from anything that my lord the king has said. It was your servant Joab who bade me; it was he who put all these words in the mouth of your handmaid. ²⁰In order to change the course of affairs your servant Joab did this. But my lord has wisdom like the wisdom of the angel of God to know all things that are on the earth."

If David was showing some signs of weakness where his own sons were concerned, he was still very much in command of the kingdom. The power and influence of the king were growing stronger as the years passed. It is worth noting that Nathan in chapter 12 and Joab here both felt the necessity of presenting their case to the king by indirect means, by spinning a fictitious story. Yet both men stood very high in the political structure of the kingdom, Nathan as a court prophet and Joab as commander-in-chief of the armed forces. It is of course true that both men wanted not only to persuade David that they were right but also to change his whole approach and attitude.

David's suspicion that Joab had prompted the woman from Tekoa (verse 19) suggests that Joab must have discussed Absalom's affairs with him previously.

From verse 1 it appears that David was in two minds about Absalom—or rather, that his heart and his mind were pulling him in opposite directions. In his mind he believed that Absalom as a murderer was rightly banned from the country, but in his heart he longed to renew close contact with his son. We should not suppose that Joab's only concern was to help the king resolve his own personal dilemma. The statements which he instructed the woman to make about Absalom show that Joab was more concerned about the kingdom than the king. He was convinced that Absalom, as David's eldest surviving son, must one day become king; David had other sons (including Solomon, of course, but he was at this stage still a child), but later events prove that Absalom had a personality which commanded respect and won him widespread popularity throughout the country. Absalom's exile, then, was an unpopular situation and, worse, it left a political vacuum in Israel, with nobody appointed as David's successor if and when he died. We must bear in mind how vital a thing to national welfare and stability a properly arranged succession can be; it was for instance a major political issue, of great concern to monarchs and counsellors alike, in the reigns of Henry VIII and Elizabeth I in English history. One can well believe that the young man who became King Edward VI could have got away with murder, literally, when he was crown prince!

The woman's story was all a pretence, but undoubtedly there were legal precedents for such a case. Here David was sitting as appeal judge in a case where the equivalent of local magistrates had already given their verdict—or so she claimed. It all seems rather complex to us; the gist of it was that her son and heir was admittedly guilty of manslaughter, but if he paid the normal penalty, which was capital punishment, she and the immediate family would suffer, by the forfeiture of all their property to distant heirs. The issue, then, was whether justice for the family did not demand mercy for the wrongdoer. By degrees the woman managed to persuade David to give his solemn oath to save her son's life.

The application of this everyday lawsuit to the case of Absalom was clear enough. He had acted very wrongly, nobody denied, but if he was punished strictly in accordance with the law, or by permanent exile, then the whole kingdom would suffer. Everybody knew that Absalom had had a just quarrel with Amnon, and it looks as if popular opinion was inclined to overlook what he had done.

Once he had given an oath to the woman concerning her son, David felt morally obliged to grant legal pardon to his own son too; and by consenting to pardon Absalom, he was tacitly agreeing with Joab's view of the political situation. To the biblical writer and to the reader, however, it seems clear that it was very undesirable that Absalom should be tacitly recognized as David's successor. Joab was wrong—he soon changed his mind!—and neither he nor David was wise to give way to popular sentiments and pressures. Both men in fact endangered the kingdom, far from aiding its stability.

There is irony as well as flattery in the way the woman described David in verses 17 and 20. David was no *angel*, and although on the whole he was a wise and shrewd king, in this instance he undoubtedly acted foolishly. Nathan's parable had led him in the right direction; Joab's protégée's parable trapped him into a wrong decision. The writer probably means us to take the lesson that David ought to have consulted a prophet and ascertained God's will about Absalom; Joab was a soldier, and not the best man to decide what was right for the kingdom. Probably too we should infer that it was David's love for Absalom which led him to accept his own ruling. He could and should have insisted that Absalom's case was not on all fours with the fictitious lawsuit: to begin with, Absalom was by no means the only possible heir to the throne.

So the woman's flattery directs us to a very important point, namely that the king of Israel needed to have superhuman wisdom; but David was beginning to show weakness in more than one respect. Good leadership requires not only shrewdness and wisdom but also the firmness to resist pressures both from close personal friends and from popular opinion, which is in any case fickle and unreliable.

ABSALOM'S RETURN

2 Samuel 14:21–33

21Then the king said to Joab, "Behold now I grant this; go, bring back the young man Absalom." 22And Joab fell on his face to the ground, and did obeisance, and blessed the king; and Joab said, "Today your servant knows that I have found favour in your sight, my lord the king, in that the king has granted the request of his servant." 23So Joab arose and went to Geshur, and brought Absalom to Jerusalem. 24And the king said, "Let him dwell apart in his own house; he is not to come into my presence." So Absalom dwelt apart in his own house, and did not come into the king's presence.

25Now in all Israel there was no one so much to be praised for his beauty as Absalom; from the sole of his foot to the crown of his head there was no blemish in him. 26And when he cut the hair of his head (for at the end of every year he used to cut it; when it was heavy on him, he cut it), he weighed the hair of his head, two hundred shekels by the king's weight. 27There were born to Absalom three sons, and one daughter whose name was Tamar; she was a beautiful woman.

28So Absalom dwelt two full years in Jerusalem, without coming into the king's presence. 29Then Absalom sent for Joab, to send him to the king; but Joab would not come to him. And he sent a second time, but Joab would not come. 30Then he said to his servants, "See, Joab's field is next to mine, and he has barley there; go and set it on fire." So Absalom's servants set the field on fire. 31Then Joab arose and went to Absalom at his house, and said to him, "Why have your servants set my field on fire?" 32Absalom answered Joab, "Behold, I sent word to you, 'Come here, that I may send you to the king, to ask, "Why have I come from Geshur? It would be better for me to be there still." Now therefore let me go into the presence of the king; and if there is guilt in me, let him kill me.'" 33Then Joab went to the king, and told him; and he summoned Absalom. So he came to the king, and bowed himself on his face to the ground before the king; and the king kissed Absalom.

Thanks then to Joab, Absalom was able to return freely to Israel, but not immediately to the royal court. It is not certain whether David's decision to keep him at a distance was made before or after Joab's mission to fetch the exile back to Jerusalem, but one can easily see why Absalom was annoyed about the situation which confronted him in Jerusalem. He was important enough to have a high official, Joab, to escort him home, but then he was treated like an outcast in his own hometown.

One can see that David banned him from the court as a punishment, but it was not really a wise course of action. From the point of view of the kingdom, it merely continued the political vacuum, since it left the succession problem unresolved; David signalled his disfavour of Absalom without naming any other son as crown prince. More serious was the fact that the action not only offended and angered Absalom but put him in a position where he could do a maximum of damage—in Jerusalem itself, but safely out of the king's immediate entourage.

Verses 25ff. provide the first physical description of Absalom the reader has been given. He was evidently a very attractive person, like his father and Saul in their youth; once again we must recognize the part this feature played in popular esteem and acclaim. The implication is that to ordinary Israelite eyes Absalom was an ideal man to be king—and the whole country knew it (verse 25).

Verses 28–33, on the other hand, give us a fresh insight into his character, and confirm our impression that he was far from an ideal person to be king: appearances were deceptive! He was not only extremely determined, which in itself might be a virtue, but also arrogant and high-handed. To destroy a man's crops was a very serious matter, as well as a dangerous action in a dry climate. His challenge to David to put him on trial (verse 32) shows too that he felt no compunction whatever over the murder of Amnon.

Yet the upshot of his arrogant behaviour was that both Joab and David meekly yielded to his wishes. The last verse of the chapter appears to describe a full reconciliation between father and son; publicly it amounted to that, and it goes without saying that Absalom resumed his former place at court, with David's blessing and approval. It is difficult to say whether David should have accepted the challenge and put him on trial; at any rate he should never have given the whole nation the impression that Absalom was the man destined to be their next king. Once again David's relative weakness and lack of wisdom are underlined by the narrative. Such faults in its leaders weaken a nation; but in the first place it was David's own position as king that was put at risk, as events soon showed. Mercy and forgiveness are thoroughly good qualities; justice should always be tempered by mercy. On the other hand, there are times when forgiveness is not made on principle but is merely weakness by another name. Above all a good leader must be a man of firmness and resolve. David's weakness with Absalom left his son unrestrained and allowed the kingdom too to drift out of control.

ABSALOM'S REVOLT

2 Samuel 15:1–16

¹After this Absalom got himself a chariot and horses, and fifty men to run before him. ²And Absalom used to rise early and stand beside the way of the gate; and when any man had a suit to come before the king for judgment, Absalom would call to him, and say, "From what city are you?" And when he said, "Your servant is of such and such a tribe in Israel," ³Absalom would say to him, "See, your claims are good and right; but there is no man deputed by the king to hear you." ⁴Absalom said moreover, "Oh that I were judge in the land! Then every man with a suit or cause might come to me, and I would give him justice." ⁵And whenever a man came near to do obeisance to him, he would put out his hand, and take hold of him, and kiss him. ⁶Thus Absalom did to all of Israel who came to the king for judgment; so Absalom stole the hearts of the men of Israel.

⁷And at the end of four years Absalom said to the king, "Pray let me go and pay my vow, which I have vowed to the Lord, in Hebron. ⁸For your servant vowed a vow while I dwelt at Geshur in Aram,

saying, 'If the Lord will indeed bring me back to Jerusalem, then I will offer worship to the Lord.'" [9]The king said to him, "Go in peace." So he arose, and went to Hebron. [10]But Absalom sent secret messengers throughout all the tribes of Israel, saying, "As soon as you hear the sound of the trumpet, then say, 'Absalom is king at Hebron!'" [11]With Absalom went two hundred men from Jerusalem who were invited guests, and they went in their simplicity, and knew nothing. [12]And while Absalom was offering the sacrifices, he sent for Ahithophel the Gilonite, David's counsellor, from his city Giloh. And the conspiracy grew strong, and the people with Absalom kept increasing.

[13]And a messenger came to David, saying, "The hearts of the men of Israel have gone after Absalom." [14]Then David said to all his servants who were with him at Jerusalem, "Arise, and let us flee; or else there will be no escape for us from Absalom; go in haste, lest he overtake us quickly, and bring down evil upon us, and smite the city with the edge of the sword." [15]And the king's servants said to the king, "Behold, your servants are ready to do whatever my lord the king decides." [16]So the king went forth, and all his household after him. And the king left ten concubines to keep the house.

After Absalom's return to the court and to favour with David, he seemed well placed to inherit his father's throne in due course. The reason why he was not prepared to wait so long is something of a puzzle, unless perhaps he doubted whether David might pass him over. Whatever the reason, he exhibited the same patient scheming and relentless determination which he had already shown when he set out to avenge the rape of his sister (chapter 13); the leopard had not changed his spots. His hatred for Amnon at least had had some excuse, but now it became clear that he had no affection for his father either. Apart from his love for his sister Tamar, he appears to have been a cold, ruthless and above all ambitious man.

He was certainly a cunning man, skilled in manipulating people. He deceived his father thoroughly; David was not only unsuspicious about Absalom's wish to go to Hebron, he was also caught totally unawares by the revolt when it broke out. It takes a great deal of time to organize a revolt as successful as this one was, and Absalom may have spent as much as four years laying his plans (cp. verse 7) but David heard no whisper of the plot.

Absalom was equally clever in misleading the ordinary citizens. No doubt the sort of episode described in verses 2–6 was only one of his schemes for discrediting David and putting himself in the best possible light, but it was highly successful. It was really sheer effrontery for him, an unpunished murderer, to express such a concern for justice, but apparently people were more convinced by his words and his friendly conduct than by memories of his past actions. Human memories are not always short but they tend to be remarkably selective.

Another example of his cunning is the way in which he inveigled two hundred of Jerusalem's leading citizens into joining him in Hebron (verse 11). He put them in a terrible dilemma; if they opposed his rebellion their lives would be immediately at risk, but if they supported him they would be held guilty of treason if and when the revolt failed. They were really in the position of hostages, and Absalom could have put a great deal of pressure on their families in Jerusalem if David had not decided to abandon the capital for the time being.

Cunning and deceit seem to have been his chief characteristics, then. By means of them he was able to induce a very large number of Israelites to turn against David. It is impossible to guess just how big his following was; he may have relied more on speed and decisive action than on numbers, but there is no doubt that he did muster a great deal of support throughout the land. It is particularly striking that David's own tribe, Judah, were prepared to give their allegiance to the rebel. It is noteworthy that Absalom's base of operations was David's first capital, Hebron, in the very heart of Judah. Perhaps David's transfer of the capital to Jerusalem had caused some offence in and around Hebron.

The story of the revolt, then, gives us further insight into Absalom's character, and makes it clear that he was very capable but utterly unscrupulous and untrustworthy. He was not the man of God's choice to govern Israel, far from it.

But David does not come out of the story too well either. He was made to look a fool, completely deceived by his treacherous son. His administration of justice evidently left a lot to be desired, to judge by verses 2f.; not that he fostered injustice, but long delays in granting justice certainly cause hardship and in fact prolong injustices. Above all, it looks as if he had become complacent, probably isolated nowadays from the common man, and was quite out of touch with the mood of the country. It is all too easy for a popular leader to rest on his laurels and lose his popularity without even realizing the fact. It is essential for a good leader to be closely in touch with those he leads.

Neither Absalom nor David, then, was an ideal ruler; but at least David showed a genuine consideration for his people that was lacking in Absalom. His first thought was to spare his capital city the horrors of either a siege or an army rampaging through it (verse 14). Absalom had pretended to a passion for justice, but he did not care how many Israelite lives might be lost in civil warfare. Actions spoke louder than words in the last resort.

DAVID'S FRIENDS

2 Samuel 15:17–37

[17]And the king went forth, and all the people after him; and they halted at the last house. [18]And all his servants passed by him; and all the Cherethites, and all the Pelethites, and all the six hundred Gittites who had followed him from Gath, passed on before the king.

[19]Then the king said to Ittai the Gittite, "Why do you also go with us? Go back, and stay with the king; for you are a foreigner, and also an exile from your home. [20]You came only yesterday, and shall I today make you wander about with us, seeing I go I know not where? Go back, and take your brethren with you; and may the Lord show steadfast love and faithfulness to you." [21]But Ittai answered the king, "As the Lord lives, and as my lord the king lives, wherever my lord the king shall be, whether for death or for life, there also will your servant be." [22]And David said to Ittai, "Go then, pass on." So Ittai the Gittite passed on, with all his men and all the little ones who were with him. [23]And all the country wept aloud as all the people

passed by, and the king crossed the brook Kidron, and all the people passed on toward the wilderness.

24And Abiathar came up, and lo, Zadok came also, with all the Levites, bearing the ark of the covenant of God; and they set down the ark of God, until the people had all passed out of the city. 25Then the king said to Zadok, "Carry the ark of God back into the city. If I find favour in the eyes of the Lord, he will bring me back and let me see both it and his habitation; 26but if he says, 'I have no pleasure in you,' behold, here I am, let him do to me what seems good to him." 27The king also said to Zadok the priest, "Look, go back to the city in peace, you and Abiathar, with your two sons, Ahima-az your son, and Jonathan the son of Abiathar. 28See, I will wait at the fords of the wilderness, until word comes from you to inform me." 29So Zadok and Abiathar carried the ark of God back to Jerusalem; and they remained there.

30But David went up the ascent of the Mount of Olives, weeping as he went, barefoot and with his head covered; and all the people who were with him covered their heads, and they went up, weeping as they went. 31And it was told David, "Ahithophel is among the conspirators with Absalom." And David said, "O Lord, I pray thee, turn the counsel of Ahithophel into foolishness."

32When David came to the summit, where God was worshipped, behold, Hushai the Archite came to meet him with his coat rent and earth upon his head. 33David said to him, "If you go on with me, you will be a burden to me. 34But if you return to the city, and say to Absalom, 'I will be your servant, O king; as I have been your father's servant in time past, so now I will be your servant,' then you will defeat for me the counsel of Ahithophel. 35Are not Zadok and Abiathar the priests with you there? So whatever you hear from the king's house, tell it to Zadok and Abiathar the priests. 36Behold, their two sons are with them there, Ahima-az, Zadok's son, and Jonathan, Abiathar's son; and by them you shall send to me everything you hear." 37So Hushai, David's friend, came into the city, just as Absalom was entering Jerusalem.

It is plain enough that David must have had enemies; Absalom's revolt would never have been a possibility otherwise. The most notable among them, a man briefly mentioned in the previous section (verse 12), was called Ahithophel, who was quite possibly the grandfather of

Bathsheba. He seems to have been the most gifted of David's political advisers, and David was not only distressed but alarmed to hear that this man was now giving Absalom the benefit of his talents (verse 31). We have no way of knowing why he turned traitor to David.

However, David was by no means without friends, and this section lists several men who were so loyal that they were prepared to risk their lives on David's behalf. This fact in itself is a testimony to David's character. He could inspire a deep loyalty in people who knew him well; it is doubtful if the self-centred Absalom could ever have won such loyalty in his followers.

The importance of these particular friends of David lies in the fact that they were men in influential positions, and events were to prove that David's eventual victory was due in large measure to their help.

(i) *Ittai* was a foreigner—in fact a Philistine (*Gittite* means a native of Gath)—who had only recently come to Israel, as the officer in command of David's personal bodyguard, who also were Philistines. (Ancient kings quite often preferred to employ foreign bodyguards, since they were unlikely to be affected by local political considerations or won over by local political factions.) David could not have kept Ittai's services in this crisis without his consent, but the soldier showed not the slightest hesitation in remaining loyal to the king. As a result David found himself supported by a small but reliable and well-trained army.

(ii) *Abiathar* and *Zadok* were the two priests in charge of the Jerusalem shrine. Their support meant that the religious authorities of the kingdom were whole-heartedly on David's side; at no point do we hear that Absalom had the support or guidance of any priest or prophet. In bringing the ark of the covenant out of the city the priests were not concerned to keep it safe—it is certain that Absalom would never have attacked it—but to provide David with this powerful symbol of God's presence in the battles ahead. However, these loyal friends were asked to go back into Jerusalem. If they quietly continued with their priestly duties they would be safe enough, but in fact they were prepared to undertake the very risky task of providing David with an intelligence service.

(iii) *Hushai* was *David's friend* (verse 37) in two senses. The title "the king's friend" was the name of a high political office in Israel, and so Hushai was one of the most senior political figures in the country. He demonstrated now that he was David's friend in reality as well as by title. He was willing to accompany the king into temporary exile, but on David's instructions he went just as readily back to Jerusalem, even though he might well have been killed by Absalom as a well-known supporter of David's regime. His role was partly to spy on Absalom and partly to attempt to counteract the masterly advice of Ahithophel; this double task was as difficult as it was dangerous.

Loyalty of such a degree is in itself a testimony to David's qualities, but it was more than that. The friendship and the courage of these men were a sure sign of God's continuing favour to David. Meanwhile David showed a commendable attitude very much in contrast to Absalom's arrogance. He was completely willing to submit to God's will (verses 25f.), whatever that might prove to be. Such willingness to surrender leadership at the right time is another hallmark of good leadership. All the same, David was right not to capitulate meekly and allow Absalom to take over the kingdom unopposed. The fact that leading soldiers, statesmen and priests all supported him with such single-minded devotion was in itself a sign that God was not taking the kingdom from him. God's will for us can often be learned by consulting the opinions of several experienced Christians.

DAVID'S ENEMIES

2 Samuel 16:1-23

¹When David had passed a little beyond the summit, Ziba the servant of Mephibosheth met him, with a couple of asses saddled,

bearing two hundred loaves of bread, a hundred bunches of raisins, a hundred of summer fruits, and a skin of wine. ²And the king said to Ziba, "Why have you brought these?" Ziba answered, "The asses are for the king's household to ride on, the bread and summer fruit for the young men to eat, and the wine for those who faint in the wilderness to drink." ³And the king said, "And where is your master's son?" Ziba said to the king, "Behold, he remains in Jerusalem; for he said, 'Today the house of Israel will give me back the kingdom of my father.'" ⁴Then the king said to Ziba, "Behold, all that belonged to Mephibosheth is now yours." And Ziba said, "I do obeisance; let me ever find favour in your sight, my lord the king."

⁵When King David came to Bahurim, there came out a man of the family of the house of Saul, whose name was Shime-i, the son of Gera; and as he came he cursed continually. ⁶And he threw stones at David, and at all the servants of King David; and all the people and all the mighty men were on his right hand and on his left. ⁷And Shime-i said as he cursed, "Begone, begone, you man of blood, you worthless fellow! ⁸The Lord has avenged upon you all the blood of the house of Saul, in whose place you have reigned; and the Lord has given the kingdom into the hand of your son Absalom. See, your ruin is on you; for you are a man of blood."

⁹Then Abishai the son of Zeruiah said to the king, "Why should this dead dog curse my lord the king? Let me go over and take off his head." ¹⁰But the king said, "What have I to do with you, you sons of Zeruiah? If he is cursing because the Lord has said to him, 'Curse David,' who then shall say, 'Why have you done so?'" ¹¹And David said to Abishai and to all his servants, "Behold, my own son seeks my life; how much more now may this Benjaminite! Let him alone, and let him curse; for the Lord has bidden him. ¹²It may be that the Lord will look upon my affliction, and that the Lord will repay me with good for this cursing of me today." ¹³So David and his men went on the road, while Shime-i went along on the hillside opposite him and cursed as he went, and threw stones at him and flung dust. ¹⁴And the king, and all the people who were with him, arrived weary at the Jordan; and there he refreshed himself.

¹⁵Now Absalom and all the people, the men of Israel, came to Jerusalem, and Ahithophel with him. ¹⁶And when Hushai the Archite, David's friend, came to Absalom, Hushai said to Absalom, "Long live the king! Long live the king!" ¹⁷And Absalom said to Hushai, "Is this your loyalty to your friend? Why did you not go with your friend?" ¹⁸And Hushai said to Absalom, "No; for whom

the Lord and this people and all the men of Israel have chosen, his I will be, and with him I will remain. [19]And again, whom should I serve? Should it not be his son? As I have served your father, so I will serve you."

[20]Then Absalom said to Ahithophel, "Give your counsel; what shall we do?" [21]Ahithophel said to Absalom, "Go in to your father's concubines, whom he has left to keep the house; and all Israel will hear that you have made yourself odious to your father, and the hands of all who are with you will be strengthened." [22]So they pitched a tent for Absalom upon the roof; and Absalom went in to his father's concubines in the sight of all Israel. [23]Now in those days the counsel which Ahithophel gave was as if one consulted the oracle of God; so was all the counsel of Ahithophel esteemed, both by David and by Absalom.

If there was encouragement for David in the loyalty of his friends, as chapter 15 indicates, chapter 16 goes on to show something of the problems that were ranged against him. The narrator presents us with three cameos, brief episodes which highlight the difficulties faced by David in the crisis which had arisen. There were the apparent hostility of Mephibosheth, the bitter enmity of Shimei, and the skilful manoeuvres of Ahithophel. Two other men, Ziba and Hushai, play low-key but not unimportant roles in the sequence of events.

(i) *Mephibosheth* was conspicuous by his absence. In the light of later information (see 19:24-30), it is doubtful if Ziba was telling the truth, but that is not particularly relevant at this point in time; as far as David knew, Mephibosheth had deserted him, in the hope of getting something for himself out of the political crisis. It is difficult to see how events could have conspired to make Mephibosheth king, unless both David and Absalom had been killed in the civil war. Even then, some other son of David would probably have seized the vacant throne. Be that as it may, one class of opponent which David had to take into account was the ambitious man. There are always politicians or army officers or the like whose only real loyalty is to themselves, and who do not mind who gets hurt so long as their own ambitions are furthered. In a crisis, the good leader must always be wary of people of this type and guard against them if possible.

(ii) *Shimei* was of a different character entirely. One must at least give him credit for his honesty and his courage; he hated David and he was not afraid to say so, even though he might easily have been killed by David's men. He represented what would today be called "sectional interest"; it would be even more accurate to accuse him of "tribalism" or indeed racism. In other words, his hostility to David was quite fanatical, and was based on the wrongs he believed that David had inflicted on his tribe (Benjamin). At the very least we must say that the so-called wrongs were exaggerated, blown up out of all proportion to the facts. The welfare of the nation as a whole did not concern Shimei in the slightest; all that mattered to him was revenge. We can still observe fanaticism and hatred of this sort in various countries today. Good leaders must be realistic enough to recognize that sweet reasonableness will never convince such men; but wisely David refrained from adding bloodshed to bloodshed, which might well have alienated the whole tribe of Benjamin permanently. Toleration and understanding are vital in dealing with such opponents.

(iii) *Ahithophel* represents the unexpected, the unpredictable enemy. We are never given the slightest idea what caused him to side with Absalom. It cannot have been ambition, since he had held as high a position in David's court as he now held in Absalom's. He was a Judaean, and cannot have shared Shimei's Benjaminite sentiments. No leader can expect one hundred per cent loyalty from all his apparent supporters, and there will always be some who surprise everyone in a crisis by the stance they adopt. Of the three men, Ahithophel was obviously much the most dangerous. His advice to Absalom in verse 21 was shrewd and practical. By such a public act Absalom would be able to demonstrate to all that there was a total and irrevocable breach between his father and himself, otherwise his support might have been half-hearted in some quarters. After all, if David and Absalom had been able to patch up their differences in some fashion,

Absalom's leading supporters would have found themselves in a very awkward position, and possibly even used as scapegoats. So Ahithophel's advice strengthened Absalom's position considerably. To take over a king's concubines was a very public claim to his throne, cp. 3:6f.

But there were two hopeful signs in all this for David. *Ziba* is an interesting character; he was just as ambitious for himself as he claimed that Mephibosheth was, but evidently he took the gamble that David would win the civil war. There were then people who were not necessarily devoted to David's cause but who were convinced that his shrewdness and experience would eventually prove stronger than Absalom's youthful vigour. The other sign of hope was the fact that *Hushai* succeeded in worming his way into Absalom's favour, and so found himself in a position to aid David's cause. In this we should see the hand of God, once more. The public humiliation of David's concubines had been foreseen (cp. 12:11), as a punishment upon David, but the fall of David was not in God's plans. Ahithophel's advice might be as sound as that of God himself (verse 23), but he was not God and he had no control over events whatever. It is all too easy to be pessimistic when we assess the size, the skill and the power of some human adversary; but as the old saying puts it, "Man proposes, but God disposes."

OPPOSING COUNSELS

2 Samuel 17:1-14

[1]Moreover Ahithophel said to Absalom, "Let me choose twelve thousand men, and I will set out and pursue David tonight. [2]I will come upon him while he is weary and discouraged, and throw him into a panic; and all the people who are with him will flee. I will strike down the king only, [3]and I will bring all the people back to you as a bride comes home to her husband. You seek the life of only one man, and all the people will be at peace." [4]And the advice pleased Absalom and all the elders of Israel.

[5]Then Absalom said, "Call Hushai the Archite also, and let us

hear what he has to say." ⁶**And** when Hushai came to Absalom, Absalom said to him, "Thus has Ahithophel spoken; shall we do as he advises? If not, you speak." ⁷Then Hushai said to Absalom, "This time the counsel which Ahithophel has given is not good." ⁸Hushai said moreover, "You know that your father and his men are mighty men, and that they are enraged, like a bear robbed of her cubs in the field. Besides, your father is expert in war; he will not spend the night with the people. ⁹Behold, even now he has hidden himself in one of the pits, or in some other place. And when some of the people fall at the first attack, whoever hears it will say, 'There has been a slaughter among the people who follow Absalom.' ¹⁰Then even the valiant man, whose heart is like the heart of a lion, will utterly melt with fear; for all Israel knows that your father is a mighty man, and that those who are with him are valiant men. ¹¹But my counsel is that all Israel be gathered to you, from Dan to Beersheba, as the sand by the sea for multitude, and that you go to battle in person. ¹²So we shall come upon him in some place where he is to be found, and we shall light upon him as the dew falls on the ground; and of him and all the men with him not one will be left. ¹³If he withdraws into a city, then all Israel will bring ropes to that city, and we shall drag it into the valley, until not even a pebble is to be found there." ¹⁴And Absalom and all the men of Israel said, "The counsel of Hushai the Archite is better than the counsel of Ahithophel." For the Lord had ordained to defeat the good counsel of Ahithophel, so that the Lord might bring evil upon Absalom.

The first phase of Absalom's revolt had been very successful, and he had taken control of the capital city without a shot being fired, so to speak. However, he had narrowly failed to reach Jerusalem in time to surround and capture David, and by now David was at the River Jordan (16:14), just within range of a fast night's march by Absalom's troops, but only just. Even now swift action could have decided the outcome in Absalom's favour, and had the very desirable effect of avoiding any fighting or bloodshed. So the second phase of the revolt was equally important, and Absalom wisely turned to his master-planner, Ahithophel, for guidance. Fortunately for David, however, Absalom **turned** to Hushai too, for a second opinion.

The first battle, accordingly, was one of words. Ahithophel

gave Absalom some very shrewd and sound advice, leaving
Hushai with the tricky task of inventing some bad military
strategy and making it sound convincing. It is instructive to
compare the two strategies and the two speeches.

(i) *Ahithophel's* plan was for speedy and single-minded
action, with the sole aim of capturing David. If David were
killed, all opposition to Absalom would evaporate; nobody
fights for a dead king. We should understand the troop
numbers as describing a force of only moderate size; very
probably the word *thousand* in verse 1 should be translated
"units". The force recommended by Ahithophel would be big
enough to make a rapid march to the Jordan without the need
for very much preliminary organization.

In putting forward this plan, Ahithophel made skilful use of a
vivid image, picturing Absalom as a bridegroom and the nation
as a *bride*, easily wooed and won. There was some flattery in
this picture, suggesting that Absalom could very easily and
naturally gain the universal affection of his subjects. The only
weakness in Ahithophel's argument was that he offered to lead
the night attack himself; no doubt he thought this a noble and
helpful gesture, but it opened the door for the criticism that it
implied some disrespect for Absalom's ability as a soldier. At
that time, the first essential in a king of Israel was his military
ability.

(ii) *Hushai* advised caution, reminding Absalom of David's
great experience in warfare. He recommended that the biggest
possible army should be mustered before any action was taken.
Then, he said, David could be located and his few troops
crushed; if necessary, any city in which David took refuge could
be besieged and sacked. There were two hidden snags in this
plan: one was the sheer exaggeration of it, for it was by no
means certain that Absalom's full army would be that much
bigger than the forces David would be able to muster. The more
serious disadvantage in it was the loss of time involved; it would
be no quick and easy task to assemble and organize a huge
army. Of course, that was Hushai's real objective; he knew that
the longer Absalom delayed, the better David's chances would

be, and that even a short delay would enable David to organize the troops available to him and to devise some military tactics.

Hushai's tactics in argument were exaggeration, vivid images, and also flattery: the vast army was to be led by Absalom in person! The writer tells us that it was God's design that Hushai's plan would be the one adopted, rather than Ahithophel's (verse 14), but Absalom and his followers accepted the inferior strategy of their own free will. They had the choice and they made the wrong one. Thus we are given another insight into Absalom's character and his quality of leadership: he was too readily moved by flattery and he did not have sufficient intelligence to size up the options correctly. All leaders sometimes make mistakes, but this was a vital decision—his whole future hung upon it. It was particularly foolish to be influenced by flattery, which is something every leader must expect to some extent, and nowhere more so than in an oriental court. Good leadership demands a cool, objective evaluation, not least of one's own abilities.

DAVID'S ADVANTAGES

2 Samuel 17:15-29

¹⁵Then Hushai said to Zadok and Abiathar the priests, "Thus and so did Ahithophel counsel Absalom and the elders of Israel; and thus and so have I counselled. ¹⁶Now therefore send quickly and tell David, 'Do not lodge tonight at the fords of the wilderness, but by all means pass over; lest the king and all the people who are with him be swallowed up.'" ¹⁷Now Jonathan and Ahima-az were waiting at En-rogel; a maidservant used to go and tell them, and they would go and tell King David; for they must not be seen entering the city. ¹⁸But a lad saw them, and told Absalom; so both of them went away quickly, and came to the house of a man at Bahurim, who had a well in his courtyard; and they went down into it. ¹⁹And the woman took and spread a covering over the well's mouth, and scattered grain upon it; and nothing was known of it. ²⁰When Absalom's servants came to the woman at the house, they said, "Where are Ahima-az and Jonathan?" And the woman said to them, "They have gone over

the brook of water." And when they had sought and could not find
them, they returned to Jerusalem.

²¹After they had gone, the men came up out of the well, and went
and told King David. They said to David, "Arise, and go quickly
over the water; for thus and so has Ahithophel counselled against
you." ²²Then David arose, and all the people who were with him,
and they crossed the Jordan; by daybreak not one was left who had
not crossed the Jordan.

²³When Ahithophel saw that his counsel was not followed, he
saddled his ass, and went off home to his own city. And he set his
house in order, and hanged himself; and he died, and was buried in
the tomb of his father.

²⁴Then David came to Mahanaim. And Absalom crossed the
Jordan with all the men of Israel. ²⁵Now Absalom had set Amasa
over the army instead of Joab. Amasa was the son of a man named
Ithra the Ishmaelite, who had married Abigal the daughter of
Nahash, sister of Zeruiah, Joab's mother. ²⁶And Israel and Absalom
encamped in the land of Gilead.

²⁷When David came to Mahanaim, Shobi the son of Nahash from
Rabbah of the Ammonites, and Machir the son of Ammiel from Lo-
debar, and Barzillai the Gileadite from Rogelim, ²⁸brought beds,
basins, and earthen vessels, wheat, barley, meal, parched grain,
beans and lentils, ²⁹honey and curds and sheep and cheese from the
herd, for David and the people with him to eat; for they said, "The
people are hungry and weary and thirsty in the wilderness."

David was by no means out of danger yet; we must assume that
Hushai sent word to him before he was sure which of the two
plans Absalom meant to adopt. Once across the Jordan,
however, David would be safer altogether, in broken terrain
where he could easily take any evasive action necessary.

Taken as a whole, this section demonstrates how the advantage swung firmly David's way; or, in other words, it shows how
the Lord looked after his own chosen king. There are four
separate topics, and each of them makes the same point in its
own way.

(i) *David's escape from immediate danger.* The vivid story
told in verses 15–22 shows how easily things could have gone
the other way. The messengers from Jerusalem only just

escaped capture; if they had been intercepted, David might well have been overtaken and defeated by Absalom's army while still on the west side of the Jordan. It was a very near thing, but the writer clearly saw God's hand in the happy outcome. The fact that the householder was prepared to help the messengers, too, shows that by no means everybody in Israel supported Absalom.

(ii) *Ahithophel's suicide.* Ahithophel's action was symbolic. It was a sign of his wisdom that he knew already that Absalom's cause was doomed; he did not wait for Absalom's defeat and for the disgrace and punishment which were certain to be inflicted upon himself. His departure and death, however, left Absalom without any reliable guide, and that fact in itself was fatal to the rebel cause. Absalom lost friends as David gained them (see paragraph iv).

(iii) *The military arrangements.* As the two armies began to prepare for battle, two things seemed to favour David. The first was that he had a secure headquarters, in the city of Mahanaim, while Absalom and his men were out in the open. By leading his army in person, Absalom was putting himself in danger, whether or not he realized it. The other factor is introduced casually but is not really insignificant: although the Israelite army as a whole seems to have supported Absalom, it was not led by its very capable and experienced commander-in-chief, Joab. (Joab was in fact loyal to David and in Transjordan with him, as we first learn in 18:2.) Absalom's chief general, Amasa, may have had little experience; at any rate, the little we know about him suggests that he was not very competent. Absalom was putting his trust in the wrong people.

(iv) *Friends and supplies.* When David had first become king in Judah, Mahanaim had been the capital city of his rival Ish-bosheth, Saul's son (cp. 2:8ff.); one might have expected this part of Israel to be disloyal to David. On the contrary, however, the rich men of this region (called Gilead) went out of their way to befriend him and to provision his army. The reasons for their attitude are not explained, but the fact that they were loyal to David shows that he had earned their support and that they saw no reason to trust Absalom. As Hushai had anticipated, the passage of time was helping the old king, not the rebel.

Two reasons can be suggested for the willingness of these men in Transjordan to assist David. One of the men, Machir, was a close friend of Mephibosheth (cp. 9:4f.), and he may well have been impressed by David's earlier generosity to Mephibosheth. The second probable reason is that Transjordan was especially vulnerable to invasion by the Aramaeans from the north, and the rich farmers of this region no doubt owed a great deal to David's strong military action against the Aramaeans. For all David's faults and mistakes, he had over many years given most of his citizens ample reason to trust him, and this fact now paid off. Good leadership is for the good of all, and it creates close bonds of trust and affection.

THE DEATH OF ABSALOM

2 Samuel 18:1–33

¹Then David mustered the men who were with him, and set over them commanders of thousands and commanders of hundreds. ²And David sent forth the army, one third under the command of Joab, one third under the command of Abishai the son of Zeruiah, Joab's brother, and one third under the command of Ittai the Gittite. And the king said to the men, "I myself will also go out with you." ³But the men said, "You shall not go out. For if we flee, they will not care about us. If half of us die, they will not care about us. But you are worth ten thousand of us; therefore it is better that you send us help from the city." ⁴The king said to them, "Whatever seems best to you I will do." So the king stood at the side of the gate, while all the army marched out by hundreds and by thousands. ⁵And the king ordered Joab and Abishai and Ittai, "Deal gently for my sake with the young man Absalom." And all the people heard when the king gave orders to all the commanders about Absalom.

⁶So the army went out into the field against Israel; and the battle was fought in the forest of Ephraim. ⁷And the men of Israel were defeated there by the servants of David, and the slaughter there was great on that day, twenty thousand men. ⁸The battle spread over the

face of all the country; and the forest devoured more people that day than the sword.

9And Absalom chanced to meet the servants of David. Absalom was riding upon his mule, and the mule went under the thick branches of a great oak, and his head caught fast in the oak, and he was left hanging between heaven and earth, while the mule that was under him went on. 10And a certain man saw it, and told Joab, "Behold, I saw Absalom hanging in an oak." 11Joab said to the man who told him, "What, you saw him! Why then did you not strike him there to the ground? I would have been glad to give you ten pieces of silver and a girdle." 12But the man said to Joab, "Even if I felt in my hand the weight of a thousand pieces of silver, I would not put forth my hand against the king's son; for in our hearing the king commanded you and Abishai and Ittai, 'For my sake protect the young man Absalom.' 13On the other hand, if I had dealt treacherously against his life (and there is nothing hidden from the king), then you yourself would have stood aloof." 14Joab said, "I will not waste time like this with you." And he took three darts in his hand, and thrust them into the heart of Absalom, while he was still alive in the oak. 15And ten young men, Joab's armour-bearers, surrounded Absalom and struck him, and killed him.

16Then Joab blew the trumpet, and the troops came back from pursuing Israel; for Joab restrained them. 17And they took Absalom, and threw him into a great pit in the forest, and raised over him a very great heap of stones; and all Israel fled every one to his own home. 18Now Absalom in his lifetime had taken and set u_ for himself the pillar which is in the King's Valley, for he said, "I have no son to keep my name in remembrance"; he called the pillar after his own name, and it is called Absalom's monument to this day.

19Then said Ahima-az the son of Zadok, "Let me run, and carry tidings to the king that the Lord has delivered him from the power of his enemies." 20And Joab said to him, "You are not to carry tidings today; you may carry tidings another day, but today you shall carry no tidings, because the king's son is dead." 21Then Joab said to the Cushite, "Go, tell the king what you have seen." The Cushite bowed before Joab, and ran. 22Then Ahima-az the son of Zadok said again to Joab, "Come what may, let me also run after the Cushite." And Joab said, "Why will you run, my son, seeing that you will have no reward for the tidings?" 23"Come what may," he said, "I will run." So he said to him, "Run." Then Ahima-az ran by the way of the plain, and outran the Cushite.

24Now David was sitting between the two gates; and the watchman went up to the roof of the gate by the wall, and when he lifted up his eyes and looked, he saw a man running alone. 25And the watchman called out and told the king. And the king said, "If he is alone, there are tidings in his mouth." And he came apace, and drew near. 26And the watchman saw another man running; and the watchman called to the gate and said, "See, another man running alone!" The king said, "He also brings tidings." 27And the watchman said, "I think the running of the foremost is like the running of Ahima-az the son of Zadok." And the king said, "He is a good man, and comes with good tidings."

28Then Ahima-az cried out to the king, "All is well." And he bowed before the king with his face to the earth, and said, "Blessed be the Lord your God, who has delivered up the men who raised their hand against my lord the king." 29And the king said, "Is it well with the young man Absalom?" Ahima-az answered, "When Joab sent your servant, I saw a great tumult, but I do not know what it was." 30And the king said, "Turn aside, and stand here." So he turned aside, and stood still.

31And behold, the Cushite came; and the Cushite said, "Good tidings for my lord the king! For the Lord has delivered you this day from the power of all who rose up against you." 32The king said to the Cushite, "Is it well with the young man Absalom?" And the Cushite answered, "May the enemies of my lord the king, and all who rise up against you for evil, be like that young man." 33And the king was deeply moved, and went up to the chamber over the gate, and wept; and as he went, he said, "O my son Absalom, my son, my son Absalom! Would I had died instead of you, O Absalom, my son, my son!"

The story of the battle is told briefly, and then, in more detail, we read how Absalom was killed and how the news was brought to David. At the outset David was quite prepared to march into battle and risk his own life, but he was extremely anxious to save Absalom's life. His men, and especially Joab, took exactly the opposite point of view: they insisted that David must take no personal risks, but they were quietly determined (or at least Joab was) that Absalom must die. Undoubtedly Joab read the situation rightly. If David were to be killed by a stray arrow,

Absalom would have won after all, and all the efforts of David's supporters would have been in vain. On the other hand, if Absalom lost the battle but escaped unharmed, David's throne would never be safe. Joab saw clearly that there was no room for two kings in Israel; politically it was too late for a reconciliation between father and son.

The truth was that David acted as a father but not as a king—as if he and Absalom had had some minor domestic quarrel which could be put right by an apology and a handshake. He failed to see Absalom as a traitor and a rebel, whose actions had caused a great deal of harm to the stability and welfare of the kingdom, to say nothing of the great loss of life in the civil war (verse 7). Yet every parent will feel a good deal of sympathy with David's viewpoint.

The narrator provides us with another of his very effective character studies in this chapter. On one side we have *David*, in his wretched dilemma between fatherhood and kingship; on the other side there is *Joab*, apparently cold, unforgiving and relentless, and yet presumably motivated by utter loyalty to David. In between the two extremes there are the ordinary troops, and especially Ahima-az, who evidently all felt a real sympathy for the king. The problem can be neatly posed in a single question—was the death of Absalom good news or bad news? It was good news for David's army and for the nation, and indeed it was good news for David the king; but it was desperately bad news for David the father, and that is the poignant note on which the chapter ends. The contrast between two heartfelt statements could not be more dramatic and effective: "May the enemies of... the king... be like that young man", said the Cushite; "Would I had died instead of you, O Absalom, my son, my son!" exclaimed the bereaved father.

The Bible does not play down the deep reality of human emotions. Nobody, king or commoner, is expected to behave like a robot; indeed, it was the very depth and reality of David's feelings that made these events a punishment to him. The loss of yet another well-loved son was a matter of intense sorrow for him. But, as a result, he was in danger of forgetting a king's responsibilities.

David's first duty was to *himself*. It is true enough that all men are equal in the sight of God, but no less true that each man is unique. David was a man with very special talents for leadership, and he held the unique position of king in Israel. His men were quite right to tell him that he was *worth ten thousand* of them (verse 3). He had given the country victory, peace and prosperity; he had given it unity and cohesion; and above all he had provided a focus for the affections of his people. The nearest equivalent nowadays to the position of king in ancient Israel might be the role of the Pope in the Roman Catholic Church—someone deeply respected and loved, looked to for guidance and leadership, both as a symbol and a genuine father-figure. David, then, was in danger of forgetting what he meant to the whole nation.

His second duty was to *the nation*. As a father, naturally David grieved over his dead son; but as a king, he had to view Absalom as just one of his subjects, and a rebellious one at that. Many others had died in the fighting, many of them soldiers who had been totally loyal to him; and much would have to be done to reunite the nation, to heal the bitterness that had arisen, and to restore Israel's self-confidence. A good leader must always put the welfare of the people he leads before his own personal interests, however urgent the latter may be. However, nobody—except perhaps Joab—would have begrudged David one moment of grief.

REUNITING THE NATION

2 Samuel 19:1–15

¹It was told Joab, "Behold, the king is weeping and mourning for Absalom." ²So the victory that day was turned into mourning for all the people; for the people heard that day, "The king is grieving for his son." ³And the people stole into the city that day as people steal in who are ashamed when they flee in battle. ⁴The king covered his

face, and the king cried with a loud voice, "O my son Absalom, O Absalom, my son, my son!" ⁵Then Joab came into the house to the king, and said, "You have today covered with shame the faces of all your servants, who have this day saved your life, and the lives of your sons and your daughters, and the lives of your wives and your concubines, ⁶because you love those who hate you and hate those who love you. For you have made it clear today that commanders and servants are nothing to you; for today I perceive that if Absalom were alive and all of us were dead today, then you would be pleased. ⁷Now therefore arise, go out and speak kindly to your servants; for I swear by the Lord, if you do not go, not a man will stay with you this night; and this will be worse for you than all the evil that has come upon you from your youth until now." ⁸Then the king arose, and took his seat in the gate. And the people were all told, "Behold, the king is sitting in the gate"; and all the people came before the king.

Now Israel had fled every man to his own home. ⁹And all the people were at strife throughout all the tribes of Israel, saying, "The king delivered us from the hand of our enemies, and saved us from the hand of the Philistines; and now he has fled out of the land from Absalom. ¹⁰But Absalom, whom we anointed over us, is dead in battle. Now therefore why do you say nothing about bringing the king back?"

¹¹And King David sent this message to Zadok and Abiathar the priests, "Say to the elders of Judah, 'Why should you be the last to bring the king back to his house, when the word of all Israel has come to the king? ¹²You are my kinsmen, you are my bone and my flesh; why then should you be the last to bring back the king?' ¹³And say to Amasa, 'Are you not my bone and my flesh? God do so to me, and more also, if you are not commander of my army henceforth in place of Joab.'" ¹⁴And he swayed the heart of all the men of Judah as one man; so that they sent word to the king, "Return, both you and all your servants." ¹⁵So the king came back to the Jordan; and Judah came to Gilgal to meet the king and to bring the king over the Jordan.

The trouble was that David's time of grief over Absalom's death was longer than a moment, and much too long altogether. While it was true that Absalom's revolt died a natural death along with its instigator, it was not the case that the country was automatically restored to David's control. David had to show

proper gratitude to his supporters and soldiers, to retrieve those
who had remained neutral, and above all to reassure and win
over those who for whatever reason had sided with Absalom; at
the same time he dared not offend one group while trying to
placate another. It was a very tricky situation, calling for
thought and diplomatic skill of a high order, but to begin with
David made not the slightest effort to do anything at all. Joab's
bold speech to the king was brutal but necessary. He even went
so far as to threaten to lead another revolt against David.

Three groups of people are discussed in this section. The first
is David's victorious army (verses 1-8); the second is the general
populace, including the survivors of Absalom's defeated army,
who had fled to their homes (verses 8ff.); and the third is the
tribe of Judah, David's own tribe, many of whom had chosen to
support the revolt (verses 11-15).

(i) *David's army.* All that was required where the victorious
army was concerned was to show them the proper respect and
appreciation. Verse 8 depicts a victory celebration, with the
king enthroned in his proper place at the city gate. A good
leader must never forget to show his appreciation, nor must he
overlook the value of ceremonial. Every nation has its pomp
and ceremony, in different ways and fashions, and Israel no less
than its neighbours. David could not take his supporters for
granted, even if perhaps Joab was exaggerating the dangers of
the situation. Human nature is very liable to sudden swings of
sentiment, and it may be that loyalty and revolt were not very
far apart.

(ii) *The general populace.* Here the initiative lay with the
people, not the king. Although there was a lot of argument,
evidently, the general sentiment was a very practical one.
Absalom was dead and best forgotten, and David had achieved
a great deal for Israel. So common sense asserted itself. A leader
cannot always rely on the common sense of his people; but he
can make sure that he serves them to the degree that they will
remember and respond to.

(iii) *The tribe of Judah.* Judah, like the other tribes, had been
divided in its loyalties; many of them must have supported

Absalom. David must have seen a danger that he, a Judaean himself, would find himself king of the northern tribes while his own tribe became estranged from him and found another leader. Perhaps Amasa, Absalom's commander-in-chief, could have become king of Judah—many a general in history has been able to seize royal power. David's decision was a clever one; it may have been partly due to his anger with Joab for killing Absalom, but no doubt his chief purpose in giving Amasa Joab's post was to demonstrate that he was planning no revenge on anybody who had supported Absalom. Judah responded warmly and positively to David's appeal. Forgiveness is an important Christian virtue, cp. Matt. 6:12–15, and a very wise and shrewd aspect of leadership.

David's deep understanding of human nature was vital to his success at this critical point in his reign, and largely made up for his failings of recent years.

DEALINGS WITH THE TRIBE OF BENJAMIN

2 Samuel 19:16–40

[16]And Shime-i the son of Gera, the Benjaminite, from Bahurim, made haste to come down with the men of Judah to meet King David; [17]and with him were a thousand men from Benjamin. And Ziba the servant of the house of Saul, with his fifteen sons and his twenty servants, rushed down to the Jordan before the king, [18]and they crossed the ford to bring over the king's household, and to do his pleasure. And Shime-i the son of Gera fell down before the king, as he was about to cross the Jordan, [19]and said to the king, "Let not my lord hold me guilty or remember how your servant did wrong on the day my lord the king left Jerusalem; let not the king bear it in mind. [20]For your servant knows that I have sinned; therefore, behold, I have come this day, the first of all the house of Joseph to come down to meet my lord the king." [21]Abishai the son of Zeruiah answered, "Shall not Shime-i be put to death for this, because he cursed the Lord's anointed?" [22]But David said, "What have I to do with you, you sons of Zeruiah, that you should this day be as an adversary to me? Shall any one be put to death in Israel this day? For

do I not know that I am this day king over Israel?" ²³And the king said to Shime-i, "You shall not die." And the king gave him his oath.

²⁴And Mephibosheth the son of Saul came down to meet the king; he had neither dressed his feet, nor trimmed his beard, nor washed his clothes, from the day the king departed until the day he came back in safety. ²⁵And when he came from Jerusalem to meet the king, the king said to him, "Why did you not go with me, Mephibosheth?" ²⁶He answered, "My lord, O king, my servant deceived me; for your servant said to him, 'Saddle an ass for me, that I may ride upon it and go with the king.' For your servant is lame. ²⁷He has slandered your servant to my lord the king. But my lord the king is like the angel of God; do therefore what seems good to you. ²⁸For all my father's house were but men doomed to death before my lord the king; but you set your servant among those who eat at your table. What further right have I, then, to cry to the king?" ²⁹And the king said to him, "Why speak any more of your affairs? I have decided: you and Ziba shall divide the land." ³⁰And Mephibosheth said to the king, "Oh, let him take it all, since my lord the king has come safely home."

³¹Now Barzillai the Gileadite had come down from Rogelim; and he went on with the king to the Jordan, to escort him over the Jordan. ³²Barzillai was a very aged man, eighty years old; and he had provided the king with food while he stayed at Mahanaim; for he was a very wealthy man. ³³And the king said to Barzillai, "Come over with me, and I will provide for you with me in Jerusalem." ³⁴But Barzillai said to the king, "How many years have I still to live, that I should go up with the king to Jerusalem? ³⁵I am this day eighty years old; can I discern what is pleasant and what is not? Can your servant taste what he eats or what he drinks? Can I still listen to the voice of singing men and singing women? Why then should your servant be an added burden to my lord the king? ³⁶Your servant will go a little way over the Jordan with the king. Why should the king recompense me with such a reward? ³⁷Pray let your servant return, that I may die in my own city, near the grave of my father and my mother. But here is your servant Chimham; let him go over with my lord the king; and do for him whatever seems good to you." ³⁸And the king answered, "Chimham shall go over with me, and I will do for him whatever seems good to you; and all that you desire of me I will do for you." ³⁹Then all the people went over the Jordan, and the king went over; and the king kissed Barzillai and blessed him, and he returned to his own home. ⁴⁰The king went on to Gilgal, and Chimham went on

with him; all the people of Judah, and also half the people of Israel, brought the king on his way.

There are two levels of interest in this section. The first is the personal angle; the story-teller has already aroused the reader's interest in Shimei, Ziba, Mephibosheth and Barzillai, and the reader wants to know how they were repaid for their earlier attitudes and actions. The more important aspect is however the historical one—the tribal angle. In putting matters to rights after the collapse of Absalom's revolt, David had to consider both individuals and tribes; but tribes inevitably assumed the greater importance.

(i) *The Individuals.* In dealing with *Shimei* in particular, David had to suppress his own feelings. He never forgave him, as we know from 1 Kings 2:8f., but he gave no hint of his anger publicly. The narrator tells us only what David said and did, not what he felt and thought. In many ancient countries Shimei would have been executed; David spared his life.

Much the same may apply to *Mephibosheth.* It is clear that the biblical writer believed his story, but it is not so clear that David did. He could perhaps have pursued the matter further and tried to find witnesses, but instead he allowed Mephibosheth to retain half his property. Even if *Ziba* had told lies about his master, his loyalty to David in a crisis had merited some reward, and David had after all promised him the whole of Mephibosheth's estates (cp. 16:4). David wanted no reprisals against anyone—that was his governing principle, and a very wise one in the circumstances.

As for *Barzillai,* his generous support had made all the difference to David, and the king naturally wanted to repay him in kind, and also to show his family public honour. In this case policy and personal feelings pointed in the same direction; but the moral of most of this section is that the good leader and the wise king must be able to suppress, even to disguise, his own feelings. David was able to do this effectively, and succeeded in reuniting the nation under his rule.

(ii) *The Tribe of Benjamin.* The important thing about

Shimei, Ziba and Mephibosheth is that all three belonged to the tribe of Benjamin; and it is noteworthy that Shimei brought with him to welcome David's return to power no fewer than a thousand Benjaminites (verse 17). Though only a small tribe, Benjamin was at that time very important in Israel, since it had been the royal tribe (under Saul and Ish-bosheth). If David had alienated Benjamin now, as he could so easily have done by harsh treatment of Shimei or Mephibosheth, the tribe of Benjamin could well have started a fresh revolt and a successful one, leaving David with only Judah as his realm. As it was, a Benjaminite did lead a revolt, though it was small and quickly crushed (see chapter 20). It was very wise indeed to attempt by all means to win Benjamin over; and it seems that David largely succeeded. History was to show that a generation later, when the kingdom split into two, Benjamin remained firmly attached to Judah.

David's abilities in leadership are emphasized by this passage. By shrewd handling of individuals, with a careful eye to wider and to future dimensions, he gave his realm new stability after the near-disaster of Absalom's revolt. It is impossible to put the clock back in life; but with care and effort, and above all with God's help, mistakes are not beyond all remedy. It is always right to take a positive attitude and to try to make a fresh start, even if the new will never be so splendid as the old.

SHEBA'S REVOLT

2 Samuel 19:41–20:10(a)

⁴¹Then all the men of Israel came to the king, and said to the king, "Why have our brethren the men of Judah stolen you away, and brought the king and his household over the Jordan, and all David's men with him?" ⁴²All the men of Judah answered the men of Israel, "Because the king is near of kin to us. Why then are you angry over this matter? Have we eaten at all at the king's expense? Or has he given us any gift?" ⁴³And the men of Israel answered the men of

Judah, "We have ten shares in the king, and in David also we have more than you. Why then did you despise us? Were we not the first to speak of bringing back our king?" But the words of the men of Judah were fiercer than the words of the men of Israel.

¹Now there happened to be there a worthless fellow, whose name was Sheba, the son of Bichri, a Benjaminite; and he blew the trumpet, and said,

"We have no portion in David,

and we have no inheritance in the son of Jesse;

every man to his tents, O Israel!"

²So all the men of Israel withdrew from David, and followed Sheba the son of Bichri; but the men of Judah followed their king steadfastly from the Jordan to Jerusalem.

³And David came to his house at Jerusalem; and the king took the ten concubines whom he had left to care for the house, and put them in a house under guard, and provided for them, but did not go in to them. So they were shut up until the day of their death, living as if in widowhood.

⁴Then the king said to Amasa, "Call the men of Judah together to me within three days, and be here yourself." ⁵So Amasa went to summon Judah; but he delayed beyond the set time which had been appointed him. ⁶And David said to Abishai, "Now Sheba the son of Bichri will do us more harm than Absalom; take your lord's servants and pursue him, lest he get himself fortified cities, and cause us trouble." ⁷And there went out after Abishai, Joab and the Cherethites and the Pelethites, and all the mighty men; they went out from Jerusalem to pursue Sheba the son of Bichri. ⁸When they were at the great stone which is in Gibeon, Amasa came to meet them. Now Joab was wearing a soldier's garment, and over it was a girdle with a sword in its sheath fastened upon his loins, and as he went forward it fell out. ⁹And Joab said to Amasa, "Is it well with you, my brother?" And Joab took Amasa by the beard with his right hand to kiss him. ¹⁰But Amasa did not observe the sword which was in Joab's hand; so Joab struck him with it in the body, and shed his bowels to the ground, without striking a second blow; and he died.

Here is a situation where future events cast their shadow beforehand. The quarrel between Judah and the northern tribes (in this passage the name *Israel* excludes Judah) resulted in a temporary readiness of most of the tribes to break away from

Judah and so from David too. It was a Benjaminite, Sheba by name, who tried to cash in on the situation and to lead a new revolt against David; if he had been successful, no doubt he himself would have become king of "Israel", making Benjamin a royal tribe once more. At first the revolt seemed dangerous, but in the end it came to nothing. However, the incident proved that Judah's position was resented by some of the other tribes; Ephraim is not mentioned by name here, but it was the most important northerly tribe and no doubt felt some jealousy of Judah's special privileges. A generation later, at the death of Solomon, these jealous feelings came to the surface again and the kingdom split permanently into two. David's grandson Rehoboam remained king of Judah and Benjamin, but an Ephraimite called Jeroboam made himself king of "Israel"; cp. 1 Kings 12.

The question that comes to mind is this: why did David succeed in holding the country together when his successors failed? Theologically, the answer is that it was God's will; at the human level, we could reply that David had talents for leadership which his successors lacked. It did not then take superhuman or supernatural qualities to hold the country together; it took wisdom and political skill, exercised in obedience to God. The message for later times was that the disunity of the nation was not beyond repair; given the right man as king, and given God's blessing, David's kingdom could be restored. The vital ingredient in David's policy was the care he took to avoid showing any favouritism to Judah (19:42). The true leader must be scrupulously fair to all his citizens; a privileged tribe, caste or class will unbalance any state, sooner or later.

David's appointment of Amasa as general was part of his plans to pacify Judah after its involvement in Absalom's revolt. This particular scheme failed, apparently because of some inefficiency on Amasa's part, and more particularly because of Joab's violent determination to retrieve his lost position. It is possible, of course, that Joab doubted Amasa's loyalty to David; whatever Joab's sins, it is at least true that his loyalty to

David never wavered over many years. David could not do without Joab. There is a reminder in this that the greatest leaders are to a considerable extent dependent on the men who are available to support them. God brought prosperity to Israel as much through Joab as through David.

THE END OF THE REVOLT

2 Samuel 20:10(b)–26

Then Joab and Abishai his brother pursued Sheba the son of Bichri. ¹¹And one of Joab's men took his stand by Amasa, and said, "Whoever favours Joab, and whoever is for David, let him follow Joab." ¹²And Amasa lay wallowing in his blood in the highway. And any one who came by, seeing him, stopped; and when the man saw that all the people stopped, he carried Amasa out of the highway into the field, and threw a garment over him. ¹³When he was taken out of the highway, all the people went on after Joab to pursue Sheba the son of Bichri.

¹⁴And Sheba passed through all the tribes of Israel to Abel of Beth-maacah; and all the Bichrites assembled, and followed him in. ¹⁵And all the men who were with Joab came and besieged him in Abel of Beth-maacah; they cast up a mound against the city, and it stood against the rampart; and they were battering the wall, to throw it down. ¹⁶Then a wise woman called from the city, "Hear! Hear! Tell Joab, 'Come here, that I may speak to you.'" ¹⁷And he came near her; and the woman said, "Are you Joab?" He answered, "I am." Then she said to him, "Listen to the words of your maidservant." And he answered, "I am listening." ¹⁸Then she said, "They were wont to say in old time, 'Let them but ask counsel at Abel'; and so they settled a matter. ¹⁹I am one of those who are peaceable and faithful in Israel; you seek to destroy a city which is a mother in Israel; why will you swallow up the heritage of the Lord?" ²⁰Joab answered, "Far be it from me, far be it, that I should swallow up or destroy! ²¹That is not true. But a man of the hill country of Ephraim, called Sheba the son of Bichri, has lifted up his hand against King David; give up him alone, and I will withdraw from the city." And the woman said to Joab, "Behold, his head shall be thrown to you over the wall." ²²Then the woman went to all the

people in her wisdom. And they cut off the head of Sheba the son of Bichri, and threw it out to Joab. So he blew the trumpet, and they dispersed from the city, every man to his home. And Joab returned to Jerusalem to the king.

23Now Joab was in command of all the army of Israel; and Benaiah the son of Jehoiada was in command of the Cherethites and the Pelethites; 24and Adoram was in charge of the forced labour; and Jehoshaphat the son of Ahilud was the recorder; 25and Sheva was secretary; and Zadok and Abiathar were priests; 26and Ira the Jairite was also David's priest.

Absalom's rebellion had been crushed in a large-scale battle during which many soldiers died; Sheba's revolt, by contrast, simply collapsed, with a minimum of bloodshed. At the start *all the men of Israel* were attracted to Sheba (verse 2), but at the finish Sheba's only remaining followers were his own clansmen, *the Bichrites* (verse 14). It is also significant that Sheba was unable to make a stand anywhere until he reached the town of Abel of Beth-maacah, almost on the northern frontier of Israel (see Map 2). Here he did make a stand, and it looks as if he was able to persuade the townsmen to support him against David's troops. So a siege became necessary. With no allies to call upon, the town would certainly have fallen in the course of time, and verse 15 shows Joab on the point of breaching the walls. If Joab's soldiers had burst in, the town would have suffered a great deal of damage and many of the citizens would have been killed. However, as the story tells, the townsfolk turned against Sheba, and in the end he was the only man to lose his life, so far as we know. All ended peacefully, with David triumphant over the whole land.

The emphasis in this little episode is on "wisdom". The woman who seized the initiative was renowned for her wisdom, and evidently the town of Abel itself had a reputation for wisdom (verse 18). Abel was a frontier-town of no very great importance, and it is probably true to say that if it had been severely damaged or even destroyed there would have been little effect on the country as a whole; Sheba's revolt would still have been crushed with relatively little bloodshed or bitterness.

However, the writer wishes to impress on us that a city noted for its wisdom ought not to come to a bad end—especially when no other city suffered in any way.

So the passage gives us a picture of wisdom in action. First of all the woman saw the problem realistically; the danger must have been clear enough to everyone in Abel, but there may have been some false hopes of rescue or intervention. Secondly, she did something about it—she did not wait for somebody else to act but took the initiative herself. Then she argued her case, challenging the rightness of Joab's actions; and he was forced to agree with what she said. So a compromise was reached; and finally she took steps to fulfil the terms agreed. In other words, wisdom was a combination of intelligent insight and bold action. The Old Testament rarely separates the intellectual from the pragmatic: wisdom is not simply knowing but also doing. The Bible has no time for armchair philosophers.

The moral of the tale then is the value and importance of wisdom. One must credit Joab with the same sort of wisdom. He was a violent man, as the chapter has already demonstrated, but he wisely took no pleasure in destroying a peaceable city. Israel benefited as much from his actions as the unnamed woman's.

One very important aspect of wisdom in the Old Testament is underlined in Prov. 1:7: "the fear of the Lord is the beginning of knowledge". The devoutness of the woman is briefly indicated in her reference to Israel as *the heritage of the Lord* (verse 19). Wisdom will often be thwarted if it is not based on a correct relationship with God; and it is bound to be thwarted in the long run if it is positively hostile to God and his plans. By contrast, when intellectual powers are blended with a sensitivity to God's ways and purposes, there is nothing that cannot be achieved, by individuals, churches, and nations.

THE FATE OF SAUL'S FAMILY

2 Samuel 21:1-14

[1]Now there was a famine in the days of David for three years, year

after year; and David sought the face of the Lord. And the Lord said, "There is bloodguilt on Saul and on his house, because he put the Gibeonites to death." ²So the king called the Gibeonites. Now the Gibeonites were not of the people of Israel, but of the remnant of the Amorites; although the people of Israel had sworn to spare them, Saul had sought to slay them in his zeal for the people of Israel and Judah. ³And David said to the Gibeonites, "What shall I do for you? And how shall I make expiation, that you may bless the heritage of the Lord?" ⁴The Gibeonites said to him, "It is not a matter of silver or gold between us and Saul or his house; neither is it for us to put any man to death in Israel." And he said, "What do you say that I shall do for you?" ⁵They said to the king, "The man who consumed us and planned to destroy us, so that we should have no place in all the territory of Israel, ⁶let seven of his sons be given to us, so that we may hang them up before the Lord at Gibeon on the mountain of the Lord." And the king said, "I will give them."

⁷But the king spared Mephibosheth, the son of Saul's son Jonathan, because of the oath of the Lord which was between them, between David and Jonathan the son of Saul. ⁸The king took the two sons of Rizpah the daughter of Aiah, whom she bore to Saul, Armoni and Mephibosheth; and the five sons of Merab the daughter of Saul, whom she bore to Adri-el the son of Barzillai the Meholathite; ⁹and he gave them into the hands of the Gibeonites, and they hanged them on the mountain before the Lord, and the seven of them perished together. They were put to death in the first days of harvest, at the beginning of barley harvest.

¹⁰Then Rizpah the daughter of Aiah took sackcloth, and spread it for herself on the rock, from the beginning of harvest until rain fell upon them from the heavens; and she did not allow the birds of the air to come upon them by day, or the beasts of the field by night. ¹¹When David was told what Rizpah the daughter of Aiah, the concubine of Saul, had done, ¹²David went and took the bones of Saul and the bones of his son Jonathan from the men of Jabesh-gilead, who had stolen them from the public square of Beth-shan, where the Philistines had hanged them, on the day the Philistines killed Saul on Gilboa; ¹³and he brought up from there the bones of Saul and the bones of his son Jonathan; and they gathered the bones of those who were hanged. ¹⁴And they buried the bones of Saul and his son Jonathan in the land of Benjamin in Zela, in the tomb of Kish his father; and they did all that the king commanded. And after that God heeded supplications for the land.

To our way of thinking, the story told here is strange and repellent. Seven innocent men were executed, with David's authority, and their bodies were dishonoured for some time. It is important to try to understand the episode in terms of the culture and attitudes of the age. First, we should recognize that there was an element of propaganda in recounting these events; since the seven victims all belonged to Saul's family, it is very likely that in some quarters David got the full blame for their deaths, and so the details are supplied here by way of explanation of David's actions. The details make it clear that David's hand was forced, by the circumstances of a famine, by the guidance of the oracle, and by the legal and to that extent legitimate demands of the Gibeonites.

Famines (chiefly caused, like this one, by lack of adequate rainfall) were all too frequent a problem in the ancient Near East—as they still are in many parts of the world. They afflicted whole communities and nations, causing much suffering and death, and were naturally interpreted as divine punishment for sins known or unknown. David was compelled by the national emergency to seek a religious reason for the famine, and as a result he was directed to consult the Gibeonites.

The Gibeonites were incorporated into Israel but were not related in any way to the Israelites (see Josh. 9). We do not know why Saul had attacked them, but apparently it was for reasons we would today describe as racist. In any case, he had killed many of them, in defiance of a solemn treaty; but under the Israelite legal system they were unable to get any redress because they were not Israelites. Morally, they were fully entitled to compensation, and probably it was expected that they would be content with damages, i.e. financial compensation, but like Shylock they were determined to have their full revenge. Saul himself was long since dead and beyond their reach, but in those days an individual's responsibilites were fully shared by his family; so it was neither unusual nor illegal for the punishment to be imposed on Saul's heirs.

David was helpless to protect the seven men, but it seems that he did what he could. He made sure that Mephibosheth was safe, and he gave the dead men honourable burial as soon as rain fell, indicating that God was bringing the famine to an end. Rizpah's loving and unselfish deed helped David to protect the bodies from desecration and dishonour.

We can put aside the aspects of the story which clearly do not apply to modern or to Christian society. It is still fair to draw the moral that we have here scriptural warrant for the protection of racial minorities inside any nation or community. It was the king's duty, even against his own inclinations and to the hurt of his reputation, to ensure that full justice was done to all his subjects. Above all, promises and undertakings had to be kept, and the law extended to cover "second class citizens". In our world, the moral duties of rich and powerful nations to their poorer brethren is a reasonable comparison to make. But it must be faced that some "first class citizens" will suffer in the process, though hardly the fate that came upon Saul's sons and grandsons.

DAVID AND HIS SOLDIERS

2 Samuel 21:15–22; 23:8–39

15The Philistines had war again with Israel, and David went down together with his servants, and they fought against the Philistines; and David grew weary. 16And Ishbi-benob, one of the descendants of the giants, whose spear weighed three hundred shekels of bronze, and who was girded with a new sword, thought to kill David. 17But Abishai the son of Zeruiah came to his aid, and attacked the Philistine and killed him. Then David's men adjured him, "You shall no more go out with us to battle, lest you quench the lamp of Israel."

18After this there was again war with the Philistines at Gob; then Sibbecai the Hushathite slew Saph, who was one of the descendants of the giants. 19And there was again war with the Philistines at Gob; and Elhanan the son of Jaareoregim, the Bethlehemite, slew Goliath the Gittite, the shaft of whose spear was like a weaver's beam. 20And there was again war at Gath, where there was a man of great stature, who had six fingers on each hand, and six toes on each foot, twenty-four in number; and he also was descended from the giants. 21And when he taunted Israel, Jonathan the son of Shime-i, David's brother, slew him. ²²These four were descended from the giants in Gath; and they fell by the hand of David and by the hand of his servants.

⁸These are the names of the mighty men whom David had: Josheb-basshebeth a Tah-chemonite; he was chief of the three; he wielded his spear against eight hundred whom he slew at one time.

⁹And next to him among the three mighty men was Eleazar the son of Dodo, son of Ahohi. He was with David when they defied the Philistines who were gathered there for battle, and the men of Israel withdrew. ¹⁰He rose and struck down the Philistines until his hand was weary, and his hand cleaved to the sword; and the Lord wrought a great victory that day; and the men returned after him only to strip the slain.

¹¹And next to him was Shammah, the son of Agee the Hararite. The Philistines gathered together at Lehi, where there was a plot of ground full of lentils; and the men fled from the Philistines. ¹²But he took his stand in the midst of the plot, and defended it, and slew the Philistines; and the Lord wrought a great victory.

¹³And three of the thirty chief men went down, and came about harvest time to David at the cave of Adullam, when a band of Philistines was encamped in the valley of Rephaim. ¹⁴David was then in the stronghold; and the garrison of the Philistines was then at Bethlehem. ¹⁵And David said longingly, "O that some one would give me water to drink from the well of Bethlehem which is by the gate!" ¹⁶Then the three mighty men broke through the camp of the Philistines, and drew water out of the well of Bethlehem which was by the gate, and took and brought it to David. But he would not drink of it; he poured it out to the Lord, ¹⁷and said, "Far be it from me, O Lord, that I should do this. Shall I drink the blood of the men who went at the risk of their lives?" Therefore he would not drink it. These things did the three mighty men.

¹⁸Now Abishai, the brother of Joab, the son of Zeruiah, was chief of the thirty. And he wielded his spear against three hundred men and slew them, and won a name beside the three. ¹⁹He was the most renowned of the thirty, and became their commander; but he did not attain to the three.

²⁰And Benaiah the son of Jehoiada was a valiant man of Kabzeel, a doer of great deeds; he smote two ariels of Moab. He also went down and slew a lion in a pit on a day when snow had fallen. ²¹And

he slew an Egyptian, a handsome man. The Egyptian had a spear in his hand; but Benaiah went down to him with a staff, and snatched the spear out of the Egyptian's hand, and slew him with his own spear. 22These things did Benaiah the son of Jehoiada, and won a name beside the three mighty men. 23He was renowned among the thirty, but he did not attain to the three. And David set him over his bodyguard.

24Asahel the brother of Joab was one of the thirty; Elhanan the son of Dodo of Bethlehem, 25Shammah of Harod, Elika of Harod, 26Helez the Paltite, Ira the son of Ikkesh of Tekoa, 27Abi-ezer, of Anathoth, Mebunnai the Hushathite, 28Zalmon the Ahohite, Maharai of Netophah, 29Heleb the son of Baanah of Netophah, Ittai the son of Ribai of Gibe-ah of the Benjaminites, 30Benaiah of Pirathon, Hiddai of the brooks of Gaash, 31Abialbon the Arbathite, Azmaveth of Bahurim, 32Eliahba of Sha-albon, the sons of Jashen, Jonathan, 33Shammah the Hararite, Ahiam the son of Sharar the Hararite, 34Eliphelet the son of Ahasbai of Maacah, Eliam the son of Ahithophel of Gilo, 35Hezro of Carmel, Paarai the Arbite, 36Igal the son of Nathan of Zobah, Bani the Gadite, 37Zelek the Ammonite, Naharai of Be-eroth, the armour-bearer of Joab the son of Zeruiah, 38Ira the Ithrite, Gareb the Ithrite, 39Uriah the Hittite: thirty-seven in all.

These two passages belong to a much earlier period of David's reign. The mention of Uriah in 23:39 proves that, for his death has already been recorded in 11:17. The episode about Bethlehem (23:13–17) mentions the Philistine encampment in the valley of Rephaim (verse 13), and is to be linked with the Philistine invasion at the start of David's reign over a united Israel (see 5:18, 22).

Most of the names given here are unknown and so of little interest to the modern reader; but we must remember that to the first readers of Samuel the names were full of interest. Some of David's heroes were the forefathers of those early readers; and the mention of place-names and clan-names in the list of soldiers will have provided additional interest for Palestinian readers.

Evidently David had two élite groups of soldiers. The smaller and more important group was *the three*; they were a sort of order of merit, accorded their status for deeds of extraordinary valour (23:8–12). The other group was *the thirty* (23:18–39), who may well have fought as an élite unit or crack regiment. Courage, strength, ability and endurance were the special virtues of these soldiers. They were the Invincibles: not even giant-sized Philistines could match them (21:15–22).

Apart from their military talents, these men were characterized by their loyalty and devotion to David. Two brief episodes illustrate this. In 21:16f. we get an indication of the protection they provided for David, as they fought at his side and later prevented him from endangering his own life. In 23:14–17 we see how willingly they risked their own lives simply to fulfil a whim of David's. There must have been a great bond of affection between them and their leader; though the mention of Uriah's name at the end of the list is a reminder that David's loyalty to them was less than one hundred per cent. No doubt we must view David's treatment of Uriah as a unique event.

Later readers could take pride in the memory of their own and their neighbours' ancestors who had helped David gain the throne and keep it, and who had under his leadership given Israel victory and political strength. No king, not even a David, can do without able and willing lieutenants. Israel's success under David was a joint operation, a matter of single-minded co-operation. No doubt some of these heroes died in battle, as of course Uriah did; all of them risked their lives time and time again. A nation cannot become great without patriotism, self-sacrifice and high ideals; and certainly a nation which loses these virtues is doomed to fall, as Israel eventually did. Great leadership is of little value without loyal followers.

Equally, brilliant lieutenants need a great leader. David was described by his own men as *the lamp of Israel* (21:17), a phrase which sums up the value of the king to his people. Without him, they would be in darkness, leaderless and rudderless, and could achieve nothing. It was precisely because Israel realized the value of the leadership provided by God for them that they were prepared to follow where David led. In today's world, with the stress we put on the equality of every man and woman and on the importance of the individual, we are in some danger of

undervaluing special talents and of misjudging the motives and
the character of political leaders. Cynicism is an easier option
than loyalty. At the same time, not every leader is God-given·
but God still overrules in the affairs of nations.

A ROYAL PSALM: GOD'S SALVATION

2 Samuel 22:1–20

¹And David spoke to the Lord the words of this song on the day
when the Lord delivered him from the hand of all his enemies, and
from the hand of Saul. ²He said,
"The Lord is my rock, and my fortress, and my deliverer,
³ my God, my rock, in whom I take refuge,
 my shield and the horn of my salvation,
     my stronghold and my refuge,
     my saviour; thou savest me from violence.
⁴I call upon the Lord, who is worthy to be praised,
     and I am saved from my enemies.

⁵"For the waves of death encompassed me,
     the torrents of perdition assailed me;
⁶the cords of Sheol entangled me,
     the snares of death confronted me.

⁷"In my distress I called upon the Lord;
     to my God I called.
 From his temple he heard my voice,
     and my cry came to his ears.

⁸"Then the earth reeled and rocked;
     the foundations of the heavens trembled
     and quaked, because he was angry.
⁹Smoke went up from his nostrils,
     and devouring fire from his mouth;
     glowing coals flamed forth from him.
¹⁰He bowed the heavens, and came down;
     thick darkness was under his feet.
¹¹He rode on a cherub, and flew;
     he was seen upon the wings of the wind.

¹²He made darkness around him
　　his canopy, thick clouds, a gathering of water.
¹³Out of the brightness before him
　　coals of fire flamed forth.
¹⁴The Lord thundered from heaven,
　　and the Most High uttered his voice.
¹⁵And he sent out arrows, and scattered them;
　　lightning, and routed them.
¹⁶Then the channels of the sea were seen,
　　the foundations of the world were laid bare,
　at the rebuke of the Lord,
　　at the blast of the breath of his nostrils.

¹⁷"He reached from on high, he took me,
　　he drew me out of many waters.
¹⁸He delivered me from my strong enemy,
　　from those who hated me;
　　for they were too mighty for me.
¹⁹They came upon me in the day of my calamity;
　　but the Lord was my stay.
²⁰He brought me forth into a broad place;
　　he delivered me, because he delighted in me."

Up to this point the books of Samuel have been fully occupied with David as a soldier and a king; only in passing has it been noted that he was also a musician (1 Sam. 16:18) and a poet (2 Sam. 1:17–27). Nowadays however, when David's achievements as soldier and king have little direct relevance to us, we remember his name above all as the Psalmist; so it is very fitting that, as the story of David nears its completion, the historian gives us a sample of his psalmody. The long poem in this chapter is also to be found in the book of Psalms, as Ps. 18.

This poem is a psalm of thanksgiving to God. Most of it is couched in general terms; only in the last verse (51) is David himself explicitly mentioned. Also, like most psalms of this type, its language is very pictorial, so that it could be applied to a whole variety of situations in which God's help was recognized and acknowledged. In the given context of verse 1, it acknowledges God as David's rescuer from his enemies, both inside and outside Israel, and gives due thanks to God for the preservation of life and limb.

The real enemy, as the Psalmist saw the matter, had been death, pictured as a violent ocean in verse 5 and as a hunter in verse 6; the *broad place* of verse 20 provides the contrast, a combination of dry land underfoot and of the open range, far away from the hunter's traps. David towards the end of his career could look back serenely on the dangers of earlier days, confident that all was now well; but he did not boast of his own prowess or skill. Rather, he remembered in humility that he had long ago turned to God for help (verse 7) and received it in full measure. The longest paragraph in this section is verses 8–16, which gives a vivid but symbolic portrait of God as he responded to David's cry for help. This picture is based on the concept of Yahweh as the God of thunder and storm—a very familiar concept in the ancient world, except that outside Israel such a deity was only one of a number of gods and goddesses. Israel's God was no *less* strong than other storm-gods; he could wield the most frightening powers of nature just as effectively as, say, Baal in Canaanite religious belief. But he was far *more* than just a storm-god; he manipulated not just thunderbolts and the like but men, nations and history, for the benefit of both David and Israel as a whole. Such reminders of God's visible power were necessary to Israelites when the nation felt humiliated by powerful enemies like Assyria and Babylon. We still need to remember the power of a loving God, in days when we are tempted to worship, or at least tremble before, the gods of nuclear power, overpopulation, economic realities and powerful nations.

David's claim that God *delighted* in him (verse 20) was no arrogant boast but a matter of experience and so a source of joy and wonder. It is just like a lover's assertion that his partner loves him; his partner's care and affection are too real and tangible to be denied.

A ROYAL PSALM: GOD'S FAITHFULNESS

2 Samuel 22:21–51

21"The Lord rewarded me according to my righteousness;
    according to the cleanness of my hands he recompensed me.
22For I have kept the ways of the Lord,
    and have not wickedly departed from my God.
23For all his ordinances were before me,
    and from his statutes I did not turn aside.
24I was blameless before him,
    and I kept myself from guilt.
25Therefore the Lord has recompensed me according to my
    righteousness,
    according to my cleanness in his sight.

26"With the loyal thou dost show thyself loyal;
    with the blameless man thou dost show thyself blameless;
27with the pure thou dost show thyself pure,
    and with the crooked thou dost show thyself perverse.
28Thou dost deliver a humble people,
    but thy eyes are upon the haughty to bring them down.
29Yea, thou art my lamp, O Lord,
    and my God lightens my darkness.
30Yea, by thee I can crush a troop,
    and by my God I can leap over a wall.
31This God—his way is perfect;
    the promise of the Lord proves true;
    he is a shield for all those who take refuge in him.

32"For who is God, but the Lord?
    And who is a rock, except our God?
33This God is my strong refuge,
    and has made my way safe.
34He made my feet like hinds' feet
    and set me secure on the heights.
35He trains my hands for war,
    so that my arms can bend a bow of bronze.
36Thou hast given me the shield of thy salvation,
    and thy help made me great.

³⁷Thou didst give a wide place for my steps under me,
  and my feet did not slip;
³⁸I pursued my enemies and destroyed them,
  and did not turn back until they were consumed.
³⁹I consumed them; I thrust them through, so that they did not rise;
  they fell under my feet.
⁴⁰For thou didst gird me with strength for the battle;
  thou didst make my assailants sink under me.
⁴¹Thou didst make my enemies turn their backs to me,
  those who hated me, and I destroyed them.
⁴²They looked, but there was none to save;
  they cried to the Lord, but he did not answer them.
⁴³I beat them fine as the dust of the earth,
  I crushed them and stamped them down like the mire of the
  streets.

⁴⁴"Thou didst deliver me from strife with the peoples;
  thou didst keep me as the head of the nations;
  people whom I had not known served me.
⁴⁵Foreigners came cringing to me;
  as soon as they heard of me, they obeyed me.
⁴⁶Foreigners lost heart,
  and came trembling out of their fastnesses.

⁴⁷"The Lord lives; and blessed be my rock,
  and exalted be my God, the rock of my salvation,
⁴⁸the God who gave me vengeance
  and brought down peoples under me,
⁴⁹who brought me out from my enemies;
  thou didst exalt me above my adversaries,
  thou didst deliver me from men of violence.

⁵⁰"For this I will extol thee, O Lord, among the nations,
  and sing praises to thy name.
⁵¹Great triumphs he gives to his king,
  and shows steadfast love to his anointed,
  to David, and his descendants for ever."

The psalm continues to praise God for his goodness to king and
to nation. Two aspects of this section are apt to worry the
modern reader. One is the apparent pride of verses 21–25,
which on the face of it make a rather arrogant claim to

sinlessness; the other is the apparent gloating over fallen enemies expressed in several verses. However, the whole psalm must be read in the light of the covenant relationship which existed between Israel and the God of Israel. The nation had entered into a solemn agreement with God at Mount Sinai (see Exod. 19:1-6); Israel had undertaken to obey God in all the laws he had imposed on them, and God had undertaken to look after his people, bringing them into the Promised Land and rescuing them from all their political enemies.

Against this background of belief, David could see that both parties had fulfilled the terms of their contract. He is not claiming a personal sanctity in verses 21-25 but confirming that as king he had maintained the laws of the covenant to the best of his ability, and brought the nation into humble obedience to them. God for his part had responded by fulfilling his ancient promises. After its many years of political weakness, struggling to defend itself against one enemy after another, Israel must have been astonished to find itself the most powerful nation in the whole area, and master of a small empire. Its response was joyful thanksgiving to God—in reality a sign of humbleness, not gloating. Such a verse as verse 28, for instance, though rejoicing at the rise of Israel and the fall of the Philistines, is in quite general terms; if Israel in turn became haughty, the Psalmist acknowledged beforehand that God would *bring them down* too.

The psalm thanks God above all for his faithfulness, to nation and to king alike; but in his meditation on all that God had achieved David was conscious of several other aspects of God's character, some of which were very much in contrast with the attributes of the gods worshipped by Israel's neighbours.

(a) He never acts without a purpose.

(b) His actions are fully just, and appropriate.

(c) His promises can be relied on.

(d) He gives light and help to his servants as they need them.

(e) He is the *living* God (verse 47). Some gods were believed by Israel's neighbours to be capable of dying, e.g. the god of vegetation in the long, dry summer. By contrast, Israel's God was always active and dynamic, caring for his people, responsive to their needs and prayers, "the same yesterday and today and for ever".

With such a God, David could end the psalm with a confident glance into the future. Israel might not always have victories (indeed, it soon became weak once more), but it would always have a God who would show *steadfast love*—better translated as "loyal love"—to the nation's leaders as the years went by. The world changes, and political circumstances ebb and flow, but God remains the same.

DAVID'S LEGACY

2 Samuel 23:1-7

¹Now these are the last words of David:
The oracle of David, the son of Jesse,
    the oracle of the man who was raised on high,
the anointed of the God of Jacob,
    the sweet psalmist of Israel:

²"The Spirit of the Lord speaks by me,
    his word is upon my tongue.
³The God of Israel has spoken,
    the Rock of Israel has said to me:
When one rules justly over men,
    ruling in the fear of God,
⁴he dawns on them like the morning light,
    like the sun shining forth upon a cloudless morning,
    like rain that makes grass to sprout from the earth.
⁵Yea, does not my house stand so with God?
    For he has made with me an everlasting covenant,
    ordered in all things and secûre.
For will he not cause to prosper
    all my help and my desire?
⁶But godless men are all like thorns that are thrown away;
    for they cannot be taken with the hand;
⁷but the man who touches them
    arms himself with iron and the shaft of a spear,
    and they are utterly consumed with fire."

This second, much shorter, poem is described as *the last words of David*. This does not mean the last poem he ever composed but rather the "legacy" which he left to Israel and to his successors; not the legacy of power and possessions, but a spiritual legacy. This consisted of two things: his psalms and his kingship. No Christian would wish to deny that *the Spirit of the Lord* was indeed active in the composition of the psalms of both David and the other psalmists of Israel, which have brought comfort and inspiration to all the generations since his time. The Psalms have been more used in Christian worship than any other part of the Old Testament.

The other legacy was kingship. David was not Israel's first king, but with him royalty had reached its peak in Israel, in two respects. At the secular level, he had provided leadership which enabled his people to gain a stable and strong position for the first time since their settlement in the Promised Land. Equally important, he had begun a dynasty which was already recognized as God's gift to the nation, stretching into the indefinite future. Thus there was both political and religious strength and stability—a wonderful legacy for Israel.

No negative note is struck in this poem; the *godless men* of verse 6 are no doubt the enemies of David, like Absalom and Sheba, who had perished. It was true that David had been a just ruler (verse 3), whose military achievements had been accompanied by social concern. Even so, there is a conditional note to verse 3: might the day not come when David's successors would themselves be *godless men* instead of just rulers? In fact, such eras did come, long before the books of Samuel were completed. We need to ask, therefore, what the biblical author who incorporated this psalm in his narrative understood by it. Almost certainly, he was looking forward to the Messianic king, that is to say the descendant of David who—as God had promised—would one day come to the throne and usher in an era of permanent justice, peace, prosperity, strength and stability (see especially Isa. 11). David's legacy, then, was to point the way forward, and to give an imperfect glimpse of what perfect leadership could achieve.

Perfect leadership is pictured in two ways in verse 4—like morning sunshine and like rainfall. Here are two universal phenomena. The writer is thinking of the gentle, beneficial effects of sun and rain—not the blistering heat of noon in tropical countries, nor the torrential and violent rains which some lands experience. Sun and rain together work the miracle of natural growth, and were viewed in Israel as gifts of God. The God-given human king, then, is designed to be like these twin blessings, quietly but constantly working for the good of all his subjects. This is the sort of leadership we all need—at every level in human society.

(*Note:* See at 21:15ff. for comments on 23:8–39.)

DAVID'S CENSUS

2 Samuel 24:1–17

[1]Again the anger of the Lord was kindled against Israel, and he incited David against them, saying, "Go, number Israel and Judah." [2]So the king said to Joab and the commanders of the army, who were with him, "Go through all the tribes of Israel, from Dan to Beer-sheba, and number the people, that I may know the number of the people." [3]But Joab said to the king, "May the Lord your God add to the people a hundred times as many as they are, while the eyes of my lord the king still see it; but why does my lord the king delight in this thing?" [4]But the king's word prevailed against Joab and the commanders of the army. So Joab and the commanders of the army went out from the presence of the king to number the people of Israel. [5]They crossed the Jordan, and began from Aroer, and from the city that is in the middle of the valley, toward Gad and on to Jazer. [6]Then they came to Gilead, and to Kadesh in the land of the Hittites; and they came to Dan, and from Dan they went around to Sidon, [7]and came to the fortress of Tyre and to all the cities of the Hivites and Canaanites; and they went out to the Negeb of Judah at Beer-sheba. [8]So when they had gone through all the land, they came to Jerusalem at the end of nine months and twenty days. [9]And Joab gave the sum of the numbering of the people to the king: in Israel

there were eight hundred thousand valiant men who drew the sword, and the men of Judah were five hundred thousand.

¹⁰But David's heart smote him after he had numbered the people. And David said to the Lord, "I have sinned greatly in what I have done. But now, O Lord, I pray thee, take away the iniquity of thy servant; for I have done very foolishly." ¹¹And when David arose in the morning, the word of the Lord came to the prophet Gad, David's seer, saying, ¹²"Go and say to David, 'Thus says the Lord, Three things I offer you; choose one of them, that I may do it to you.'" ¹³So Gad came to David and told him, and said to him, "Shall three years of famine come to you in your land? Or will you flee three months before your foes while they pursue you? Or shall there be three days' pestilence in your land? Now consider, and decide what answer I shall return to him who sent me." ¹⁴Then David said to Gad, "I am in great distress; let us fall into the hand of the Lord, for his mercy is great; but let me not fall into the hand of man."

¹⁵So the Lord sent a pestilence upon Israel from the morning until the appointed time; and there died of the people from Dan to Beersheba seventy thousand men. ¹⁶And when the angel stretched forth his hand toward Jerusalem to destroy it, the Lord repented of the evil, and said to the angel who was working destruction among the people, "It is enough; now stay your hand." And the angel of the Lord was by the threshing floor of Araunah the Jebusite. ¹⁷Then David spoke to the Lord when he saw the angel who was smiting the people, and said, "Lo, I have sinned, and I have done wickedly; but these sheep, what have they done? Let thy hand, I pray thee, be against me and against my father's house."

We might have expected the book of 2 Samuel to end either with the peaceful death of David, or else with some grand climax, some outstanding achievement in the latter part of his reign. Instead, we find here a situation of fresh trouble for king and country, placed in a setting of God's *anger* against Israel (verse 1). Moreover, the story is puzzling for modern readers; it is never explained why God was angry, nor why David's census was considered to be an evil thing. Also, the statement that God *incited David* raises moral and theological problems for Christian readers.

The best starting-point for understanding this chapter is to pick out the historical facts, at the same time observing that the narrator is considering them retrospectively. The basic facts were as follows: (a) David held a census; (b) a major epidemic occurred soon afterwards; (c) Jerusalem more or less escaped the effects of the epidemic. (The sequel in verses 18–25 was the most important event of all to the writer.) The story explores the links between these separate events, and sees God at work behind them.

(i) *The Census*. The first event, then, was the census, carried out on David's orders for the purposes of efficient military administration. We are not told why it was wrong, but evidently Joab was uneasy about it and David afterwards had a conscience about it, so clearly it was the sort of thing which roused serious misgivings in ancient Israel. Why? Perhaps because it was felt that to assess the army's potential in this fashion was an act of arrogance and of lack of trust in God; the Old Testament insists more than once (see for instance Judg. 7:2ff. and 1 Sam. 14:6) that victory in battle depends not on big battalions but on God's plans for his people. In fact, the exact numbers produced by David's census were at once drastically reduced by the effects of the pestilence that ensued!

The fault was shared between king and people; but God's purpose was nevertheless fulfilled in the sequel, so the writer is convinced that God was active even in the sinful deed.

(ii) *The Epidemic*. Plagues were all too common in the ancient world. Without the aid of scientific medical knowledge and techniques, all ancient peoples would naturally seek divine guidance. It is no surprise that a prophet comes forward with precise recommendations.

(iii) *Jerusalem's Escape*. The *angel* whom David saw in a vision or dream was the destroying angel of current Israelite belief—God's "messenger" (the literal meaning of the Hebrew word for *angel*) inflicting the punishment of death; David saw in his vision that Jerusalem was to be spared. This was not because of any special virtue in the capital city or its inhabitants but because of God's sovereign choice and decision; the reason will become clear in verses 18–25.

There are two lessons in this passage for Jerusalem: (a) God had special purposes for the city; (b) the city was nevertheless in danger of God's anger. This twin message was true for centuries after David's time. It can be illustrated by the miraculous deliverance of the city when the Assyrians besieged it (2 Kings 19:32–36) and by its utter destruction when the Babylonians besieged it (2 Kings 25:8ff.).

This combination of the promise of blessing and the threat of disaster is a permanent lesson for the Church too. We too can be sure that God has his purposes for the Church universal, for his people engaged on his mission; but the individual local church may well face decline, schism and fall—as did the church at Laodicea in Rev. 3:14–17. The Church must always march forward, or else face defeat and decay.

AN ALTAR TO THE LORD

2 Samuel 24:18–25

18And Gad came that day to David, and said to him, "Go up, rear an altar to the Lord on the threshing floor of Araunah the Jebusite." 19So David went up at Gad's word, as the Lord commanded. 20And when Araunah looked down, he saw the king and his servants coming on toward him; and Araunah went forth, and did obeisance to the king with his face to the ground. 21And Araunah said, "Why has my lord the king come to his servant?" David said, "To buy the threshing floor of you, in order to build an altar to the Lord, that the plague may be averted from the people." 22Then Araunah said to David, "Let my lord the king take and offer up what seems good to him; here are the oxen for the burnt offering, and the threshing sledges and the yokes of the oxen for the wood. 23All this, O king, Araunah gives to the king." And Araunah said to the king, "The Lord your God accept you." 24But the king said to Araunah, "No, but I will buy it of you for a price; I will not offer burnt offerings to the Lord my God which cost me nothing." So David bought the threshing floor and the oxen for fifty shekels of silver. 25And David built there an altar to the Lord, and offered burnt offerings and peace offerings. So the Lord heeded supplications for the land, and the plague was averted from Israel.

God's purpose in the whole sequence of events now becomes clearer: David's vision of the angel in verse 16 and the prophet Gad's instructions to him in verse 18 both concerned the same place just outside the city, an open space then used as a threshing floor and owned by a non-Israelite named Araunah. Every Israelite reader will have known that it was here, on the site of Araunah's farming estate, that in due course Solomon's temple was built. So the disaster of the epidemic finally resulted in the discovery, or the creation, of a new place of worship for Israel, a shrine which would be the most important of all and would eventually displace every other Israelite sanctuary.

The books of Samuel leave the reader, then, with a picture of peace after storm (looking back) and of God's continuing presence (looking to the future), symbolized in the place of his own choosing. It is impossible to exaggerate the importance of this shrine to the citizens of Jerusalem, to all Israelites and their descendants the Jews, and to the Christian faith in turn. God is not tied to places, nor to buildings, and indeed the temple would prove to have its drawbacks (as Stephen recognized very clearly, cp. Acts 7), but as a sign and symbol of the reality of God's deep involvement with human beings and with his people in particular, and of his commitment to them, the temple would be of tremendous significance.

God had been at work in all that had happened since before Samuel's birth. He had been there in Israel's defeats as well as their victories. He had helped Samuel to lead Israel; he had at first helped Saul to do so, and then when he had washed his hands of Saul he had brought David to the fore; now for a generation he had given Israel unprecedented success and prosperity through David. Even in famine and plague God had been there; and still he was there, in touch with the people who could now bring him their offerings and their worship in the place God himself had indicated.

So the books of Samuel end with an unfinished story. Much changed for Israel as the generations and centuries passed; and much more changed with the advent of Jesus Christ and the start of the new people of God, the Christian Church. The

Jerusalem temple has long since perished, but as Heb. 10:1–18 explains in detail, the whole sacrificial system by then had become obsolete. However, the Christian has no less a duty to worship God than did the Israelite of old, as the Epistle to the Hebrews again indicates: "Let us continually offer up a sacrifice of praise to God, that is, the fruit of lips that acknowledge his name. Do not neglect to do good and to share what you have, for such sacrifices are pleasing to God" (Heb. 13:15f.). Our world is far from stable politically, but we have one King, who never changes, and we can enjoy a communion with him which will remain constant throughout the many vicissitudes of this life and this world.

FURTHER READING

P. R. Ackroyd, *The First Book of Samuel*; *The Second Book of Samuel* (Cambridge Bible Commentary)

J. Bright, *A History of Israel* (Old Testament Library), chapter 5

H. W. Hertzberg, *I & II Samuel* (Old Testament Library)

P. K. McCarter, *I Samuel* (Anchor Bible) (*II Samuel* is forthcoming)

W. McKane, *I & II Samuel* (Torch Bible Commentaries)

J. Mauchline, *1 and 2 Samuel* (New Century Bible)

MAPS

1. AREA MAP

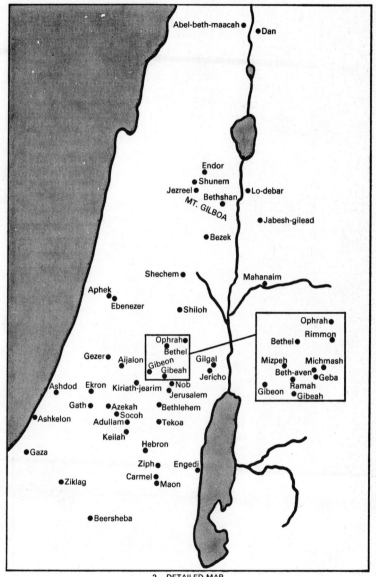

2. DETAILED MAP